FOXY

FOXY

My Life in Three Acts

PAM
GRIER

with ANDREA CAGAN

SPRINGBOARD

New York • Boston

I have modified the identities and certain details about some of the individuals described in this book.

Springboard Press
Hachette Book Group
237 Park Avenue, New York, NY 10017
www.hachettebookgroup.com

Printed in the United States of America

First Edition: April 2010

Springboard Press is an imprint of Grand Central Publishing.
The Springboard Press name and logo are trademarks of Hachette Book Group, Inc.

10 9 8 7 6 5 4 3 2 1

Library of Congress Cataloging-in-Publication Data

Grier, Pam, 1949–
Foxy: my life in three acts/by Pam Grier with Andrea Cagan—1st ed.
    p. cm.
ISBN 978-0-446-54850-2
1. Grier, Pam, 1949–   2. Actors—United States—Biography.   3. African American actors—Biography. I. Cagan, Andrea. II. Title.
PN2287.G6875A3 2010
792.02'8092—dc22
[B]
                                                      2009030547

For Gwen, my mother, and
Gina, Rod, Gaël, Bronson, Koleman, and Michael
and my guardian angels who watch over me every day

Contents

ACT ONE

The Early Years

1949–1970

CHAPTER 1

Stunt Work

I was snuggled in my mother's arms in the backseat of the old Buick. My dad's Air Force buddy was at the wheel, driving us from Fort Dix Air Force Base to Colorado, where Dad was being transferred. I'd been born into a military family, making my first move by car at three weeks old, since blacks were rarely seen on trains. And, of course, there was no way we could afford to fly, even if planes had been available.

I was born in Winston-Salem, where my dad's family lived. My parents had expected their visit to North Carolina to last three to four days before they returned to Colorado, where Mom would give birth to me. But it seemed that between the intense heat, the long hours of relaxation, and the large mouthfuls of ripe, juicy watermelon she ingested, my mom went into early labor with me. She was uncomfortable having her baby in Winston-Salem. She'd wanted to be safe and sound in Colorado when I was born, with her own family around her. Apparently I had other plans.

Now Dad was in the passenger seat, riding shotgun, while his buddy drove the old '48 crank Buick with no seat belts, which no one had as yet. In the backseat, the driver's wife was carrying a goldfish in a bowl of water, and Mom was carrying me. As we rode along the New Jersey Turnpike, a car sped down the on-ramp, passed us, and suddenly shot out onto the road right in front of us. As Dad's friend swerved to miss the car cutting us off, our Buick rolled over three times and came to a stop at the side of the turnpike, its wheels beneath it. We all got out. Mom had never let go of me, and everyone in the car walked away without a scratch—except the goldfish, who died from oxygen inhalation.

That was my first stunt.

Of course I don't remember that happening. My first memory was in Columbus, Ohio, where my father was stationed at the Air Force base there. I was in diapers, about a year and a half old, and I recall my mother's colorful skirt and the gauzy white strings that hung off the bow of her apron. Her legs looked impossibly long, and I marveled at her wedged shoes that made her taller than she really was. She was at the kitchen sink, and I was on the floor beside her, when I heard an engine roar outside the house. We both turned to look past the black and white Formica kitchen table out into the courtyard to see my dad driving into the garage.

"Daddy's home," my mother practically sang, as I tried to climb up the table leg to see outside. Mom, pregnant with my brother, Rod, hoisted me up onto the kitchen table so I could watch my father get out of the car and come into the house. It makes my mom absolutely insane that I can remember these things in such minute detail from before I was two. But I do. I also remember sitting on the front steps, eating a slice of fresh tomato, and dropping it on the ground when my dad walked toward me. I was standing on shaky legs, my arms raised for him to lift me up, when I slipped on the tomato slice. I bounced once before my dad caught me. Back then, there was no one more amazing and strong in all the world.

My dad, Clarence Grier, was a strappingly handsome man with tremendous strength in his hands. I could literally feel youthful energy shoot through his fingers. He was kind and loving to me, and the scent of his cologne combined with the crisp, starchy smell of his clean Air Force uniform delighted me. A loving, carefree man, he was my mom's hero. He was so light-skinned, he could pass for white, which caused him a lot more trouble than if he had clearly looked black or white. His mom was mixed, and his blue-eyed dad was mixed but looked white, so he never really fit in anywhere.

Remember the old term *mulatto*? Today we call it biracial or multicultural, but back then, being a mulatto was a major obstacle. At the base in Columbus, for example, where segregation was at an all-time high, blacks had to live in apartments off base because they were offered substandard living on base. That was where Dad suffered the confusion of his superiors, who thought he was white when they first met him.

When we arrived, we had been awarded a lovely place on base to live, because they thought Dad was Caucasian. But before we ever moved in, they discovered their mistake and told us that since we were Negroes, we had to make other living arrangements. Dad felt comfortable living among whites, and the indignity of being asked to move out affected his self-confidence. He had dreamed of going to officer training school. He had what it took, and Mom wanted that for him, too. But he lacked the necessary confidence. He had hit the racial wall so many times, I guess he just gave up, and we lived in an apartment off base that was shockingly inferior to the living quarters on base. In fact, everything was different.

If you lived on base, you had decent facilities, good food, and current entertainment, including movies and music. If you lived off base, the public bus system hardly ever stopped for you, particularly if the back of the bus was full. On base, shuttles took you shopping or wherever else you wanted to go. Off base, you felt the humiliation, embarrassment, and sting of segregation, like when you were shopping with your family and the bus sped right by you, as if you didn't exist. In this era, we had to make sure we didn't look at someone the wrong way—it was a constant tension—or we could end up having our lives threatened. It seemed that while Air Force whites had access to whatever they needed, blacks had to make do, and there was no bucking against the status quo. The makeshift apartments where blacks lived (we called ourselves Negroes back then) were some distance from the base, and if you didn't have a car, you had better have a pair of sturdy legs.

One afternoon—I was about five and my little brother, Rodney, was four—Mom and us kids were carrying shopping bags home from the grocery store. The walk was a few miles, and my mom usually didn't mind it, but it was so hot that day that we were walking from tree to tree, stopping in the shade to catch our breath and drum up the courage to walk under the blistering sun to the next tree. Laden with shopping bags, my mom, dripping with perspiration, looked longingly at a nearly empty bus that drove right past us.

"It's so hot out," I said. "Why won't the bus stop for us, Mom?"

"Because we're Negroes," she said.

Mom was gasping for air, she looked like she was ready to pass out, I was beyond uncomfortable, and even my little brother was panting. Another bus, completely empty, sped by us, and then another. When a fourth bus was about to drive on past us, it slowed, pulled over to the side of the road, and stopped. Mom walked cautiously to the stairs as the white bus driver opened the door. She looked in questioningly, glancing at all the empty seats, hoping against hope that we might be able to ride home.

The driver said nothing and neither did my mom. She just hustled us to the back of the bus and we fell onto the seats, breathing heavily. We sat quietly in our private chariot, grateful to be out of the hot sun. Mom knew this man was risking his personal security by picking us up. He obviously had a big heart under that white skin. He never looked at us, and we kept our eyes straight ahead as we neared our apartment complex. Mom told him when we got close to home, and he stopped to let us off.

She knew she was not allowed to speak to him, and she fought the urge to show her appreciation with a light touch on this kind man's shoulder. That could have gotten her into trouble. We faced these kinds of issues every day when the grocery clerk put our change on the counter instead of in our hands to avoid physical contact. How my mom managed to hold on to her dignity in such a condemning and shaming society, where we had to take what we were given, I will never know. But somehow she was able to turn everything around and convince us it was a blessing.

Instead of touching the bus driver, she said, "Thank you," as they looked into each other's eyes, sharing a moment of grace and true humanity. He drove away, never looking back. She turned to Rodney and me and said, "We just got a beautiful gift. Never forget it. God is taking care of us." And she never mentioned it again.

As a little girl, I wondered what it would have been like to wait for a bus like anyone else, to go into any restroom anywhere, and be welcomed into any restaurant we chose. I imagined Mom saying, "Hey, let's take a break from shopping and go have lunch," like any other citizen of the world. But that was not our world.

When I think back about why we didn't end up feeling inferior every day of our lives, I give credit to my loving family. We were very close, my parents made sure we had good manners and morals, and my mom always had several white friends who were sympathetic to contemporary black issues. While a few white women were still stuck in racial prejudice, most of Mom's friends, the white women who were married to NCOs (noncommissioned officers), never believed the ridiculous and denigrating myths and lies surrounding Negroes. After all, the men worked in close proximity, whether they were white or black. And Mom's ability to create dress patterns and sew beautiful clothing gave her a special standing among her group of friends.

Mom was so good at sewing, they could show her a dress on the cover of *Vogue* magazine and she could create that very dress and make her friends look classic and rich. My mom's white friends knew that we were good people and that she wanted the same things for us that they wanted for their own children. Today, I see what a great role model my mom was. She didn't believe in prejudice and she didn't want us to grow up hating or fearing white people.

In the segregated area of the city where we lived, we could only socialize with other people of color. We couldn't sit beside whites at movies or eat with them in restaurants. We couldn't use public transportation, and it was so bad that just chatting with white people could get us in trouble, so we avoided it.

When we spent time on base, however, our best friends were both black and white kids. We were invited to join them in the sandboxes, in the swimming pool, and on the bike trails. Some bases were more liberal than others, and at our base, the military complex worked hard at creating the "look" of equality. That meant we were allowed to enjoy the company of color-blind friends who accepted us just the way we were. It was an important lesson to learn that not all white people hated us for being different.

Mom went through nursing school during that time so she would have an occupation that felt worthwhile and would help her pick up the financial slack if it was necessary. She believed very strongly that women needed to know they could fend for themselves if push came to shove, such as in case of a death, disablement, or illness. And she could add income to the family coffers. Dad loved his Air Force work, where he focused on aviation, which was his calling. He was an NCO, which meant he had enlisted. He held on to his dream of becoming an officer, but he was holding out until "things" got better. That was the African American mantra—"Waiting for times to get better"—as we tried to envision a world with fewer obstacles, apprehensions, and hostility.

Up to the time I was six, when my day-to-day existence would change drastically, I had a bubbly personality and a zest for life. We had no home of our own since we were constantly being transferred from base to base. But I was always eager to laugh and hungry to learn, and I adored the early days when we lived with my grandmother Marguerite, whom we called Marky, and my grandfather Raymundo Parrilla, of Philippine descent, whom we called Daddy Ray. Marky was a music enthusiast, cleaning house to the sounds of Mahalia Jackson, gospel, and Elvis's "Blue Suede Shoes," which she played over and over again. Every day, each family on the block had a pot of vegetables, beans, or black-eyed peas and collard greens simmering on the stove. Food aromas wafted down the street all the time, which gave a homey, warm feeling to the neighborhood.

I was thrilled when Daddy Ray gave me a dime one Saturday so I could go to the movies with a few of my friends and cousins. My aunt Mennon, my mother's sister, had four children, and I recall my excitement when we headed off to the neighborhood movie theater to see *Godzilla*, a film clearly chosen by the boys.

The truth is that the film could have been about anything under the sun. I wouldn't have cared. It was my first movie, and I was ecstatic over the darkened theater and my very own nickel bag of popcorn that I didn't have to share. There were no segregation restrictions for the kiddie matinee, so we were free to frolic, scream, and munch on candy and popcorn. It felt like an indoor playground where kids could bounce on the seats, yell, giggle, laugh, and play with abandon, reacting to what was on the movie screen.

Our group of about ten kids felt safe, since the older cousins and neighbors watched over us younger kids, and we all cheered and booed in the appropriate places. But when I told the other kids that the monster wasn't real, they refused to believe me.

"His tail was made of rubber," I insisted. "I could tell. I saw the crease."

"It was not!" they said, unwilling to believe that the magic of Hollywood was in play here. They didn't want the monster to be made of rubber, while I was fascinated by rubber monsters with fake tails. I decided then and there that, one day, I would work in the movies in some capacity.

Marguerite and Daddy Ray spent time between their farmhouse in Cheyenne, Wyoming, and a modern cinder-block and brick home in Denver, Colorado, where we stayed sometimes when Dad was stationed nearby. This sleepy, bucolic neighborhood was fashioned in Craftsman style, its streets lined with century-old majestic oak and maple trees. The sidewalks were slabs of granite and redstone, no cement; the structures were built to last. No one had garages then, so everyone parked their Edsels on the streets with no worries about them getting stolen.

In the house, there were chrome faucets in the bathroom, and every time we used the sink, we had to wipe the water spots off the chrome. If we didn't, my grandmother went berserk and raised holy hell, since she was meticulous to a fault. After dinner, the floor had to be swept and the dishes had to be washed, dried, and put away. Then and only then could we sit down to tackle our homework.

My grandfather had a station wagon and an army jeep for hunting. While Dad taught us to play tennis and other games he enjoyed on the base, Daddy Ray taught us how to survive. As I mentioned, the army bases were sometimes color-blind as to our attending activities and eating good meals. But out in the civilian world, particularly in public school, we had to deal with civil rights, racial prejudice, and the accompanying self-hatred. Daddy Ray wanted us to be prepared.

Best of all was my grandparents' farm up in Wyoming, where my grandfather and my grandma specialized in growing sugar beets and raising goats. My favorite place in the world. We went there on weekends. The farmhouse had a big old barn where Daniel, one of my American Indian uncles, lived. Uncle Daniel had a long white braid, and he mainly survived on canned peaches from the farm. He lived to be 107.

The farmhouse had no indoor plumbing, so we used an outhouse that was stocked with corn cobs and a coffee can full of vinegar to disinfect and disguise the smell. Our grandparents had used corn cobs for toilet paper back in the day, but by the time we got there, we had toilet paper, so the corn cobs were just a reminder of days gone by. Since there was no electricity and it was pitch-dark at night, Daddy Ray set up ropes that we could hold on to that led from the house to the outhouse. We used a kerosene lantern to see our way, and when the wind blew up in swirling gales, if we didn't grasp the rope tightly, we could get blown away.

The farmhouse kitchen was one big room with a slab of slate with a hole in it for the sink. The actual sink was underneath in the form of an enamel basin sitting on a small table. At the end of the table was the pump primer that we would pump a few times to get water flowing from the spigot into the sink. We heated water there for our baths. The farmhouse eventually became the cabin where the men stayed during hunting season. A small slice of heaven on earth, this wonderful farm was precious and charming, and I felt safer and healthier there than anywhere else, even as we dealt with the harsh and sometimes cruel elements of the wild, such as high winds and extreme temperatures from hotter than hot to freezing cold. In fact, the wind-chill factor was so extreme that when it reached up into the higher registers, the force of the gales could actually crack metal.

My favorite time of day was the early morning when we would help Daddy Ray in his organic garden. Gardening was the norm in that area, and neighborhood families took great pride in competing with each other. Who could grow the biggest and tastiest squash, pumpkins, cucumbers, and "ter-maters"? Just about every home in this little town had a working garden—they took up at least half of the large yards—and our white and black neighbors traded vegetables, freshly caught fish, and venison to help each other out. As a result, we always had fresh lettuce with Italian dressing and ripe, pungent tomatoes that were bloodred on the inside. We grew our own onions, scallions, radishes, and carrots, and on the far side of my grandparents' house was a big strawberry patch. In the middle of the patch was a tree that bore golden freestone peaches with little clefts in the sides that turned orange when the peaches were ripe. Beside the peach tree were a prolific black walnut tree and a cherry tree, full of dark red bing cherries that weighed the branches down when they were ready for picking.

We ate like royalty back then because everything was fresh. This was before the emergence of the massive supermarkets where we buy our food today. We got our protein from the Korean deli around the corner, where they sold freshly killed chickens and recently caught fish. Some of our neighbors had chickens on their property and a cut-off tree stump for slaughtering them. They would catch a chicken, wring its neck and lay it across the stump, chop off its head like with a guillotine, and drain the blood. Then, to remove the feathers easily, they would drop it into boiling water for a few seconds.

When the men took off on hunting expeditions into the high country of Colorado or Wyoming, they brought back pheasant, game hens, wild turkeys, elks, and antelope. They fished for river catfish, bass, and lake trout, and my grandfather taught us kids to fly-fish. Daddy Ray was obsessed with teaching us to be self-sufficient, and we all had to learn to tie flies onto the hooks with pieces of carpeting and feathers and shiny wool. Then we were taught to cast a fly rod so we could catch German brown, rainbow, and speckled trout. We also took turns learning to steer the fishing boat through the water.

Some of the girls said, "I'm scared, Daddy Ray. I don't know how to steer a boat. I can't."

"You can't be scared," he told them, "or you can't come with me. If something happens to me, you have to be able to bring the boat back to shore." We also loved waterskiing and we needed to steer a boat for that, too. I was always the first in line to learn whatever he showed us.

As primitive as life was on this farm, I loved how people treated each other and how we all shared our crops with our neighbors. It seemed like cities were prohibitively expensive because people tried to make money off of each other instead of lending a helping hand. Out in the farmlands, in contrast, no one went hungry because we traded raspberries for cherries, and tomatoes for corn. I learned how many ears of corn usually grew on a stalk, and Daddy Ray showed me how to dig deep down into the soil to determine if it was rich enough for the crop we wanted to plant.

"The roots of the cornstalks need to be at least four feet in the ground," Daddy Ray told me, "and the stalk will measure about eight to ten feet high. The longer the roots, the more ears of corn it will produce."

We were taught to respect and cherish the earth, something that has stayed with me for my entire life. When I hear the famous Joni Mitchell lyric "They paved paradise and put up a parking lot," I nod my head. I may not have been raised like a privileged city kid with a ton of new clothes and toys, but that means nothing, because when I was growing up, I got to live in paradise.

CHAPTER 2

Marky and Me

Pammy. Tudot," Marky, our grandma Marguerite, called out to me. Tudot was a Native American nickname she called me, and I still don't know why. "Can you do something for your grandma?"

"Yes, ma'am," I said, always anxious to please. I stood and waited. We were back in the city house in Denver now.

"Did Daddy Ray leave for work yet?"

"Yes, ma'am."

"Okay, then. I need you to go to the store for me like a big girl. Can you do that?"

"I can do that," I said, puffing out my little chest. I was about to turn six.

"Here's twenty-five cents," she said. "Go ask Helen for a can of Coors beer." Helen, a Korean woman whom we all loved, owned the deli that was in walking distance from my grandparents' house. Marky made me repeat the name "Coors" several times to make sure I would remember.

"But don't tell Daddy Ray," Marky cautioned me. "This is between us. It's our little secret. Can you be a good girl and not tell anybody?"

"I can do that," I said. I was getting my first instructions on how to lie from my grandmother. This stood in stark contrast to the other adults, who never stopped reminding us kids about the pitfalls and consequences of telling lies. But I wanted to be a big girl and win approval from my grandmother.

Today, I understand that Marky, the grandmother whom I so wanted to please, had some deep and troubling issues that she refused to acknowledge. As a farmer's daughter, she had worked herself to the bone when she was young, and she'd had enough of it. Now, she preferred the life of a high-society woman (even though she wasn't one). She kept her house spotless and was paying off a fur coat she had put on layaway. And she liked her beer.

Instead of becoming self-sufficient, which was the focus of most members of my family, Marky wanted to be the helpless female so my grandfather and everybody else would be forced to do things for her. They had married when she was fifteen and he was eighteen. That sounds painfully young for marriage, but the truth was that in the world of farming and agriculture, people married young because they were ready. They knew how to build a home with their hands so they would have a roof over their heads. They had been driving tractors since they were ten, and they knew how to grow food and hunt so they would never go hungry. Out of necessity, they grew up a great deal faster than city folk, and they were ready for marriage and families when they were quite young.

Rumor has it that my grandmother might have been pregnant at age fifteen when she married my grandfather, but no one knows for sure. She never admitted it to anyone, and we never pushed her to tell us. All we knew was that when Marky wanted something, she made sure that someone else got it or did it *for* her. She didn't want for much, and she was pretty good at getting away with her games and manipulations.

"Why don't you learn to drive a car?" Daddy Ray asked her over and over.

"I'm too scared," was her usual response.

"But you could be independent and do things on your own," he said. "Wouldn't you like that?"

"I'm too scared," she repeated. "I don't want to." And that was that.

I began my secret outings to the Korean deli for my grandmother that day, buying beer for her from Helen, sneaking it home, and watching Marky hide it from my grandfather. I knew it wasn't right, and keeping secrets from my grandfather made me feel bad. But I was torn, because I liked having something special with my grandmother.

One day, after this had been going on for several months, my dad was away at the air base, my mom was working, the other kids were with friends, involved in summer activities, and I was at the house, sitting on the front porch steps, waiting for Daddy Ray to come home after work. As always, I was delighted to see Daddy Ray. I ran toward him for a hug. After he picked me up and swung me around, he said, "Hey, Pammy, tell me what you did today."

We sat together on the front steps, and I said, "Well, I had breakfast and I made my bed."

"That's a good girl," he said. "What else did you do?

"Then I went over to the store and bought the beer for Marky and we—"

"Whoa. Back up," said Daddy Ray, "What did you just say?"

I looked into his face, which was appearing more troubled by the second. I felt afraid, but I repeated, "I went to Helen's and I bought the beer for Marky."

"Did you now?" he said. He stood and took my hand. "Where did you get the money?"

"Marky gave it to me," I said honestly. "And I gave her the change like I always do." I didn't want him to think I kept the change.

Daddy Ray took my hand. "How about we head over to Helen's right now and have a little talk with her?"

"But Grandma is making lemonade," I said. I wasn't sure what I'd done wrong, but heading over to the deli sounded serious.

"That's okay," he said. "We'll be back before she even knows where we've gone."

"Okay," I said reluctantly. When we walked into the store and greeted Helen, Daddy Ray asked her calmly if she had ever sold me beer. She said she had.

"How long has this been going on?" he asked.

"A few months," she said.

On the way home, Daddy Ray's silence scared me.

"I don't want to get anybody in trouble," I said.

"You didn't do anything wrong." That was all he said. He patted my head and remained silent until we got to the house. "Pammy," Daddy Ray told me, "I want you to stay outside for a little while. I'm going in the house to have a grown-up talk with Marky, and I don't want you to come inside until I come out and get you. Okay?"

"Yes, sir."

I walked over to the swing set and started swinging while Daddy Ray headed into the house, closing and locking the door behind him. I swung back and forth, letting my feet skim over the earth as I lifted my head to the heavens, trying to lose myself in the breezy motion. I was scared, and I wasn't sure why. The next thing I heard was my grandfather's low, gruff voice and my grandmother yelling back as they got into a screaming fight. I swung higher and higher, trying to reach the sky with my legs and leave everything else behind.

I slowed down when I heard the back door slam. Suddenly I had to pee really bad. I ran to the house and banged on the front door, but nobody could hear me. Or if they did, they didn't care. I wished we were up at the farmhouse, where I could get to the outhouse without bothering anyone. I banged louder. Still no one. I was too afraid to go around the house to the back door, where I imagined Marky was standing outside, crying. I sat on the front stoop and crossed my legs. The back door opened again as I heard screaming and more door slamming.

By the time Daddy Ray got to the front door to let me in, it was too late. I had wet my underwear and my shorts, and I was embarrassed and crying.

"What's wrong, Pammy?" he asked. "Come on in." He looked angry.

"I had to go the bathroom and the door was locked," I said through my tears.

"I'm so sorry, honey," Daddy Ray said, softening up a little.

"Your grandma will help you change. Go and see her. She's in the bedroom."

I walked slowly to the bedroom at the back of the house. I stood at the doorway and watched Marky sitting on the bed, crumpling a tissue in her hands. She lifted a swollen, angry face toward me, the tears still spilling down her cheeks. "I told you not to tell," she said to me through clenched teeth. "I thought this was our secret."

"Am I gonna get a whoopin'?" I asked, backing away.

She reached over and jerked my arm, pulling me toward her. "You're a bad girl. You broke your promise." When she felt the wetness on my shorts and realized that I had peed myself, she made a nasty face and instructed me to get some fresh clothes from my room and to change in the bathroom.

She avoided me for the rest of the afternoon, and I was terrified about what would happen when my mom got home. If I hadn't gotten a whooping yet, I figured it was only a matter of time until someone laid into me.

When Mom got home, I ran to meet her, but Marky was right behind me. "She's a bad girl. She lied to Daddy Ray," Marky told my mom. "She said I was drinking, and it isn't true. She's a liar."

"No, she isn't," boomed Daddy Ray's voice. He appeared in the doorway and said, "Pammy told the truth. Marky lied."

He was resentful that my grandmother was so helpless and that she acted so entitled, like she was better than the rest of us. I guess that was the last straw for him. That night, Daddy Ray moved out of their bedroom and into the guest room. He never slept in his wife's room again, but they refused to divorce since they were both Catholics. I continued to get a lot of positive attention from Daddy Ray, but the sense of safety that I had always felt around my grandmother was gone.

When Marky turned against me, she began to do outrageous things, like hide my homework the morning it was due. Marky was just too insecure to let go of her resentment toward me. I remember having to go to my teacher, Mrs. Oma, and explain that I had finished my homework last night, but when I woke up, it was gone. I was Mrs. Oma's best student, and she knew I always did my homework. I think she believed me, but my life had become stressful and dangerous living around my grandmother.

I was relieved when we moved to my aunt Mennon's house in the projects in Denver. She lived in Platte Valley in an all-black area called the Five Points. This was where the black ballrooms emerged, and people were serenaded by Duke Ellington, Nat King Cole, B.B. King, and Count Basie, a veritable mini-Harlem in the West.

Aunt Mennon's four children, my first cousins, and our family had a real ball together. I was six, enrolled in Mitchell Elementary School, when my mom found a job as a nurse's assistant to supplement our income. The older kids watched over us younger ones and kept us safe, but once again, the adult who was supposed to watch us had her own set of major problems.

Remember the movie *Five Easy Pieces*? Well, Aunt Mennon, a hot, sexy, smart waitress who reminds me of Karen Black's character, worked at the local food joint, Buster's Barbecue. Buster's secret, which we all knew, was in the gravy, as he slow-cooked spices with honey and cloves. Then he poured in a little orange juice and let it all simmer. When it was done, we dipped soft pieces of white bread into the sauce to sop it up. We called that a "Slap Yo' Mama"–good barbecue. That meant if she tried to eat off your plate, you would slap your own mama to save it for yourself. And then your mama would slap you right back for your audacious behavior.

The most popular restaurant in town, Buster's Barbecue was always jam-packed, with lines of people down the block waiting to get in. The smell of fresh beef, pork, and chicken, swimming in the savory sauces, wafted into the projects at dinner hour, and whenever anyone went to a concert or a club, they always ended up at Buster's afterward, drinking, eating, and dancing. When Mom got home after a night out, her perfume (Tabu was her favorite) was always mixed with the smell of Lucky Strike cigarettes and the smoky aroma of barbecue.

I remember many a Saturday night when I was fast asleep and I heard Mom calling, "Kids, come on downstairs. We have ribs for you."

We'd run down for the ribs they had brought home for us. We went back to bed and they woke us up bright and early the next morning, ready for church, no matter how late they'd gotten home. Robust and lively, my parents went to church on three hours of sleep, and you could never tell. They liked their partying, but there were no excuses for missing church.

But my aunt Mennon hardly went to church (she liked to sleep in). She was smart as a whip and had an explosive temper. When she got angry at a woman in a club one night for messing with her boyfriend, she followed her to the bathroom. In the next moment, the unsuspecting woman's head was stuffed down the toilet and my aunt kept on flushing.

Aunt Mennon had a pugnacious personality and she was a fierce fighter, especially when she was drinking. When she drank, she became irrational and everyone who knew her tried to stay out of her way. She got so wild and out of control, she would jump on the back of some guy's Harley, a guy she barely knew, and they would take off. Then the older cousins were stuck with watching us younger kids. It made my mom furious whenever she got home from work and Mennon was nowhere in sight.

CHAPTER **3**

Keeping Secrets

It was mid-summer in the projects and I had just turned six. Some of my cousins and my brother had gone to the local public swimming pool, but I didn't like it there. I once cut my foot on a piece of glass on the bottom of the pool, so I stayed away. The girls in Aunt Mennon's home—including me, my cousin Krista, and my other cousin, Becky—shared a bedroom. My brother and his male cousins shared a room, too, and Aunt Mennon had her own bedroom. When she stayed at her boyfriend's house, Mom and Dad took her bedroom. When she was home, they stayed with my grandmother.

On this particular afternoon, I was home while my mom was at work. Aunt Mennon was supposed to be there, but she'd taken off on one of her wild rides so, as usual, there was no adult supervision. Three boys were in the bedroom when one of them appeared at the top of the staircase. He looked down at me. I was drawing in my coloring book.

"Come upstairs, Pammy," he said with a smile on his face.

I looked up, excited. I was bored and I thought we were about to have a sock fight.

Sock fights were one of my favorite games, partly because they weren't allowed. Before these fights were banned, my cousin Krista, my brother, Rodney, and I used to gather some kids from the block and turn the beds on their sides to create a bunker. Then we crumpled our socks into small balls of cotton and put a marble in the center of each bundle. When we tossed the socks over the bunkers at our opponents, if they hit their mark, it hurt. Of course it drove the adults crazy because we turned the bedroom into complete chaos. We weren't exactly crack shots, so we hit mirrors, lamps, and windows, often breaking them, not to mention how worried our parents were that a marble could take out somebody's eye.

Whenever they left the house, their last words of warning were, "You better not have any sock fights."

We promised, kissed them good-bye, and before they were down the street, the beds were on their sides and we were hurling sock bundles with marbles all over the room. I thought that was what the boys wanted to do now, so I ran upstairs, thrilled they were including me.

I stopped at the door to the bedroom. The beds were not turned over. "Aren't we gonna have a sock fight?" I asked. "Don't you wanna wait till Krista and the other kids get home?" There were no girls around at all, and Aunt Mennon had taken off for God only knew how long.

"We're not having a sock fight," one of the guys said. "Come on in, Pammy."

"Whacha doin'?" I asked, suddenly feeling shy.

"We want you to come in here and lie down on the bed. We have something to show you."

My face lit up. "What is it?" I asked.

"Come and find out."

I walked into the room and stood at the side of bed. "Why do you want me to lie down?"

"Just do it," one of the boys said harshly.

His voice sounded impatient, so I did as I was told. I smiled at him, until a boy started to pull at my slacks. "What are you doing?" I asked him. "Why are you pulling my pants down?"

When he got them down, one of the boys climbed on the bed beside me, shifted over on top of me, and started to push my thighs apart with his knees. I felt several hands holding my arms and legs down. I had no idea what was going on, so I just waited. After all, I had no reason to mistrust these boys, but I was starting to feel some pain.

I heard the boy unzip his pants. Terribly confused, I felt him probing at my crotch, I saw his eyes squint, I heard him moan, and then the searing pain came. I was too afraid to protest when the first boy moved off and the second one climbed on. I was hurting, and I didn't understand the feelings. I was sobbing, and all I could see was this boy's yellow, blue, and green striped T-shirt on my face as he pressed himself inside of me. His chest was cutting off my breath, and I managed to mumble, "Stop hurting me." He was beyond hearing anything besides his own grunts of pleasure. I could hardly breathe because that ugly striped T-shirt was pressing down on my nose.

When he was through, someone else was about to jump on when we all heard a noise in the house. Everyone froze. We heard the unmistakable sound of someone running up the stairs. I couldn't stop crying, and when I looked toward the door, a white repairman pushed it open. Aunt Mennon had forgotten to cancel a telephone service appointment. It seems she had not locked the door, either, and when no one answered his knock, the worker had pushed open the front door and heard my cries of distress.

"What the hell is going on here?" he bellowed. He rushed over to the boys and pulled them off of me. "Get away from her," he ordered them. When I saw how upset this adult was, I began to really freak out and cry even louder. I knew something weird and bad had happened, but I didn't get the full gravity of the situation until I saw the horror and anger on my rescuer's face. I was six. I knew nothing about sex and I hadn't even known I needed rescuing. I only knew that these boys, supposedly my friends, were hurting me.

"Put on your clothes," he said to me. "Go into the bathroom."

I grabbed my pants, disappeared in the bathroom, and shut the door. What had just happened? Why did it hurt so much? And why didn't any of my cousins help me?

The repairman called into the bathroom, "Are you okay?"

"I don't know," I said weakly. I heard him yelling at the boys, and then it sounded like they all left and he went about his business fixing the phone, the real reason he was there. A short while later, he left, too, probably afraid that if someone came home, he would be blamed for hurting me.

I climbed into the empty bathtub, rolled up into a ball, and sat there for a good hour, confused and crying. I knew something was wrong, but I didn't know what it was. When all the outer sounds were gone and I was sure everyone had left, I came out of the bathroom. I hurt so badly, I could hardly walk. I left the bedroom and was startled to see one of the boys sitting on the stairs, waiting to talk to me.

"Pammy," he said in a whisper. "You better not tell. If you do, I'm gonna whoop you. Do you understand? We all will, and you'll be really sorry."

"I won't tell," I said. I knew if I told, he wasn't the only one who would punish me.

When my cousin Krista got home, she took one look at my face and asked me what was wrong. I looked back at her a moment, debating what to say. When I finally opened my mouth, I said, "N-n-n-nothing's wrong. I'm f-f-f-fine."

In the space of an afternoon, I had gone from being a lively, self-confident young lady, excited about life, to a shy girl soon to be known as "Quiet Pammy," a frightened, insecure child who stuttered whenever she tried to talk.

CHAPTER 4

Big Horse

Leave her alone," everyone said. "She'll come around. She's just shy. She'll stop stuttering all by herself."

I didn't come around. And I didn't stop stuttering. In fact, my stuttering escalated because when I opened my mouth to say anything, I wanted to talk about the assault. I guess the words were in my mind, but my brain would pull them back and I ended up stammering to get any words out at all. I never told a soul about what happened to me, and I didn't completely stop stuttering until I turned twelve, with a few reprieves when I was deeply distracted. For the most part, however, I was so afraid and silent after the rape, I hid in my bedroom closet when people came over to visit.

Krista loved having her friends over, and they all knew me and liked me and would ask, "Where's Pammy?"

Krista didn't know why I was hiding in the closet. She just knew I had nothing to say to anyone. "Haven't seen her lately," Krista said. I became known as the quiet girl with no personality. How could anyone understand that my heart and soul were so overburdened from holding on to my painful secret, it was all I could do to stay in a room where a group of people were gathered? If anyone looked at me too directly or gave me the smallest bit of attention, I dropped my eyes and willed the floor to open up and swallow me whole. Or I found a way to make my exit and I'd "forget" to come back.

No longer the happy, eager, precocious child I once was, I found my only comfort zone was being alone and reading fantasy books like *Peter Rabbit* and *Alice in Wonderland*. I liked nothing better than disappearing into my room and diving into a book that featured somebody else's story and had nothing to do with me and my life. That was a good way to pass the days, while socially, instead of getting better as time passed, I got worse. I was so wounded by what those boys did to me, to this day when I see a striped shirt, I become paralyzed with fright. Since then, I've learned that although we find ways to cope, trauma never heals completely, and it seemed to get worse the longer I was in school in Denver.

As I was already traumatized beyond repair, it was unfortunate when a strange young boy in my class became fixated on me. He had a name that no one could pronounce, his long, thick dark eyebrows curled upward on the ends, and his head was way too big for his body. A stutterer like me (maybe that fueled his fixation), he was mentally challenged, physically unkempt, and highly unattractive, and the other kids teased him mercilessly. They also teased anyone he paid attention to.

To my horror, he would wink at me and walk up to me in school (we were both six years old) and try to give me things like an apple, a pen, or some other little trinket he had picked up. I wanted none of it; I wouldn't take his gifts or talk to him. I wouldn't talk to anyone back then, but this boy obviously took it personally and he pursued me every day for attention and conversation. He got nothing back, but he never stopped trying.

One afternoon when we were in the classroom waiting for the teacher, he got so frustrated that I wouldn't pay attention to him, he began calling my name out loud repeatedly. When I wouldn't acknowledge that he was talking to me, he picked up a steel chair with a wooden seat and hit me over the head with it. I fell to the ground and nearly passed out. The teacher, who had just entered the room, rushed over, and after she made sure I was okay, she asked Strange Boy why he did it.

He had no idea. He just stood there and shook his head. I understand now that he got violent with me because I was ignoring him and he was mentally unbalanced. But back then, it scared and confused me and made me not want to go back to school. My parents met with his parents, they tried to talk things through, but nothing changed. All I could do was try to stay away from this kid while his fixation gained momentum, probably because it was unrequited.

On my walk back to the projects after school one Friday afternoon, it seemed that the coast was clear—until Strange Boy appeared as if out of nowhere. He stood in front of me, making me stop short. In the next moment, he slugged me in the head, knocked me to the ground, and sat his big, fat butt on top of me. Then he turned over and began bouncing and rubbing himself against my body, until a white man who happened to be on the street pulled him off of me. I lay on the ground sobbing. What the hell was going on? I never asked for any of this. Why didn't everybody just leave me alone?

When my mom explained that this boy probably thought I was cute and that was why he was acting so badly, I made a decision. Being cute and getting attention were not good things, I decided. Cute girls got into trouble with boys. I would make sure I was not a cute or a pretty girl, and I cringed when my parents took me to church functions and I'd hear people say, "Isn't she a pretty child! Look at her hair."

I would mess up my hair and do what I could to throw off the "pretty girl" label. Pretty girls got all the attention, which made them targets. At the tender age of six, I'd had enough of being victimized because I was pretty and naïve. It never occurred to me to fight back, and I withdrew more and more, becoming a scared, withdrawn, stuttering little girl—except when I was on the back of a horse.

I climbed up on my first horse on the family farm in Wyoming. We went there on weekends, and it felt like every day was my birthday, as I walked through the pastures and fields. I loved that farm as much as any place I've ever known. Several hundred feet from the rustic farmhouse was a great big barn where my uncle Daniel stayed. Sometimes he let me ride with him in a cart that was led by wagon-pulling horses.

"C-c-can I ride the big horse? P-please?" I asked.

"No, Pammy," Uncle Daniel said, "he's not a 'riding' horse, and there's a dangerous bull in the next pasture." I'd seen that big old bull with the ring through his snotty wet nose and I wanted to pet him. "It isn't safe," Uncle Daniel warned me.

I thought the bull looked gentle and safe enough. In fact, I was drawn to the bull partly because of the sweet copper smell of his nose ring. But I did what Uncle Daniel told me—most of the time.

When we got back to the farmhouse and the horses were grazing in the pasture, we went inside to have lunch. I finished eating quickly, and when the adults excused me from the table, I wandered over to the pasture fence and watched the horses munching on grass. I looked at the tallest draft horse, whom I called Big Horse. He was about twenty years old and very gentle. He was leaning up against the fence where I stood, and I reached my arm toward him and stroked his mottled gray and brown coat, and the white feathering on his legs. He leaned toward me, letting me touch the soft spot on his muzzle. I knew he was responding to me, and I was mesmerized by his hay-scented breath and his huge liquid eyes.

I started to climb the fence. I looked all around me. I was alone. The adults were still in the house, finishing lunch. I got to the top of the fence and Big Horse stood completely still. I lifted one leg carefully and threw it over his back. I looked around again. No one was coming. When Big Horse didn't move, I pulled myself all the way on top of his bare back, settled on him, let my other leg hang down, and grabbed hold of his mane. I was sitting astride him now, and I felt the warmth of his body and the energy shooting between us.

Big Horse took a step and then another as he rocked me gently from side to side. I had no fear of falling as I held on to his mane, feeling like I was soaring with each step that Big Horse took. Rocking from side to side with him, I was sailing through the sky as he glided slowly along. Then he turned his neck to look back at me, as if to say, "I'm gonna show you one of my favorite places." Entranced with the way Big Horse was moving underneath me, I let him walk me through the pasture and up a small rolling ridge. We passed the old bull, and I waved at him. He looked unimpressed as he swished his tail around, swatting away files. Hawks circled the hills, and wild turkeys and pheasants scratched at the ground, looking for food while a murder of jet-black crows called out their cawing sounds as they hunted their prey.

Big Horse walked over to a massive oak tree and stopped there beside a small pond. I was amazed when I looked into the water and saw my reflection—a tiny girl on top of a huge horse that stood at least eighteen hands. For anyone who doesn't know much about horses, that's really tall for any rider, let alone me, a six-year-old, who reached the horse's kneecaps when we stood side by side. And I had no saddle.

Big Horse leaned his head down slowly so I wouldn't fall off his back, and he took a long, cool drink from the livestock pond. I waited patiently on top of him. Then he walked a few steps to the shaded area under the tree and exhaled. Clearly, he was ready for a nap. But what about me? I looked as far back as I could see, but the fence was out of my view. How was I supposed to get off his back without a fence to hold on to?

Mr. Horse, I was thinking, *you really need to take me back to the fence. It's a very long way down to the ground.* He didn't read my mind, so there was nothing to do but wait while he napped. I leaned forward a little, rested my head on his soft neck, and began to doze right along with him. I was completely comfortable and must have been sleeping like that for fifteen minutes when I felt a pair of large hands grab me around my waist.

"Pammy, Pammy," called out Uncle Daniel and Daddy Ray, who had been searching for me on foot. "Are you okay?" Uncle Daniel lifted me up off the horse and put me safely back on the ground.

"I'm fine," I said. "Big Horse and I were taking a nap." I had just completed two full sentences without a stutter. It seemed that when I was with horses, I could speak clearly and directly. It was being away from them that perpetuated my speech problems.

Daniel led Big Horse beside us as we slowly walked back toward the farmhouse. "We've been looking everywhere for you," he said. "We didn't know what happened to you. You know better than taking off like that."

I didn't answer.

"I told you not to ride that horse, Pammy," Uncle Daniel scolded. "You could have fallen and hurt yourself badly."

They both continued to scold me as we walked across the field, but I didn't care. Riding Big Horse had made me ecstatic, and all I could think about was the next time I could get back up on his back. Daddy Ray and Uncle Daniel both fell silent, and we strolled quietly for a little while. Then Uncle Daniel asked me, "Were you scared up there, Pammy?"

"No. I wasn't scared." Then I got up my nerve to say, "Can I please ride him again? Please?"

It was not lost on him that I was speaking without a stutter, but I never expected Uncle Daniel's answer. "Well, since you weren't afraid, I'm going to give him to you."

I looked at him in disbelief. Did he just say Big Horse was mine? I searched Daddy Ray's face, but he wasn't saying anything.

"That means you have to take care of him," Uncle Daniel cautioned me. "You need to wash him, groom him, check his shoes, and feed him. Do you think you can you do that?"

"Yes, sir," I said.

There was no saddle for Big Horse since no one ever rode him because he was so huge. Daddy Ray and Uncle Daniel gave me a halter for him and they let me walk him and then ride him around the pasture, as long as an adult was overseeing. I washed him and groomed him, and I searched around for pop bottles for refunds to pay my share of Big Horse's food and care. At this point, my stuttering didn't show up when I was around the horse. He had healed me temporarily, and I only stuttered when we were back in Denver, mostly around the cousins who had attacked me. In fact, my stuttering flared intermittently when I was around angry boys and striped T-shirts, anything that triggered the nightmarish memories that forced my throat to close off and my speech patterns to scramble. I realized later that my stuttering had also flared when I was angry or wanting to defend myself but couldn't.

When we had reached the end of our two-year stay at Lowry Air Force Base in Denver, it was time to move again. I was relieved since so many bad things had happened during the past couple of years. Sometimes, being an army brat had its upside, like the move we were anticipating. We began to make plans to move to another town and another school and build new memories, but this time we were moving far, far away to another country and continent altogether—England.

While we packed up our clothing and got ready for our first cruise on a real ocean liner, I was enthusiastic and ready to start life all over again. When I went to say my good-byes on the day we were scheduled to take to the seas, I realized that so far, my short life had not been that kind to me. As we left the past behind and headed for new horizons, in the end, Uncle Daniel, Big Horse, and the big old bull with the wet ringed nose were all I would miss.

CHAPTER 5

A New Perspective

Bags packed? Check.

Immunity shots for overseas? Check.

Train tickets? Check.

Ocean liner reservations? Check.

Passports? Check.

Pammy and Rodney? Check.

It was 1956 when we piled into my grandfather's car and he dropped us at the train station in Denver amid tearful good-byes. Dad was already in England. As a military family, we were accustomed to saying good-bye, leaving places, and moving around the country, but we had never gone this far away. Now we were on the initial leg of the longest journey any of us had ever taken—first a train ride from Denver to New York City. Then we would cross the ocean on the USS *Darby*, a massive ocean liner, heading for England. Finally we would arrive in Swindon, an English market town adjacent to the air base where Dad was already working.

When we got off the train in New York and made our way over to the dock, I stared in awe at the huge smokestacks and the length of the massive ship that never seemed to end. I had been revved up all morning, asking if we were there yet, knowing we were heading for an exciting new world. But now, at seven years old, feeling dwarfed and insignificant beside the largest ship imaginable, I was terrified by the loud noises, the acrid smells of oil and smoke, and too many people shuffling around and shouting over each other. I was looking at the sloping gangplank and the murky blue waters between the boat and the dock, when my stomach lurched and I took off running down the dock. I was *not* getting on that ship.

Mom asked a few male passengers to run after me as she called out my name, ordering me to come back right now. I couldn't make my legs stop moving away from the boat until a man caught me. I freaked out, screaming, crying, and kicking as he handed me over to my mother. There was no way I would give in.

I tried to fight my mom, who grabbed both of my hands and started pulling me toward the USS *Darby*. I shrieked when we got to the gangplank and looked up to see my brother, already on the ship, waving down at me. I stood firm until my mom put her strong hand on my small back and pushed me up the ramp ahead of her while I screamed and cried like I was being led to my death.

When she finally got me safely on board and I stopped crying, I realized what had scared me so much. It wasn't the ship itself. It was the water between the ship and the dock. I was sure that if I walked up the gangplank, I would fall into the ocean and drown. But I'd made it, and there I stood, alive and breathing, ready to take off for Europe, which felt like a million miles away.

I can only imagine how exhausted my mom must have been when we finally got on board, between packing, getting us ready, and putting up with my tantrum. She went straight down for a nap, but as soon as we left the dock, I got a second wind. I was suddenly ecstatic being at sea, and I fell in love with the oily smell of the ship and the people there who took care of me. The crew treated my mom, my brother, and me with dignity and respect, even though we were the only blacks on the ship.

So while my mother and my brother were green faced and seasick the entire time, throwing up every day from sunup to sundown, I didn't get sick for a minute. Instead, I ran around the ocean liner, energized and feeling great, exploring the nooks and crannies of the USS *Darby*. I especially loved the library. I had never seen so many books in one place that I could access. And I loved talking with the stewards and the crew who came from all over the world and were eager to teach me anything I wanted to know.

I enjoyed the trip so much, I didn't want to disembark, a minor miracle compared with how I'd fought against boarding the boat three days earlier. We took the sixty-mile train ride from London to our new destination, Swindon, a suburb where we would be staying for the next two years, and I was fascinated by everything we saw. Eventually we clattered along a cobblestone street and stopped in front of a two-story brownstone at 101 Clifton Street, which was close to Swindon Air Base, where my dad was stationed. We had reached our new home, and Dad was there, waiting for us.

We threw our arms around him and began to explore our new digs. Mom had done her research, and Dad had rented the upper rooms of a duplex from our new landlady, Carrie Lofton, a sweet British woman who lived on the floor beneath us, and her husband. I was enchanted the moment I saw the flat, and we learned quickly, partly from how kindly Mrs. Lofton treated us, that American-style racial segregation was not an issue in our new home. We saw right away that Mrs. Lofton embraced all of us, and I will never forget her gentle nature and her consistent generosity.

There were fruit trees in her backyard, and the aroma of sweet apples wafting through the air became odd bedfellows with the musky odor of coal in this small market town. Early in the morning, when the sun was still rising, a horse-drawn wagon pulled a huge load of coal past our home. We had no hot water, so when we heard the bell and the clip-clop of the horse's hooves (the sounds reminded me of Big Horse), we ran outside and bought a couple of large lumps of coal for the day, which we put into the furnace to heat the house and give us hot water for bathing and cooking. Then we fed a shilling into a meter box in the house that would release the gas and electricity. When it stopped, we had to put in another shilling. It was a pay-as-you-go system that worked very well in this town.

In the afternoon, the same horse-drawn wagon returned, this time with exotic citrus fruits from Egypt, as well as dates and bananas. We also had a daily visit from a local vendor, a veritable farmer's market on wagon wheels, where everything was fresh and delicious, like potatoes, onions, leeks, and brussels sprouts that came straight from the earth. We had no refrigerators, but the air was so cold that we kept our fruit and dairy products on the window ledge, where they stayed fresh until we ate them.

Finally, a vendor pushed a large rolling cart of local fruits and vegetables as he called out, "Fresh tomatoes and lettuce," in his singsongy lilt. We would buy his wares, and we got fresh products from a nearby dairy. Back then, milk was packaged in thick, clear glass bottles with the cream sitting on top, and to me, it tasted like ambrosia.

When we took the double-decker bus to Piccadilly Circus in London, we got to eat fish and chips (my favorite) and drink American Coca-Cola as we visited bazaars where they sold imported fabrics and spices. Back home on Clifton Street, in our multiethnic neighborhood, I learned how to make authentic Russian borscht, cabbage rolls, and Polish sausages from scratch. On our street alone, there was our family and several families from the Mediterranean, as well as native Britons. However much our traditional diets varied, we all baked our own bread, and you could smell the aroma all the way up and down our street in the mornings. You could also smell fresh meats simmering in exotic spices. At mealtime, the various ethnic herbs and spices all blended together just like the people did. It was a generous lifestyle where everyone helped everyone else, regardless of color or race, and neighbors watched over each other's children like we were one big, happy family.

It was nothing short of a wonderful life for us. Mrs. Lofton, whom we adored, babysat when Mom went shopping. She loved to read books, so did I, and she taught Mom and me to knit and crochet. When we spent time together practicing my "knit two, purl two," Mrs. Lofton asked me a ton of questions about America, where she had never been. She was genuinely interested, and I loved talking about the family farm in Wyoming and the house in Denver but left out the painful parts of my life that I was still bound and determined to keep secret. I feared polluting the beauty and flow of my new life with bad memories and agonizing stories. Now that we were in Europe, so far away from my troubles, it felt like they had floated away—as if they never existed. I felt free and happy, with no desire to dredge up the past.

Even going to school felt better in England. Each morning, we enjoyed the charm of the holly-lined cobblestone streets that led to the village center, where the school marm stood outside a brick schoolhouse and rang a large brass bell to gather us all inside. On my first few days, I wore an expensive-looking dress that Mom had picked up for a song at a Goodwill store. The dress had a large bow in the back, and the other kids must have thought we were rich. But that ended when I got my school uniform the very next week, which was one more way of discouraging class prejudice or any other kind.

Every day at school, wearing a uniform that gratefully made me feel like everyone else, I concentrated on learning new things, like the metric system and other languages. They taught us about world history, math, and the English, Middle Eastern, South American, and European cultures that were merging. When your neighbors are uniquely separate European countries rather than interconnected American states, there is an opportunity to experience life from a variety of cultural points of view.

School was not the only place that offered lessons. When we drove through the countryside, we got to see the consequences of World War II right in our own backyard. Evidence of violence and destruction were everywhere. I saw areas that had been utterly destroyed by bombs, and people rebuilding their broken worlds with integrity and respect for each other. London was close to flattened after the war, and there were signs of ruin and destruction everywhere we went. I learned at a young age, by seeing it with my own eyes, what a war could do to people, their families, their culture, and their homes.

When I met my dad in Germany or France during those two extraordinary years, I saw it there, too, where people were exerting tremendous efforts to rebuild. This was a large dose of international politics for a young girl, and I came away with understanding and feelings that were well beyond my years. In the meantime, my mom and Mrs. Lofton educated us kids about Nazism, socialism, and Communism. I was now a member of a global society where war-torn countries were visibly struggling to rebuild their land and their communities.

But if you think these people were depressed, discouraged, or complaining, it was quite the opposite. It was a testament to the human spirit to see my mom and Mrs. Lofton dancing in the living room to American music by artists like Patti Page, Fats Domino, and Nat King Cole. Mrs. Lofton often invited a group of women over to knit and dance, and my mom and I showed them all the latest dance steps. A seed of cultural creativity was sprouting that had begun in America and had crossed the ocean, where it was slowly opening into full bloom.

Mrs. Lofton's friends loved Americans and our music, and nearly every afternoon there was a dance-a-thon in our landlady's living room. The ladies, always feminine and conservative, wore long skirts, hand-knitted or crocheted cardigans, and shirtdresses that were popular at the time, with a full skirt and a big pleat in the back. In winter, they wore rusts and browns, and in summer blues and pastels. But whatever the weather, they wore crisply starched white blouses with long sleeves.

As they danced around in their hand-knitted socks and their high-heeled pumps, they imagined what it would be like to go to an American record shop where they could buy their favorite music, like Ella Fitzgerald, Duke Ellington, the blues, and the boogie-woogie. Then we'd have crumpets and tea with clotted cream, orange marmalade, and freshly churned butter.

These women impacted me deeply. I watched them having a ball and cooking dinner together while they danced and laughed. I listened carefully as they carried on deep discussions about power struggles between the genders and how to survive the oppressive and aggressive ways of their mining and military husbands when they got home from a grueling day's work. They all agreed with my mom that getting an education made all the difference in the world for a woman. The women's movement was expanding globally, while these women discussed the care and feeding of their hardworking husbands, which usually started with giving them a tall glass of ale before they talked about anything. Or sometimes the men joined their mates at a local pub.

At school, I learned to play cricket while I taught the British kids how to play double Dutch jump rope and baseball. Though somewhat shy, I felt more secure than back in Denver because no one persecuted me here, and I hardly stuttered at all. But I was disappointed to see what was happening to Heidi, a white friend of mine from Norway, who was relentlessly pushed around by the other kids.

It broke my heart when they beat her up, which they did as often as they could get away with it. Heidi was a smart and proud young girl, and I started sticking up for her and tried to make the kids stop hurting her. Sometimes I even fought for her. How could I not when I'd been in her position so many times?

"You're my only real friend," she said to me when we were alone. "You stand up for me."

"I just don't get it," I told her. "You're white and so are they. Why on earth would they want to fight with you?"

"It's my name. They think I'm German."

"What's wrong with being German?" I asked.

"They think all Germans are Nazis."

Once again, prejudice was rearing its ugly head at school, but this time, not at me. They didn't care that I was black since they hadn't been raised to hate blacks. Instead they'd been raised to hate Germans. The irony was that Heidi was Norwegian, not German. But because her name sounded German, she became a target for the kids' cruelty, the token "nigger" on the block. I learned that day that prejudice went beyond color, and I felt a deep connection to and compassion for Heidi.

She wanted to know why we Americans had so much racism, lynching, and violence. I had no idea how to answer her. It seemed to me that wherever minorities lived, they were held in contempt by others who feared anything different. It was difficult to assimilate into a new culture if everyone pushed you out when all you wanted was to fit in. The human race had a long way to go in this regard; people flocked to their own and were suspicious of those who looked, spoke, thought, or acted differently.

In the end, our time in England was valuable on multiple levels. The school system was superior to the public schools in Colorado, and my brother and I both advanced academically. I learned the metric system and other languages, and our school uniforms created a feeling of connectedness among kids of different cultures and moved us away from flaunting our class differences.

Maybe the best part of all was that my dad did not have to face the American stereotypical "black man" prejudice. With so much newfound acceptance and freedom in our lives, it felt like the bar had been raised and we could create a wonderful life for ourselves with brand-new opportunities and loads of encouragement. When people are urged to reach higher, we usually do so, and if you expect more from people, we will most likely give it to you. All we really need is an open door and some help along the way.

CHAPTER **6**   # Home Strife

Although I loved Swindon, I wasn't unhappy when it was time to return home. My family had been moving every two years since I was a baby, so I'd learned to accept my present environment, wherever we were, and then make the best of moving on. Now, at eight years old, I had more courage than I'd had before our stay in Europe and a lot more understanding about life in general. Not only did I see things and meet people in England that changed my world view, but it was also powerfully liberating to not be condemned and insulted at every turn, just for being born with dark skin.

When we returned to the States, we went straight to Denver for a brief visit, where we reconnected with family and told our amazing stories of life on another continent. We talked until we could hardly speak anymore, and we had so many tales to tell we constantly interrupted one another. We spoke so fast and told so many stories at once, Ebonics was like the Queen's English compared with how my family talked when we were revved up. We described Mrs. Lofton, the dancing, our neighbors, the war-torn streets, the wonderful schools, and the sense of being accepted everywhere. Our stories sounded like fairy tales to the rest of the family, and they couldn't hear enough about our European adventure. I had even come back with a slight

British accent, and they never stopped making fun of me.

Then we were off to Travis Air Force Base in California, where I enrolled in the third grade. I'd been so welcomed in England, I had erased all memories of racial prejudice—until I was back in the States, where I quickly remembered, whether I wanted to or not. As I worked to reassimilate into school, I tried to stay on target by concentrating on my studies, but it seemed that the school system was not my friend. My mother was enraged when I was forced to go to remedial reading classes, not because I was bad at reading. Quite the opposite. I was way ahead of my age group since our stay in Swindon, and they should have skipped me a year forward. Instead, all the blacks were thrown together in remedial classrooms with no books for the students to take home. That meant that the teacher had to read to us in the class-room. Then, when we got home, since there were no books, we had no homework and very little opportunity to learn and grow.

Mom constantly had to fight for me as she advanced in her nursing studies. The old sense of struggling against impossible odds was back, and although my life so far had taught me not to waste time missing people and things, I have to say that I missed the ease of my English school, the lack of competitiveness, the constant mental stimulation, and the dance parties, and I really missed Mrs. Lofton. When her letters came, Mom and I read them aloud over and over, but we had to keep looking and moving forward.

I spent the rest of the year running track, which I liked, and refusing to talk, which I hated. Even the gym teacher had trouble getting me to open up. But I found solace when a friend gave us a sweet little cocker spaniel puppy named Spooky. I loved that little dog so much, and he transformed me, as I became happier and more outgoing the longer I took care of him. The thing was, I had no idea how to train him. One day, after he tore up a brand-new chair with his teeth, my dad decided there was no room for the dog in our home any longer. Instead of looking for a family to adopt him, he abandoned Spooky in a field and drove away with me in the car.

I sobbed my heart out and yelled at him. "You're m-m-ean," I accused him.

"Stop crying, Pammy," Dad said to me, looking annoyed. "He's a dog. He can take care of himself just fine."

"But I'll miss him. What if he dies? What if no one finds him or feeds him?"

How would he eat, and where would he sleep? Dad obviously didn't care, and I was so traumatized and angry at him, I refused to speak to him. Mom tried to explain that Dad was on edge since he was about to retire and he didn't know what he would do next, but I stayed mad. In fact, I was so traumatized about losing Spooky, I started wetting the bed, which was humiliating for a girl of ten.

Mom had a lot on her hands then as she and Dad argued pretty regularly while she kept up her nursing studies. But when she suddenly announced she was pregnant again, she was set on us owning a home of our own in Denver. Dad suggested that when Mom got close to her due date, we could move to another base nearby with more up-to-date birthing facilities and better living conditions than at Travis. But Mom was determined to have her baby in Denver with her family around her, and she wanted to find us a permanent residence there.

She didn't make it back in time for Gina to be born, but soon afterward, she took us three kids to Denver to find a house. When Dad retired, she wanted him to come home to a wonderful place that was all ours where he could get his bearings and plan for the next part of his life.

I fantasized about having our own home just like Mom did, but when we went to Denver to house hunt, we had to stay with Marky and Daddy Ray. Not only did I miss Spooky, but now I had to live with Marky again, who still resented me because of the beer incident so many years earlier. I think she blamed me for turning her husband against her, and she never forgave me. But Marky eventually came through for us when she offered my mother a loan to buy a home in Denver. Whether it was a gift from the heart or a way to get us to move out of her place, I'm not entirely sure. I only know Mom was thrilled.

So while Dad stayed at Travis to complete his military work, my mom, my brother, my baby sister, and I stayed in Denver. In a matter of a few weeks, with a combination of her work money and the loan from Marky, Mom found us a beautiful tri-level brick home on Eudora Street in a lovely neighborhood on the east side of Denver.

This was about a year before the assassination of JFK. Though on the surface there seemed to be calm, underneath, politics and civil rights were reaching a boiling point. For example, that year a riot occurred on the campus of the University of Mississippi in Oxford because of desegregation. Two people were killed and at least seventy-five were injured. Hundreds of troops were brought in to join federal forces already stationed in Oxford as the violence spread to its streets.

As a result of this and other desegregation efforts, many neighborhoods across the country became victims of "white flight," including our little neighborhood. Whites left in droves when blacks started purchasing the houses next door. Remember the old expression "There goes the neighborhood"? White people who previously loved their neighborhoods were selling their homes at rock-bottom prices and moving elsewhere, which allowed us to move in. Add to that the case of *Brown v. Board of Education*, in which segregation in schools was made illegal, and now we were also facing the controversial issue of busing, as it was being implemented for the first time. The foundation that we had hoped to build in our peaceful little neighborhood was now a bubbling well of political unrest.

Although Dad sent us money each month, sometimes the envelope contained as little as five dollars. Mom never complained. She was a real Buddhist in that way, accepting things as they were, rejecting the idea that if the man of the house didn't bring home the bacon, the whole family would starve. Rather, she embraced a new school of thought, the women's movement, where you earned the bacon yourself if need be, you protected your family, covered for your husband any way you could, and you did your best never to flaunt that in his face. Mom wanted Dad to have the luxury of retiring to a lovely new home with his family all around him. She didn't care that she had to work the graveyard shift in the hospital ER at the University of Colorado in Denver to keep up the payments.

When Dad finally retired and arrived in Denver, he had never seen our new home. Mom had told him it was gorgeous, brick, tri-level, with lots of bedrooms and land, but he was stunned. I don't know what he was expecting when the taxi pulled up, but he told the driver, "Please wait here. This can't be the right place."

The taxi idled while Dad rang the bell. He knew how little money he'd been sending home and that we could never afford a house this nice. But sure enough, there we all were, throwing our arms around him as we welcomed him to his new life. Mom never asked why he had sent so little money. She avoided battling with him or reprimanding him. Instead, she greeted him with open arms and proudly showed him the big, beautiful kitchen, the brand-new carpeting, the new glass table in the dining room, and the stereo system, with everything freshly cleaned and painted. It was our dream home, and we were ecstatic when Marky told Mom she didn't have to pay back the loan. She and Daddy Ray had not sent Mom to college like they did her sister (who drank her way through school) because they had had no money at the time, so this was how they intended to make up for it.

Dad slowly tried to adjust to his retirement, working the land with his friend, gardener-landscaper Hank. The grass in front of our home was like a soft green carpet, and I loved lying down on it and staring up at the clouds. Quite a few Korean families had moved into the neighborhood, since they were worldly and accustomed to living around people who were different. Their homes and yards were magnificent and so were those of the Japanese families who owned the landscaping companies. In this way, our block reminded me of our life in Swindon, where people from diverse ethnic backgrounds were living harmoniously and helping each other.

While Mom continued to work the night shift at the ER, Dad was like a lost soul. If he could have passed a simple test, he could have worked for good money in a nearby military finance center as an administrator, a common job for a retiree. But Dad didn't follow through, since he was so ill-prepared to be a civilian. I tried not to judge him. Mom said, "People are who they are, and I guess being a financial administrator is not right for your father."

Mom wanted Dad to be the best man he could be and to find his way, no matter how long it took. But the reality of life made her goad him gently. "I don't mean to push," she said, "but we have three growing children now who all get hungry. We have a home where we can settle and get them ready for college. That was our dream for our kids. Remember? All these opportunities are opening for people with better educations these days. Getting an education is the only way our children will ever earn the respect they deserve. You really need to work now so we can give them what they need."

A long time passed in this way, while Dad considered going to work for the post office. Government jobs paid well, and many military retirees took those jobs. But he was not drawn to that, either. As he tried to build a new life for himself and floundered, the guilt was eating him alive. It didn't help when his friends said, "Hey, man, that's some house you bought your family."

"I didn't buy it," he said. It was a bitter pill to swallow and to talk about. A military man through and through, Dad couldn't accept his wife making more money than he did. Mom had encouraged him to take the officer training course so he could get that finance job, even if it was only for a little while, but he had no confidence in himself.

"Clarence," Mom said, "you're very intelligent. No one ever tells you that, but I know you are. You can do anything you want if you put your mind to it." Dad loved aeronautics more than anything, and he desperately wanted to remain working in that field, but his racial identity, once again, was making it impossible.

Mom did not get through to him, partly due to his stubbornness and partly because she had no skills to communicate such sensitive issues with the right kind of tact and gentleness. She must have scared him and made him feel inferior because she was so scared herself. Soon, their bickering escalated into full-blown shouting matches, which they tried to confine to times when we kids were in school. But when their rage and resentments got out of hand, we often took my little sister, Gina, next door so she wouldn't have to hear their screaming and name-calling.

❀

One afternoon when I was about thirteen, I came home from school to hear my parents going at each other from inside their bedroom. I was tiptoeing down the hall, trying to get to my room before they saw me, when Mom ran into the hallway, a look of deep pain contorting her face. I stepped close to their bedroom door and looked in. Dad was packing a suitcase.

"Where you goin', Dad?" I asked, suddenly frightened.

He looked at me with rage in his eyes. "I'm moving," he said, "and you're never gonna see me again."

I fell to the floor, sobbing, as Mom tried to calm me. "He doesn't mean it," she said, holding me. "He loves you. Of course you'll see him again."

"He just said I wouldn't," I said through my sobs. "Where is he going? Why is he leaving us? What did I do?"

About twenty minutes later, Dad stomped out of the house, carrying his suitcase. I remember sitting on the bed with Mom and two-year-old Gina, all three of us crying. Although they still loved each other, Mom and Dad could not resolve their issues because of the terrible things they had said to each other in the heat of anger.

Dad never moved back home again. He went to live with a roommate in an apartment, and he finally took a job working at the post office. We kids hoped Mom and Dad would make up and at least become friends, but that didn't happen. There was very little family therapy available back then and no books or TV shows with advice on how to communicate with the opposite sex. Mom and Dad had no idea how to mend their wounds enough to get back together and start over. Or to be friends. And so we all chipped in as best we could to make ends meet and deal with the sudden blow of losing our hero: our father.

CHAPTER **7**

Going Gospel

We were on our own now, and when we needed help, Mom had to call on our neighbor Hank. Or we went to the hardware store and tried to fix things ourselves. Mom had let Dad go without demanding much money from him. She figured she was making more money than he was and we kids could chip in as well. But the less Mom called on him, the less he showed up, until we rarely saw him, if ever. Maybe he couldn't face us. Maybe he was ashamed and embarrassed. Whatever the reason, he was moving on, dating other women, and making himself scarce among us kids.

It was disappointing that my years at school in Denver were laden with the same old prejudice and judgments from the past, and sometimes I got into fights with the other kids. I never provoked anyone or started the fights myself, but my deep silence scared people, and sometimes they became aggressive to get a rise out of me. One particular fight stands out. The irony of it was that I'd never met the girl named Christine who supposedly sent a message through a friend, Gail, that she would "see" me in the school yard when class was over.

"Who?" I said. I was feeling tense and anxious.

"Christine."

"I never even heard of her. What does she think I did?" I asked.

"Well, you must have done something," Gail said. "She's really upset."

When I arrived at the school yard to see what was going on, sure enough, there stood a tall, big-boned blonde girl I'd never met, waiting for me. Apparently, it was Christine, and she looked mad as hell. This had to be some kind of mistake, so I tried to nip it in the bud. I walked right up to her and said, "I don't know what I did, but I apologize. I don't know you, and I have no idea what's going on."

In response, she shoved me hard, knocking my books out of my hands. She wanted to fight. I couldn't believe it. Who the hell *was* she, and what did she have against me? The other kids pushed us toward each other and egged us on, forming a circle around us as we began to exchange blows. Suddenly, it was white against black, and Christine, completely deranged and angry, started circling her arms round and round like a windmill. The principal and a few teachers heard the sounds, but they couldn't get through the tight circle of kids that were keeping us barricaded.

I had studied karate and jiu-jitsu at one of our military bases, so when I saw that she was mentally losing it, I used my training to put an end to the fight with one shot to Christine's side. I took her down, and for a moment I thought I'd killed her. I guess there had been plenty of rage behind my punch. But she began to stir as the crowd dispersed and the adults came running in. We both got into trouble, but everyone had seen her start the fight by shoving me.

Later, Christine and I realized that we both had been victims of our peers, who had manipulated and provoked us so the could watch us fight. We had nothing against each other, and we became friends for a while, based on the fact that someone had wanted to see me beat her up, aware that she had no fighting skills at all. Unfortunately, these were the mean pranks that junior high school kids liked to play on each other. But I refused to act in ways that were destructive to my own race. I was trying to remember the things that many of us had forgotten along the way: Everyone deserves respect, and fighting is not the way to achieve it.

❧

As if Mom were not being tested enough as sole head of a growing family, shortly after Dad and Mom separated, Aunt Mennon's three kids moved in. Mennon was drinking and partying so hard her kids had no supervision, and they came over to our house one day in tears. Mom would've been justified in explaining to them that she was in over her head already, that her husband had left her and she was working overtime. But that was not her way.

"You move in with us," she told my cousins. "I have a big house, and I can do this. I know I can. You're my nieces and nephews, and if everyone does their share, we can get through this together."

We got bunk beds to accommodate three more kids, and I happily moved my cousin Krista into my room. From that day on, she was my sister, not my cousin. I also began to do some lawn jobs with some of my other cousins and my brother. Or I would babysit. I did anything I could to be able to contribute to the family bills. My oldest cousin, Raymond, became man of the house. He did the repairs my father used to do, and we all kept the place immaculate and cooked great meals for Mom when she got home from work. She didn't have to lift a finger around the house, and we always had a flourishing garden of fresh vegetables and a ton of love. More than enough to go around.

It was a good thing that Mom could rest when she got home, because she was completely torn apart by the divorce. I know she had some sleepless nights, and so did I. But my cousins moving in with us helped to distract us both. Mom had never been one to sit around and feel sorry for herself. She said soon after the cousins moved in, "I don't have any more time or energy to cry every night over my husband. I have to feed and clothe all these kids."

Sometimes there were eight of us (including a few friends) gathered around our dining room table, eating spaghetti and venison. When my mom would take Krista to buy a new sweater, in the spirit of cooperation, Krista would ask me what color I liked so we could share it. During this time, Mom worked her butt off at the hospital and raising us kids. I can see now that she was the role model I used for the industrious nurse in my movie *Coffy*.

In the meantime, Aunt Mennon was my character in *Foxy Brown*, a wild and uncontrollable woman with a lot of rage. Mennon resented the fact that her kids were safer and happier in our house than in hers, and one night, when she was drunk out of her mind, she tried to tear the front door of our house off the hinges. A few days later, when I got home from school, I heard Mennon and Krista in the bedroom that we shared, shouting at each other. Apparently Mennon had staggered over to our house, full of gin, and tried to get her kids to come home. She had only her daughter Becky, who was still young, left with her. "Who's going to watch Becky for me when I need to go out?" was Mennon's argument—not a very alluring or convincing one for her kids.

When I rushed upstairs and opened the bedroom door, Krista and Mennon were physically duking it out. The room was in shambles, the closet was torn apart, clothing was strewn everywhere, and blood was dripping down Krista's blouse. I ran to alert Raymond, who had just gotten home from his road construction job. He flew into the room and pulled them apart like they were wild dogs. Then he guided his own intoxicated mother down the stairs and out the door, and he locked it behind her. She shrieked obscenities before she staggered away, and that was the last time Mennon was ever allowed in our home.

❈

I tried not to be angry at my dad for leaving us with so much trouble, but the longer he was gone, the more shy I became. Mom hoped that involving me in music and dance would help—that is, until racial prejudice reared its ugly head once again. It didn't take long for me to realize that strangers in a foreign country had treated me better than my fellow Americans did.

For example, I tried to take riding lessons, but the equestrian center treated us like the hired help. Literally. When Mom and I entered the front door of the riding school, the barn director thought we were there to clean out the stables, and he directed us to a back entrance.

"No, no. I'm here to sign up my daughter for riding lessons," said Mom, trying to stay calm.

The barn director looked amused. "The class is completely filled up," he said out of the corner of his mouth.

We walked away discouraged. We knew that he was lying. There was always room for one more student in the equestrian world.

Mom and I continued our uphill battle against racial rigidity to find some diversions for me. It was more of the same. When I tried to take dancing lessons, the teacher discriminated against us and refused to let me join the dance academy. The same thing happened with the music academy. I already knew more about music than all the other kids my age. At seven years old, I'd studied the fundamentals of classical music in England, and we'd compared the excellence of top jazz musicians like John Coltrane to the sounds of contemporary classical artists.

Still, the music teacher told my mother in hushed tones that she'd love to teach me, but the other parents would withdraw their kids. We were discouraged and might have given up if one amazing woman had not stepped forward on my behalf. A German piano teacher from school, Mrs. Heinemann, approached my mom when she heard I'd been turned away. "I'll give your daughter private lessons at home if you can get hold of a piano," she offered.

Mom and I smiled ear to ear. My grandfather had a piano in his house because he moonlighted as a drummer and bassist with a popular Polynesian band to supplement his income. The group met at his place to practice, so he had all the instruments there.

"When can I start?" I asked excitedly.

A few afternoons later, Mrs. Heinemann, her long, soft gray hair pulled back in a bun, arrived at my grandfather's house with a stack of sheet music in her wonderful old beaten-up leather briefcase. She placed her cane against the wall and we got to work. After I'd done my exercises, she played for me, and the neighbors would all sit out on their front porches to listen. It seemed that she'd dreamed of joining a symphony orchestra—she was a superior musician—but her husband had prevented it. Maybe between Germany suffering its own share of prejudice and her husband keeping her on a tight rein, Mrs. Heinemann understood how it felt to be judged and left out.

For whatever reason, once a week like clockwork, cane in hand, she took the bus from the white side of town to the black side to teach me. When it started to get dark early, my grandfather drove her home so she didn't have to take public transportation at night in an all-black neighborhood.

In June, when the kids from school were having their end-of-the-year recital, Mrs. Heinemann talked to the school principal about letting me take part. "She's a really good student," she coaxed. She had her personal motives for wanting me to participate because she was so proud of my progress around so many obstacles. But he wouldn't budge, afraid of angering and distancing the other parents.

"It doesn't matter," Mrs. Heinemann told me. "You play very well, and you're going to be a great musician one day." She was angry, but she tried to make the recital seem unimportant, which I really appreciated.

As we continued to search for ways to make my life fuller, we heard about a black family, the Ryans, who lived just down the street and whose six kids sang like a choir of angels. They played the piano, too, with no formal lessons, and when we met them, they told us about a fantastic choir leader in their church.

During that era, a large gospel movement was spreading like a welcome epidemic. It was no surprise to see the likes of Billy Preston hanging out in Reverend James Cleveland's church. A gospel singer and arranger born in 1931, James Cleveland was the driving force behind the creation of modern gospel. In fact, he was the first man to go beyond the basic gospel sound and break it down into classical harmony and melody components that unveiled and invited in a whole new level of consciousness. The tones reached peoples' hearts and bolstered them with enough faith to believe in themselves.

Reverend Cleveland was a role model for civil rights because he paid no attention to the color of a musician's skin. White, black, yellow, pink, or green, he didn't care. He refused to let other people define him and tell him whether he had value. While racial prejudice still hung heavy, the first seeds of integration and color-blindness were also in the air, especially in the area of the arts. When we heard Reverend Cleveland sing, it felt like Jesus himself had opened his mouth, and we all raised our voices to join him.

When Mom took my brother and me to the red stone church that the six talented Ryan kids attended, we couldn't believe our eyes or ears. When the praying started, so did a whole lot of rocking, thumping, tribal chanting, and dancing. Everyone was on their feet, playing instruments like drums and bass guitars, belting out songs from two of the most well-known gospel quartets, the Mighty Clouds of Joy and the Blind Boys of Alabama. When they played, I couldn't breathe or speak, I was so moved. I would give anything to be a part of the choir.

And they accepted me immediately. The founders, Mr. and Mrs. Ryan, had started the choir, and when one particular son, Eugene, sang, you could fall to your knees and weep, his voice was so heavenly. Mrs. Ryan was giving the neighborhood kids something to do with their after-school time, helping them find themselves, and giving them purpose. Any child of any color or gender could join, even if they had no voice. But the rules were clear: If you disobeyed the leaders at any time, you were out. If you were late, you were out until you brought a parent to make a decent excuse. In this way, potential problems were nipped in the bud, because no one wanted to be asked to leave the choir, it was such a fantastic place to be. We had minimum discipline problems, and anyone who created havoc or didn't listen to the adults was immediately let go.

There was so much talent in that choir, almost every kid in the city of Denver, if not in the state of Colorado, wanted to be part of it. Black kids, that is. The white kids were free to join, but we had very few because if they sang with us, the community would call their parents "nigger lovers."

That didn't stop them, however, from inviting us to sing at their white churches. In fact, every church in the state wanted us, and they gave us a 10 percent tithe from their collection baskets. We kids were amazed at how much money we started taking in, and our directors were ecstatic. Hayward Hobbs, our music director, did our arrangements and could play any instrument and all kinds of music: classical, jazz, blues, gospel. Mr. Ryan, our founder, used our tithing money to buy us burgundy choral robes, with yellow sashes to complete our costumes. And soon, since we were invited to sing at so many churches, both in and out of state, I'd heard that Mr. Ryan mortgaged his house to buy us our own 1954 Greyhound touring bus.

We could hardly believe our luck when an invitation arrived from California—one that would help shape my view of the world forever after. I remember the Ryan kids and me cheering when we were told that we would be traveling in our trusty bus all the way from Denver to Southern California. It was the summer of 1965, and we'd been invited to the towns of Compton and Watts to perform in several of their churches.

When we arrived in Los Angeles after a day and a half of driving, we were road weary and checked into a residential part of a church in Bellflower. There we basked in the Southern California sunshine and we prepared for our performances by pressing our robes, doing our hair, and rehearsing some of our songs. We wanted to be at our absolute best since we were booked at some of the finest churches in the city, with choirs that were so outstanding, they were already known around the world. We could not have been more excited.

After a good night's sleep, we spent our first day in Compton singing in churches ranging from huge and upscale in wealthy neighborhoods to slightly smaller churches in lower-income neighborhoods. We were surprised at the Spanish architectural influence, which we had never seen before, and our trip was an eye-opener architecturally, socially, and politically. We were received with so much love and respect that the tithing baskets were passed several times and we were making more money than we ever imagined. Now we could upgrade our transportation, clothing, and our dreams for the future of our group. We remained dedicated to the initial goal of the choir— keeping kids off the streets.

Then, on August 11, 1965, as our bus was entering Watts for our next group of performances, something happened that would rock the city to its core. Los Angeles police officer Lee Minikus, a white

California Highway Patrol motorcycle cop, pulled over Marquette Frye, a black man, in the Watts area, the heart of the black 'hood. Officer Minikus thought Mr. Frye was intoxicated due to his erratic driving, so he stopped him. When Frye failed two separate sobriety tests—walking a straight line and touching his nose with a specific finger—Minikus called for a squad car backup, and the black man was arrested.

Frye's brother, Ronald, and his mother had been in the car with him, but Minikus refused to allow Ronald or the mom to drive the car home. Instead, he radioed for it to be impounded, leaving Frye's family to fend for themselves. When Marquette and Ronald began to argue with Minikus about the car, a group formed around them, swiftly swelling into a crowd of more than a hundred people. When the cop started shoving Frye around, the witnesses became an angry mob, shouting obscenities and throwing rocks at the police officers. Amid this riotous struggle, Frye, his brother, and their mother were all arrested.

Our bus was heading into Watts as the police drove the family away in their squad car, its lights flashing. The cops had figured everyone would disperse and go on with their day, but the incident was only beginning. Community rage had been triggered, and for nearly a week, Watts broke out into full-scale race riots.

We couldn't have timed it better if we'd planned it, as if anyone would plan such a thing. It just so happened that as we turned onto the main drag of Watts, heading for one of the churches where we were scheduled to perform, shots were fired at our bus. We'd planned to stay in nearby Bellflower, but as the gunshots zinged by our bus, just missing the windows, we were not about to keep driving. We were literally stranded in Watts during the most bloody California street riot in history.

Police in riot gear blocked the streets and we were rushed to a parishioner's apartment. All forty of us stayed in two apartments for the next several days, camped out all over the floor.

We heard the gunshots.

We saw the helicopters.

We breathed the smoke.

We were terrified, our eyes like saucers, wishing to be anywhere else.

Obviously, our performances were canceled as we worked to scrape together enough money to pay for the gas to get home. But we still had to wait until it was safe enough to get back on the road. When the blood and dust settled seven days later, 34 people were dead, 1,032 were injured, and 3,952 people, mostly black, were arrested. It was the worst riot the city had ever seen to date, and we were there.

When I think back, I realize that we spent the first day performing and the next few days dodging bullets. We'd been gone about five days, and once we headed for home, all of us were a little wiser for the wear. As terrifying as the experience was, I feel lucky to have been there and lived through it. It helped me find the courage to venture out into the world where people, cultures, and languages were different. Whether it was Watts or Swindon, I was getting a universal kind of education that was not and never would be available in schools or in books. If you're so frightened of the great big world out there that you refuse to explore and learn about it, then you're limiting your experience and living only half of a life.

Thank you for your support!
Go to: www.epj.org\donate
Buy books, CDs, and DVDs.
Help the Evanston Library
Donate to fund for Excellence

Current time: 11\15\2017, 20:53
Call number: B Crick,p Crick,p [15]
Item ID: 31182014289250
Author: Crick, Pam, 1949-
Title: Foxy : my life in three acts
Date due: 12\13\2017, 23:59

Current time: 11\15\2017, 20:53
Call number: 302.8 Robel,D
Item ID: 31182020923813
Author: Roberts, Dorothy,
Lics, and old
Title: Fatal invention : how science, pol
Date due: 12\13\2017, 23:59

Visit www.epj.org
Sign up for email notices,
Phone renewal 847-550-8108
Evanston Public Library

Date due: 12/13/2017,23:59
Title: Fatal invention : how science, poli
tics, and big
Author: Roberts, Dorothy.
Item ID: 31192020637813
Call number: 305.8 Rober.D
Current time: 11/15/2017,20:53

Date due: 12/13/2017,23:59
Title: Foxy : my life in three acts
Author: Grier, Pam, 1949-
Item ID: 31192014589210
Call number: B Grier.P Grier.P
Current time: 11/15/2017,20:53

CHAPTER **8**   # Beauty and the Beast

found a verse in the Jewish Talmud that is very special to me:

Every blade of grass has an angel that bends over it and whispers, "Grow, grow."

In the face of trouble, I remember that verse, which was my mantra all through high school, even when Mom and I discovered that making ends meet on our own was next to impossible. I would invoke the angels and continue to grow, grow, grow, no matter the obstacles I encountered along the way.

My stuttering was long gone when I enrolled at Metropolitan State College, an independent accredited city college. There, I was premed, studying psychology and sociology with the dream of becoming an anesthesiologist or a veterinarian. I wanted to go to an East Coast college as soon as I graduated high school, but I couldn't afford it yet. This would do in the meantime.

Then I got several jobs so I could help build my college fund, working at things like ironing clothes, babysitting, receptionist jobs, and anything else I could find. While I focused on studying psychology and sociology, I vented my frustration by riding my bike and running.

My family called me the "filly," as I raced around town on my thin little racehorse legs with my ponytail waving behind me. I was on the move, running, studying, and always looking for better-paying jobs, such as becoming the receptionist at the KHOW radio station office, which was close to my school campus.

I showed up at the radio station every day. By the time I was eighteen, I was still quiet, but people told me I was very pretty, whatever that meant. I had little awareness of my own beauty, but my hair was healthy and long and my looks were exotic, since I was multiracial. I guess I knew I was pretty because men were drawn to me. But inside, I felt unworthy of the attention and I feared it much more than I appreciated it. Pretty was dangerous. I had learned that early on. And now it confused me.

I had women friends who were much darker skinned than I was. They had noses that were more ethnic, full African-style lips, and they were not considered beautiful in the mainstream world. I didn't get it. My cousin/adopted sister, Krista, was called a "high yellow" girl, which meant her skin was not that dark, and she was called "pretty." What about the darker girls? I thought they were pretty, too, and I didn't want to get compliments if they didn't, which made me even more shy when guys got crushes on me.

I pretended not to notice them as I went to Metropolitan State, worked my jobs, and helped take care of the house and of Mom. The good news was that Mom was making friends with an Air Force captain named Edward Samuels. I guess it was about three years after Dad left when this well-educated, soft-spoken, kind and loving man we called Sam started to become a familiar and welcome sight in our home.

A tall, handsome African American man with processed straight hair and a profound love of family, Sam was encouraging and loving, and he believed women could do most everything men could do. He thought they just needed to be "feminine" about it, which made sense to me. He bought us a German shepherd puppy, which helped heal my old wounds from abandoning Spooky, and he let me get a white bunny named Seymour, who slept on my bed with me. He and Mom pleaded with me to keep the bunny in the cage, but I didn't follow their directions. He told me, "If you want a bunny, you can have it, Pam, as long as you clean up after it," and I agreed.

He absolutely adored my mother, and when she became ill and needed a hysterectomy, he took care of her and kept up the house while she recuperated. It would be a few more years before they would marry, but in the meantime, Papa Sam (that's what we called him when he was happy) became Mom's friend and constant companion and we loved him. So did the neighbors. A strict disciplinarian, Captain Crunch (that's what we called him when he was angry) helped us through the next phase of our lives and was a communicative partner for my mom. Of course they had disagreements. All couples do. But he hung in there and was willing to work things out. That was great for my mom, and it was also valuable for us kids to see adults staying cool and handling their differences with respect instead of calling each other names and running away in a heated rage.

We missed Dad, but he had remarried and we only saw him when we attended funerals or other family functions. He had a new wife and family now, and Mom suggested we stay away so his wife wouldn't feel uncomfortable.

I did what I was told, focusing on school and work—until one day someone at the radio station made a pivotal suggestion.

I had just turned eighteen when a disc jockey at KHOW approached me at my reception desk. He said, "Pam, you know you're really pretty."

"Thank you," I said dismissively. I didn't like being called "pretty," and I went on with my work.

"You should enter the Miss KHOW Beauty Contest," he went on. "I bet you'd win."

He was referring to a beauty pageant the radio station was holding to name a Miss KHOW for publicity purposes.

"Right," I said, laughing.

"I'm not kidding, Pam," the DJ said. "You can win money for school." Everyone knew I was obsessed with making money so I could get into a great college.

"How much?" I asked, suddenly interested.

"Enough to help you out," he said. "About a hundred bucks, I think."

"I don't even know how to put on makeup."

"The people in the beauty pageant do your makeup," he told me. "They give you false eyelashes and they do your hair."

The employees from my second job, at Mac's Record Rack, also encouraged me to compete for Miss KHOW.

I can't begin to tell you how terrified I was to enter that contest. My shyness was so paralyzing, and I was so flustered that I was about to strut in front of hundreds of people who would be staring me up and down and judging my looks, I put my one-piece swimsuit on backward during the actual pageant! It was my mistake, but I guess it looked fine that way because I walked away with the title and a check for a hundred dollars, which went straight into my college fund. Maybe I won because I was the only participant, but that's beside the point. This is what women did during this time and I joined right in.

Suddenly I was somewhat of a celebrity at Mac's Record Rack, the hottest music store in town, where I sold records in the afternoons. Air Force cadets came in all the time when they were on leave, and there was one cadet in particular from Colorado Springs who drove up most days in a red Corvette convertible. I can only describe his amazing skin color as cinnamon, and he gravitated to me, the quiet one in the white go-go boots who had won a beauty contest. I expected he would become an astronaut or a physicist, he spoke so beautifully and he seemed so intelligent. But I shied away from his attention. I felt immature—I didn't have the right clothes and I was taking the bus to work while he was cruising around town in an expensive, fancy new Corvette. I wore no makeup, not even lipstick or mascara, and I kept my focus on my job, selling music and watching the guys from afar.

One day, the cinnamon cadet in the red convertible told me, "Pam, my friend has a crush on you."

He was referring to another good-looking cadet named Bruce who had a brand-new green Oldsmobile, and he wanted to take me out. I told Bruce, "Look, I'm really flattered that you're interested in me, but you're an Air Force cadet, and I sell records for a buck twenty-five in the daytime, and I'm a receptionist at a radio station on the weekends. I really can't date anybody seriously until I finish school."

I knew that any other girl would have jumped at the chance to date this man, fall in love, get married, and have babies. But that was just not me at this time.

Bruce backed off, but another cadet from Denver named Colin, who was attending Annapolis Military Academy, came into the store one day when he was on vacation. I have to say, he was devastatingly handsome. He asked me out, but when I gave him the talk I'd given Bruce, he wanted to go out with me anyway. How could I refuse him? He came from a good family. He had light skin like my dad, sandy hair, and a soothing voice. He was a reserved man, so I wasn't afraid of him, and I decided to go on a date with him, a dinner, which we both enjoyed a lot.

When Colin went back to Annapolis, we corresponded, and one day he invited me to a big ball they were throwing there. He offered to pay my way to visit him in Maryland, but I felt like Cinderella because I didn't have anything to wear or enough money to buy something new. Ashamed to admit my problem, I told him I'd have to think about it.

"Maybe you could wear my wedding dress," Mom suggested.

"I already wore it for Halloween at Travis," I reminded her, "and it's pretty faded and outdated."

"I can *make* a dress for you," she offered. But even if we got the dress done, I couldn't afford to buy the shoes, the purse, and whatever else I needed. I was terribly disappointed, and I declined the invitation casually, like I was too busy, since I was too ashamed to tell Colin the real reason. Dating was not going so well for me, and my next encounter with Brian, a family friend, made things a great deal worse.

Brian was a dark-skinned pro athlete with the physique and strength to go along with it. He was a massive, good-looking man with very broad shoulders, golden eyes, and an engaging smile, and his family had known my family for years. When he called me for a date, as usual, I didn't want to go.

"You never go anywhere, Pam," he urged me on the phone. He had seen me at Mac's recently. "Just come to a party with me. All the players will be there, and you can meet their girlfriends."

Mom talked me into it. "Go with him," she said. "What can happen? He seems like a nice enough guy, and he knows your stepdad would come after him if he got out of line. And our cousins and uncles would join in."

I wore a red dress and the go-go boots because I didn't have any other party clothes. I also wore a purple suede designer coat I got from Lerner's for thirty-nine dollars, a major purchase at the time. When I looked in the mirror, I decided I looked okay, but I was still scared when Brian drove up in his brand-new car with the fresh leather smell. I just wasn't used to dating.

Brian wore a black tweed blazer, which made him look conservative, and he was a perfect gentleman, promising Mom to get me home early and opening the car door for me. We exchanged pleasantries as we headed to a large hotel in the shape of a tower that was located just off the freeway. His friends greeted me respectfully, but I could see they wondered which boat I'd just gotten off. I glanced around the overcrowded room at the women who were a great deal more sophisticated than I was. It was obvious they were all sleeping with their boyfriends, hoping to become the wives of these powerful athletes who were raking in the bucks.

Brian's cologne smelled expensive, and I observed people dancing and kissing each other. There were empty liquor bottles all over the place as people lounged, smooching and whispering on the two king-size beds, one of them piled high with coats. Brian tried getting romantic with me at one point, but I politely pushed him away. When he persisted, I said, "Stop it. I'm not into it. I hardly know you."

Brian gave me a hard look. It was getting late and people were starting to leave when Brian strode over to me and knocked me back on one of beds, on top of people's coats and purses. The bedroom was empty of people by then, and I was stunned when he threw his body on top of mine. Grabbing both of my wrists, he held my arms down as I yelled out, "No, no! Please help me!" The music was loud in the other room, or maybe people heard me and refused to ruin Brian's good time. Maybe he told his friends to ignore whatever they heard.

I let out a piercing scream, but he put his huge hand over my mouth to shut me up. "Oh, no," I moaned to myself. "Not again." I bit his fingers.

The bite enraged him even more as he let his dead weight crush my chest, taking my breath away. I was very slim at the time, and his body felt like a huge building lying on top of me. There was no getting him off of me with my physical strength—I was much too overpowered—so I tried another tack. "I'll tell my family if you don't let me go," I threatened.

He looked into my eyes, which were wet with tears. "But, Pam, I like you. I want us to be together."

I tried to go along with it. "So wait," I said. "Let's do it after we date a while."

"But I *have* to fuck you now," he said, panting, as he reached up my skirt and tried to pull down my panties.

"Please," I said, "I'm not on birth control. I can get pregnant. Please don't do this."

He suddenly smiled. "I have birth control," he said. He held me down on the bed with an arm that was stronger than both of my legs put together. Then he reached into the pocket of his pants (he never took them off), and he came out with a cardboard sheet of pills that had been laminated in plastic. Using one hand, he grabbed a cardboard square and stuffed it up inside of me, pushing out one of the pills. I screamed with pain as his fingernail scratched me.

"Stop being such a baby," he said. "I got it in there. Now we have birth control."

"Oh, my God, you idiot," I said as I tried to wriggle out from underneath him. I simply couldn't move, and as I made a last-ditch attempt to throw him off of me, a terrible pain shot up my spine.

"Pam, you're going to hurt yourself if you keep this up," he said.

I surrendered because he was right. There was no way to fight him and walk away afterward. When he felt me calm down, he said, "It's okay. I'll be good to you."

I can get through this, I told myself. *I* will *get through this. I'll tell Mom and Papa Sam, and he'll really be sorry. I'll turn this into a church scandal, and his family will never forgive him.*

When it was over, he jerked me up off the bed. "C'mon, let's go. I'm taking you home," he said. I sat up, red-eyed, in pain and freaked out that he had ejaculated inside of me. All I wanted was to get his semen out of me as I pulled myself together, searching for my clothes among the coats on the bed. *I have to get the hell out of here and get this shit out of me as fast as I can,* was my only thought.

He grabbed my hand. "We're walking out of here like best friends," he ordered, throwing my purse and coat at me as he roughly grabbed my hand. I held the coat bunched up in my arms as we walked through the crowded room, hand in hand, while he greeted his buddies and said he'd be coming back soon. My hand was sore, as he'd been squeezing it very hard, and I pulled it out of his as soon as I got in the car. It was snowing outside and I couldn't exert the effort to put on my coat. I just sat there, shivering and silent, like I'd been struck dumb.

"Say something," he ordered me.

I remained silent.

"Why aren't you saying anything?" he demanded after a few minutes.

I continued my silence.

"You think you're gonna go tell your folks, don't you? Well, you better not. Wanna know why?"

I stared straight ahead.

"Why won't you talk to me?" he demanded, getting angrier.

My body temperature was flashing hot and cold. "I'm too warm," I muttered, still shivering. "I can't breathe."

"Then roll down the damned window."

I did, and just as I was reaching out my arm to open the door from the outside, he grabbed my hand closest to him and pulled my arm hard. "Don't you dare try to jump out of this car!" he shouted, forcing me closer to him.

"Stop hurting me," I cried, trying to pull my hand away from his, wrenching my shoulder. "I won't jump out. I promise to sit here. Just let go of me."

"Here's how this goes," he said, letting go of my hand. "I'll be letting you out in front of your house in a few minutes. You're going to get out and I'll walk you to the door. Then you're going to go inside and not say anything to anybody. Do you understand?"

He slowed the car at a red light, and, unable to stay in the car with this beast for another second, I got the door open and jumped out.

The last thing I heard him say was, "Get back in this car, bitch," as he rushed out to follow me. I ran down an alley and was out of sight in a few seconds, slipping and falling on the ice and snow. I figured I was safe because he wasn't about to leave his precious car in the middle of an intersection to catch up with me. Still, I didn't stop running until I was standing in front of my house.

My shoulder was sore and I was hurting badly on the inside when I realized I had rushed away from my attacker without my coat or purse. I'd left them both in his car, and I had no keys to get inside the house. As much as I wanted to scream and cry and wake up the whole family, I had second thoughts. If I told on Brian, well—I knew the wrath of my family. I could pretty well count on someone getting shot or killed (probably Brian) and someone going to jail for life (probably my stepfather, my brother, or a cousin).

I walked to the side of the house and threw a few small pebbles at the window of my little sister's bedroom, which we shared since Krista had moved out. Gina looked out the window with sleepy eyes. "Pammy? Is that you?" she called out.

"Shhh," I called up to her. "Just open the door. Don't wake Mom or Papa Sam."

Sleepy-eyed, she opened the front door. I stood there completely disheveled, with no coat in the freezing cold. I rushed inside and got Gina up to the bedroom. Before she could say a word, I told her, "Listen, Gina, don't tell Mom I woke you up to let me in. I'll buy you a bunny, a bike, anything you want. Just promise not to tell."

She didn't ask any questions. She slid back into bed and I filled up the bathtub with warm water, praying the splashing sound would not wake Mom or Papa Sam. I *had* to get the beast's smell off of me and his body fluids out of me. I lay there in the tub, remembering so many years earlier when I was six, rolled up in a ball in an empty bathtub, wishing I could disappear. I knew I could say nothing to my family, because if any one of them found out, they would have put out an all-points bulletin to every male family member from Colorado to Wyoming and parts north. It would have been full-on war as they hunted my attacker down and did their worst to him—and his precious car.

Instead, I sobbed and cried silently while I held on to the sides of the tub, exactly like I had done when I was six. The differences were that this time I was eighteen, not six, the tub was full of water, and I knew exactly what had happened to me.

CHAPTER **9**

Westward Bound

I hid my pain at breakfast the next morning, responding to Mom's questions about my date with Brian in one-word answers. He hadn't struck me where it showed, and I pretended to be distracted because I was late for work. When I got out the door and headed for Mac's Record Rack, my mind was racing with thoughts like, *Did he even like me a little bit? Why did he have to take it from me? Couldn't we have dated like regular people before we had sex? Did it have to be rape?*

Though I was glad I would never have to see his sorry ass again, being raped wounds more than the body. So does keeping secrets, and I knew deep in my heart that there was another reason I would never tell on Brian, besides keeping the family peace. I was afraid that men would consider me damaged goods once they found out I'd been raped, not once but twice, and they would have no interest in me.

When I got to Mac's, a coworker named Betty asked me, "Where's that beautiful purple suede coat you always wear, Pam?" Betty was three hundred pounds of pure kindness and heart, someone whom I adored. It seemed like she had dreamed of losing enough weight to fit into that coat.

"Oh, I got tired of it," I said. I didn't expect her to believe that, but before she could say another word, Mac, the store owner, came walking toward me carrying that very coat and my purse from last night. I was stunned. "How did you get these?" I asked him, afraid to hear the answer.

"Some guy brought them in earlier."

"Thank you," was all I said, refusing to meet Betty's gaze after I'd just told her I was tired of my coat. I couldn't believe that Brian had come to my workplace to return my things. How dare he? What an invasion. Was he asking for trouble? Or did he dislike me so much that he wanted to humiliate me even further?

Mac must have seen how upset I looked. "Pam, do you need some help? You can tell me. Do I need to get my gun?" he asked.

I nearly burst into tears because he was being so kind to me. "Mac," I said, choking back my emotions, "it's okay. I'm okay."

He looked me over to see if I had bruises or anything else. It seemed that in the midst of attacking me, the beast had covered his own ass. Satisfied that I looked unharmed, Mac left me alone, but he assured me that if I needed his help, he was there. Later, when Mom asked me where my coat was, I told her I spilled something on it and I would have to clean it before I wore it again. Mom knew something was wrong, but she didn't press me. She had enough trouble in her life without goading me to bring up more.

I continued at Metropolitan State, where a psychology professor took a genuine interest in me. He must have seen my passion for learning and he asked me what I wanted to do in life. "I'm interested in what you want," he said, "not what other people want for you."

"I'm interested in TV and film," I told him. I had let go of dreams of becoming a doctor—there were just too many racial, gender, and financial obstacles—but dreams of filmmaking had taken their place.

"Well," he said, "there are four colleges in the country that have good film schools. You could transfer to one of them."

"I'd love to go to film school, but I don't have enough money to transfer. I'd have to live in an apartment or a dorm, and I can't afford it."

I kept dreaming, though, especially when I was working at the record store. I was still the quiet one, but since I'd won the beauty contest, I could pretend to be exotic rather than shy. I was sure my pageant days were over since it was so against my nature to compete like that. But when I heard that they were holding auditions for the Miss Colorado Universe Beauty Pageant and the prize was several thousand dollars, I rose to the occasion once again with Mom urging me on. This pageant, however, was not as simple as entering the Miss KHOW contest. It cost money to enter an international beauty pageant, and we needed to find a corporation to sponsor me.

Once we convinced a major supermarket to put its money on me, I had to choose a foreign country to represent. We could choose whatever we wanted and was available. I asked to be Miss Africa, an obvious choice, but someone had claimed that already. Clearly, I couldn't choose Miss Norway or Miss Japan, so I chose Miss India—partly because it suited my looks and partly because no one else had taken it yet.

Now we had to figure out what to do about a dress. I knew that Mom was a terrific seamstress, but still I was amazed at her expertise when she made me a gorgeous sari for ten dollars. She also made me a crepe, empire-waist, pink and green gown with white spaghetti straps. Once I had the outfits worked out, I began my research on India, focusing on Mahatma Gandhi and Indira Gandhi.

The Vietnam War was raging, and the Kent State riots were exploding as I tried to represent the best parts of India. I researched Indian history and I studied makeup for African American women in some beauty magazines. I also studied how Indian women wore their hair. I was terrified to be in front of thousands of people, but I showed up for all the publicity that began about two months before the pageant, with my goal in mind—money for film school.

We all donned our gowns and arrived at various locations for publicity and photo ops. The other women had spent hundreds of dollars on their formal evening wear, and there was no way I could have matched them. But I felt great in my handmade gown, and after I got over my fear, I actually started enjoying our appearances. We were sparking more and more interest with each PR event, and local promoters were touting our charms and competitive natures. We were showing the world that we could celebrate our beauty and be smart and strong women as well.

We opened the actual pageant by floating across the stage in our gowns. I imagined I was a ballerina, and I developed a way of walking with a straight back that made me feel grand and beautiful. I had huge Liz Taylor–style Grecian curls framing my face while I strutted in my dress, and as the pageant progressed, I won the swimsuit division. (This time, I'd managed to get my suit on frontward!) That gave me five hundred dollars and some encouragement for the rest of the pageant. Then I won the formal gown competition. That was another five hundred dollars and almost a guarantee that I would win the entire pageant.

When it came to the crown, however, an amiable white girl named Ann Bell won. They crowned her Miss Colorado Universe, while I was first runner-up. I agreed that Ann looked great, but many people felt I should have won because I won the first two divisions. In fact, it nearly caused a riot when the audience decided the judges were being racially prejudiced.

We were all back in our gowns, ready for the finale, when I realized that my dress had not been hemmed. I'd stepped on it when I got off stage earlier. Mom thought I'd hemmed it and I thought she'd done it. No one had done it, and there were raggedy strings hanging off the hem that could easily trip me as I walked around in my heels. And so, a few seconds before I was ready to strut across the stage as first runner-up, Mom and my sponsor were busy folding and taping my hem into place.

I may not have won, but I was grateful to be part of the global community in which women were making great strides toward our independence. And the pageant helped me get over my extreme shyness and fear of being in front of people. When the winner was named,

I realized I had participated in something I loved, and I had made some great new friends. In essence, I did win, even though I lost.

❁

When the pageant was over, I was approached by two agents, David Baumgarten and Marty Klein. I hardly knew what an agent was, but they invited me for lunch at the Broadmoor Hotel in downtown Colorado Springs, where I got my first taste of Hollywood power players who hung around the swimming pool in Gucci loafers with no socks. Didn't they do their laundry?

David Baumgarten was an eloquent, well-manicured man in a herringbone jacket, and he represented many of the actors who were appearing in the blockbuster variety show *Laugh-In*. "The way you spoke in the pageant and carried yourself was extraordinary," David said. "You have something special. Unique. I watched you come alive when you were talking about India. You took me there with you."

Marty Klein agreed. While I ordered lunch they called my mom so she wouldn't worry about where I was. Marty told me, "There's a movement in Hollywood right now, Pam. I represent an emerging black actor named Richard Roundtree. We just signed a movie for him called *Shaft*. We think he's going to be a huge star. There are lots of opportunities for black actors right now in music and film. This would be a perfect time for you to come to Hollywood and become an actress."

An actress? I nearly laughed out loud. Acting on TV or film was for other people. In our community, we knew that black people mostly got subservient roles, like blue-collar workers or maids. It had been such an ordeal to get myself onstage for a beauty pageant. How would I ever overcome stage fright enough to act? But it was another way to raise money for school, and so I kept an open mind, even though I thought the suggestion was ridiculous.

When I got home, though, Mom picked up where David and Marty had left off. "They think you have outstanding qualities. They like that you're unassuming and unaware of your beauty."

"Do you really think I should go to California?" I asked her. "It sounds awfully expensive." Mom was no stage mother, but she recognized an opportunity when she saw one. "We'll figure it out. You can go to school there." She paused. "Pam, this could be the chance you've been waiting for, an opportunity to find out who you really are. You can always come back home if things don't work out."

I spent the rest of the day thinking about the cadets and how inferior I'd felt around them. I thought about the beast who had attacked me, and I wondered why I would stay here in Denver. What opportunities did I have in a state like Colorado? I wanted to expand my understanding of the world and find out what was out there. I wanted to move to Hollywood and take my chances. I always had a safe home and loving mother to come back to, so what did I really have to lose?

I've noticed that when we make life-changing decisions that are right for us, the universe seems to give us a helping hand. The moment another aunt—her name was Mignonne—learned that I was considering moving to Hollywood, she offered to drive me there.

And so, while the sun was rising in the east very early one Friday morning, I grabbed my suitcase with my single pair of jeans and my purple coat, and I kissed Mom good-bye. Then Aunt Mignonne and I bought a bucket of fried chicken and, with thirty dollars for gas, off we went in my blue Pontiac. I was leaving the people I loved behind me, and I felt a sense of free fall, as if I had cut myself loose. I was slipping through the rabbit hole, and there was no turning back. But that was fine, because I didn't want to turn back. I knew that as scary as it seemed, I could not resist the powerful draw to head west, and I didn't intend to return until I had satisfied that pull, made my fortune, and discovered my version of utopia.

ACT TWO

'Fros and Freaks
1970–1989

CHAPTER **10**

Going Hollywood

Aunt Mignonne and I drove west until we were too tired and hungry to go on. We'd polished off the chicken along the way, and then, as the sun was setting, we ate at a roadside diner and then continued traveling along the famous highway Route 66. "Get your kicks on Route 66." So went the lyrics in Nat King Cole's hit song. There was great romance and promise connected to the image of Route 66, and there we were, driving down the highway that was beckoning us farther and farther west.

The sun was setting on the Painted Desert with its magentas, golds, and coppers. Overlooking the mesas, we could see the statuesque cacti and scrub oaks, while a fragrance of sage and desert flowers filled the air. We stopped and picked some sage for cooking and burning for its musky aroma.

When we were too exhausted to see straight, we got a room with two double beds and a gadget called "Magic Fingers" that vibrated the bed if you fed it a nickel. I lay back and dropped off to sleep amid Aunt Mignonne's storytelling. Though in her mid-seventies, she was still lively and fun, and we both woke up early the next morning, ready to devour bacon and eggs and get back on the road. It was a great adventure, between the motel, the dives where we ate, and the sense of freedom and possibility as we headed into the unknown west.

When we finally pulled into Los Angeles, I was awestruck by the luxurious palm trees, the blinding sunshine, and the deep blue skies. Not at all like Watts! People cruised around in their convertibles, tops down, their skin glowing a healthy golden tan. We found Sunset Boulevard and drove along the Sunset Strip, a mile and a half of storefronts, restaurants, and clubs made famous by the huge numbers of hippies who walked the streets all day and night in the sixties. We drove beneath the huge billboards that reached toward the heavens and practically shouted out the latest blockbuster movies that were opening within the next week or two.

When we drove through a section called Pacific Palisades, we passed sprawling mansions, exotic greenery, and restaurants that exuded wealth and elegance. We had never imagined anything like it. We followed the curving boulevard all the way to the Pacific Coast Highway, where we stopped at the beach, parked the car, and took a barefoot walk along the shore. It was like a dream come true as we inhaled the salty air, buried our feet in the clean, fine white sand, and sat together, side by side, staring out at the vastness of the Pacific Ocean.

For a moment, we were silent, musing on the journey that had gotten us where we were—truly another world from Denver's majestic mountains, pine trees, and rivers. We were in a brand-new world. Aunt Mignonne took out our lunch that she had bought at a deli at our last rest stop—corned beef sandwiches, kosher dill pickles, and sauerkraut. As a caterer for wealthy Jewish families, she had developed a taste for their ethnic food. Believe me, I wasn't complaining as we wolfed down the biggest sandwiches I'd ever seen while we watched surfers, people on boats, and soaring seagulls that gathered their courage to fly nearer and nearer to us, hoping we might leave them some scraps. The ocean was a foamy blue, the air smelled marine salty, and the sand was warm and comforting under our feet.

I stared at a boat swaying back and forth in the ocean and wondered what it would be like to just keep on sailing forever. I could have sat there all day long and into the night, dreaming and fantasizing. I understood why so many people were drawn to the sea; it was hypnotic. Eventually Aunt Mignonne gathered up our stuff and we reluctantly headed back east toward the part of Los Angeles where I would be staying for a while. A cousin on my father's side had a home there, just off of La Brea Avenue, with a pool house that had an adjoining bathroom. This low-ceilinged little apartment had been converted from a garage, and after I tearfully said good-bye to Aunt Mignonne, I unpacked my few articles of clothing.

When I looked around at my new digs, I smiled to myself at the rules and regulations my cousins had given me: no boys, no drinking, and no acting crazy. This one tiny room I'd be calling home was not exactly an ideal place to bring a date home. It didn't matter anyway, because that was the last thing on my mind.

First on my agenda was getting a job, so I contacted David Baumgarten, the agent I'd met in Denver after the beauty pageant. He proved true to his promise to help me, and he hired me as the receptionist in his office, allowing Mom some peace of mind. The job description was simple: answering phones and directing the calls to the right people. That was perfect for me, a young woman with very few business skills. What I did have, though, was discipline and consistency. I showed up every day, taking calls and looking for more work to pick up the slack while I tried to settle into a world that moved very fast, cost a great deal more than I was accustomed to, and was extremely unfamiliar to me.

Despite the obstacles, I kept my sights set on attending film school at UCLA. There was no way I could afford it yet, but I heard about some students who were meeting on their own to do what they called "guerrilla filmmaking." I took a risk, striding onto the campus, my back straight, my eyes focused directly ahead; I acted like I was part of the school. I found the group that was making films and pretended like I belonged there, as I learned all aspects of filmmaking, including directing, doing stunts, how to hold lights, and how to check for sound. We would stage scenes on Hollywood Boulevard and see what happened when we started shooting. It was so stimulating and creative, my interest in filmmaking was piqued even more than before.

I would have been content being a part-time student, but I couldn't even afford that. I dreamed of becoming a legal resident of California so classes at UCLA would be inexpensive, and I continued to work and study, hoping for the best. It was very discouraging at first. I remember calling my mom one night, crying. "Mom, I don't think I'm gonna make it. It's so expensive here. I have two more jobs, I'm working three in all, and I still can't bring in enough money to save for school. Gas is high, I'm paying seventy-five dollars a month for my room, and I need to live here for two years to be a resident so I can afford classes in case I get accepted at UCLA."

"You have to keep trying, Pam," she said soothingly. "You never know what will happen, and you can always come back home."

I decided to keep moving forward, and I met new and fascinating people each time I covertly attended the film lab along with many other off-campus students starving to learn the film business. Although I wasn't actually enrolled in UCLA, I had a sense of community since I knew people there who were like-minded. While I wasn't getting an accredited education, I *was* getting a life education, and I was eager to learn even without pay or credit. I was the kind of student who was willing to go anywhere, just to learn something new.

I'd been in Los Angeles only a few weeks when I stood outside Judy's, an upscale women's West Los Angeles clothing store in Century City—the most beautiful store in the world, as far as I was concerned. I'd just been hired as a receptionist at a highly respected theatrical agency called the Agency for the Performing Arts (APA) on Sunset Boulevard, and I needed some appropriate work clothing. I gazed at the luxurious window designs featuring the hippest styles as I took a deep breath and got ready to walk inside. My hands were shaking. I suddenly wished my British coworker from the office had come with me. She'd offered, but I'd declined, deciding to do this one alone. I wanted to spare her and myself the ultimate embarrassment and humiliation.

Shopping for work clothes should have been business as usual, and it probably would have been—if I didn't have dark skin and hadn't grown up when I did. Back then, in the early sixties, blacks were *not* allowed to try on clothing in any store in Denver or a lot of other U.S. cities. We could go through the racks and choose what we liked, but we were barred from entering the dressing rooms. We had to buy the outfit (that eliminated choosing from several different things, because we didn't have enough money), take it home, and try it on. Apparently it was okay to try on the clothes, as long as the general public didn't have to witness it. Then we could keep it or return it—if it was still in the original bag with the receipt. No exceptions. If we lost a receipt or the bag, we didn't bother trying.

It was the same thing with shoes. What did we think—that we could put our common black feet into brand-new shoes in front of a white woman who might eventually purchase them? We had to buy the shoes, too, and try *them* on at home, out of view. Imagine the humiliation we went through just to go shopping. But then, hundreds of years ago, before the Civil War, an early Congress had deemed a black person to be three-fifths of a human being. These perceptions and labeling leave their scars, so I couldn't believe I was standing outside of Judy's, about to buy clothes like a regular adult.

I was accustomed to wearing jeans and Krista's hand-me-downs, which mostly consisted of wool sweaters, heels, and Timberland hiking boots for temperatures that would freeze your butt off. These boots were functional back then, not the fashion craze that they are today. The irony is that I was ahead of my time, wearing Timberlands when they cost $9.95 at Sears instead of $175 at Nordstrom. But no one wore wool or heavy boots in balmy Southern California. I needed something new and different. Since the secretaries at APA didn't bat an eyelash when they heard I was heading over to Judy's, maybe it was true—they really *did* let anyone try on clothes here.

I exhaled, pushed the door open, and stepped inside the store. I remained skeptical, even when a young white saleswoman walked toward me with a big smile. "Can I help you?" she said pleasantly.

"Well," I almost whispered, "I'm looking for a white blouse and a black skirt. Something simple, comfortable, not expensive, that I can wash by hand and iron. They're for work."

The saleswoman continued smiling as she took a moment to look me up and down, not to judge me but rather to assess my size. Then she began gathering several blouses and skirts for me to try, casually chatting all the while. "The fitting rooms are right over there," she said, pointing behind the checkout counter. "Oh, here's something you might like." She pulled a few more outfits from the rack, walked toward the fitting rooms, and hung the clothes on the hooks inside, expecting me to follow her.

"Really?" I said, standing where I was. "Are you sure?"

She looked confused as I stood there, hesitating. "Just go ahead," she said, "and let me know how they fit."

I tried to look nonchalant, covering my amazement as best I could. When I stepped inside the fitting room and the saleswoman pulled the curtain closed, I had to catch my breath. My mother would never believe it, and neither would my friends back home. This is what we'd been protesting and marching for—to be treated like anyone else— and it was actually happening. I stood in the fitting room, holding back tears. This was how it *should* be in the world, the way my mom had envisioned it, and I couldn't wait to tell her.

CHAPTER 11

A Tall Gentleman

One of the first jobs I got in Los Angeles was being a backup singer for R&B artist Bobby Womack. I had sung most of my life, and I got the gig when I called Rosey Grier (not my cousin, by the way!), whom I already knew from radio promotion. He offered to call Bobby Womack for me, and I figured, why not? Rosey's word was enough. Bobby hired me without hearing me sing, and he paid me the huge sum at the time of three hundred dollars a session. I could hardly believe my luck.

As if that weren't exciting enough, Bobby said to me, "I have a friend, Sylvester Stewart, who needs some backup singers for a recording session at CBS studios. Do you want another gig?"

I agreed, but I had no idea that Sylvester Stewart was actually Sly Stone. I only found out when I arrived for work and there he was. It was good thing I didn't know who this man was because I might have backed out from intimidation. I sang with Stevie Wonder's backup group, Wonder Love, and the guest drummer was legend Buddy Miles. Late into the night, Jimi Hendrix himself walked into the studio to jam with Sly. I could barely tolerate so much celebrity in one room. Remember, I was the girl from Colorado, and truly had just gotten off the turnip truck.

I didn't do much more recording at that time, but I was busy

83

moving among my three jobs, and my friends were concerned that all I ever did was work. They were right, but I couldn't figure out how else to survive. I was in a fog of desperation, working to make as much money as I could at every waking moment and avoiding dating. It wasn't easy to make ends meet in an expensive city like Los Angeles, while I also tried to save money for my future college tuition—the goal that mattered to me the most.

During this time, I downplayed my looks as much as I could. Well, to be perfectly honest, I wanted to dress like a fashionable, sophisticated woman of the world instead of a starving student, but I had no money at all for clothing or makeup. And I looked like it! I had a vague idea that I looked good to men, but since being attractive meant being a vulnerable man magnet, I was in self-protection mode, and I must have been getting pretty boring.

"You need to get out, girl," some friends told me. "Start having some fun. It's no wonder you look depressed."

Two rapes in my past, one that had occurred only nine months prior, might have had something to do with it. But I never talked about that. "I don't have any clothes," was all I said. "All I have is my white blouse, a black skirt, and some sensible shoes."

"Go put them on, then, and we'll pick you up."

They took me to a smoky nightclub in the Crenshaw District called Maverick's Flat, a favorite meeting place for contemporary black luminaries like Lionel Richie and the Commodores and basketball player Wilt Chamberlain, reputed to be an insatiable womanizer. Since trying on clothing in a store was a revelation for me, imagine how it felt to learn that wealthy, well-educated blacks were living in the Crenshaw District with sprawling mansions, swimming pools, and housekeepers. Instead of cleaning other peoples' homes and doing their yard work, they were hiring nannies, cleaning ladies, and gardeners of their own.

When we entered Maverick's Flat, crowds of revelers in chic and glitzy clothing and women with long, red, elegant nails, teetering in chunky platform heels, were buzzing around, all gathered to dance, to listen to music, to see and be seen, and to brush elbows with prominent black movie stars, musicians, and sports figures. My friends got a drink and headed for the dance floor while I sipped on a soda and sat in a corner, a wallflower, completely curious about everything and everybody. Then I noticed the tallest man I'd ever seen approaching me. I'd been watching him dance, and I have to say, as long and lanky as he was, he had great rhythm and he knew all the moves. God, was he tall! And he was wearing shades inside the club, in the evening, in the semidarkness! He looked like a basketball player. At his towering height of seven feet two inches and the way he moved, what else could he be?

He leaned forward so his mouth was close to my ear. "Would you like to dance?" he asked, trying to make himself heard over the din of loud conversation and drum beats.

"O...kay," I said, cautiously, wondering if he felt sorry for me.

"You're not from around here, are you?" he said.

I shook my head. Of course I wasn't, since I had on no makeup, I was dressed like a Sunday school teacher, my heels were only two inches high, I was drinking soda, and my hair had a simple, rather conservative curl to it. Clearly, this man was not looking for a glamorous girl to dance with. They were all over the place like a scene out of *Soul Train*, in their Rudi Gernreich miniskirts and mod platform shoes, ripe for the picking, if that was his pleasure. But he was talking to me, and he wanted to dance.

"You can really move out there," I said.

"I love to dance, and I love listening to jazz," he offered as he led me onto the dance floor.

During the evening, I learned that my dance partner's name was Ferdinand Lewis Alcindor Jr. "Call me Lew," he said. A burgeoning basketball star who was completing his last year at UCLA, he'd been drafted by the Milwaukee Bucks and would be moving to Wisconsin in less than a year. I told him I was trying to survive in Los Angeles, living in my cousin's garage that had been converted into a small pool house. It had faux luau decor with a sofa bed, a tiki bar, and soft lighting. "The garage door goes up and down sometimes while I'm asleep," I told Lew, "when the gardener comes in to get the lawn mower. 'It's just me,' he tells me, 'go back to sleep.'"

Lew laughed. "Is the rest of your family here in town?" he asked. "No, my mom's in Colorado."

"There are black people in Colorado?" he asked with a slight smile.

"Last time I checked, there were," I bantered with him.

I told Lew I'd attended Metropolitan State College in Denver for a year. "I came here to try and get into UCLA, but it's very expensive. In order to lower the cost of classes, I'd have to be a resident of California."

Out on the dance floor with Lew, I began to move to the music, and I hoped I would see this gentle man again. It happened when we were both invited to the same party in a frat house on the UCLA campus.

When my towering admirer saw me there, he came right over and we started talking. I was happy to see him, partly because I didn't know anyone else, but also because I really liked him. True, he was the tallest man I'd ever seen, and his enormous feet looked more like snowshoes than human appendages, but he was surprisingly gentle and intelligent, and he made me feel safe. He was well-spoken. His dad was from Trinidad, and as an only child, Lew had attended a prestigious Catholic school in New York. He was a gangly, gawky adolescent, and the other kids had made fun of him as he continued to shoot upward—until he strode onto a basketball court and showed them what he was born to do.

Lew and I started dating, and I often met him on campus, entranced with him and with everything I saw there. For me, walking around UCLA was pure nirvana, with its imported palm trees, vivid California poppies in yellows and oranges, and the smell of newly mowed lawns. I was in awe of the black student union and the constant discussions about free speech, civil rights, and the Vietnam War. The women's movement, which my mother had championed in her own small way, was alive with wisdom and messages from the likes of feminists Angela Davis, Coretta Scott King, Gloria Steinem, Betty Friedan, Germaine Greer, and Bella Abzug. Whenever my mom found an article in the Colorado newspaper about women's rights, she sent it to me.

It was 1970 when a group called the Third World Women's

Alliance published a piece called the "Black Women's Manifesto," which sought to reframe the idea of black feminism to better combat oppression. Black feminists Gayle Lynch, Eleanor Holmes Norton, Maxine Williams, Frances M. Beal, and Linda La Rue cosigned the manifesto, which opposed both racism and capitalism. It stated:

> *The black woman is demanding a new set of female defini-*
> *tions and a recognition of herself as a citizen, companion and*
> *confidant, not a matriarchal villain or a step stool baby-maker.*
> *Role integration advocates the complementary recognition of*
> *man and woman, not the competitive recognition of same.*

In the midst of these powerful social demands and changes, Lew and I were getting along really well. He had attended a private boy's elementary school and now, at UCLA, he had become educated and adventurous.

He and I had so much in common. As an army brat, I'd lived in England and my father had exposed me to jazz, classical music, and opera. Lew found these interests attractive since he'd been raised to be worldly. We both loved a variety of music as well as travel, exploration, books, culture, anthropology, and Egyptology. We also shared a love of art, architecture, photography, and filmmaking. And we both loved the martial arts. I'd studied karate and jiu-jitsu when I was young, and Lew and I loved watching Bruce Lee films. He eventually became a student of Bruce Lee's, and we must have watched Kurosawa's *Seven Samurai*, the inspiration for the Hollywood classic *The Magnificent Seven*, at least a dozen times.

Now, let me tell you what it's like to have a sexual relationship with an athlete. Their bodies are amazingly strong, their body temperatures are hotter than the average man's, and their scent is refreshingly clean from working out. While most men take a shower in the morning and maybe another before a date in the evening (maybe not), an athlete takes many showers during the day. Lew was diligent about his cleansing rituals, his cologne, and his patchouli oil, and he always smelled fresh and light because he cherished and protected his body, inside and out.

I admired his way of life, and I really liked his mom and dad, Cora and Lew Sr., to whom he proudly introduced me. I liked his friends, too. I appreciated Lew's taste in home furnishings, especially his sumptuous Persian carpets that made his new Malibu apartment feel like a Middle Eastern mosque. He let me cook him exotic foods, and he listened tirelessly to my stories about farming, raising horses, and nurturing the land. He hung a stunning collection of antique swords on his walls, and he loved Siamese cats. A man after my own heart. I always believed if someone had the desire and the wherewithal to care for animals, they could take care of people, as well.

I let Lew know from the very start, however, that I simply couldn't get emotionally involved at this stage in my life. I was determined to go to school, so I didn't want the heartbreak and malaise that so often accompanied love to distract me from what I felt I needed to accomplish. He said he understood, since he was leaving for Milwaukee within the year. We could just enjoy the summer together.

With this clarity established between us, we had a romantic sex life. There are things people want to know, but I've never been one to kiss and tell. Let's just say that whatever you're imagining, he measures well beyond that. The truth is, though, nothing beat just being in his company and sharing our stories and dreams. I've always been the kind of woman who values honesty, companionship, and fun first. Then comes sex.

I want to be clear here that I appreciate good sex as much as the next person. But in my opinion, women are not valuing or appreciating sex enough. When girls start having lots of sex at young ages, they wear their vaginas out. Literally. What do you expect if you have intercourse four or five times a week with different partners starting when you're fifteen years old? By the time you grow up and meet a great guy, you're all stretched out. When a marriage or relationship is based on sex alone, there's nothing to keep it together when the sexual blush fades from that hypnotic, euphoric, in-love phase.

Lew and I had a really good balance in these areas.

We saw each other a lot, and at some point during the summer, I remember he asked me to start calling him Kareem Abdul-Jabbar.

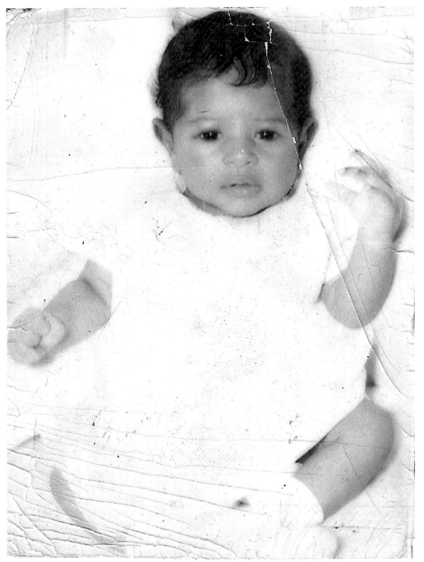

Me at three months.

Mom and Dad in 1962 at her sister Aunt
Mennon's house.

Baby brother, Rodney, a few months old; Aunt Mignonne; and
me, barely two, in Denver.

Me, Dad, and Rod, ready to go for a ride.

Me, Mom, and Rod, at church on Easter.

Me in junior high—seventh grade.

Me in the Miss KHOW Beauty Contest. I was so nervous during the contest that I put my swimsuit on backward!

My senior high school photo. I'm wearing the sweater I shared with Krista.

The morning after the Miss Colorado Universe Beauty Pageant, where I won first runner-up.

My Levi's billboard, from the streets of Manhattan.

A fight scene from *The Big Doll House*.

My friend Jack Silverman took this picture of
a marquee in Chicago—a surprise to me.

Kareem and me. It was the eighties. After all we lived through, being apart, he never judged me in my decisions not to convert or to do nude scenes in films. We became true friends—not lovers, but friends to share our lives and laugh.

Pam,

I hope this note finds you well. This place is out of sight but I'm glad to be going home.

Peace
Kareem

PAM GRIER
1647 Sunset Plaza Dr.
Hollywood California
90069
USA

Kareem had been on a journey to Egypt, the land of pharaohs and kings. I was working on a Roger Corman film in the Philippines and missed him dearly.

"Why?" I asked him.

"I'm changing my name."

"Okay." I knew that a lot of black UCLA students were changing their names because they wanted to be rid of what they called their "Anglo-Saxon slave names." But unbeknownst to me, Lew was changing his name for a different purpose—his new religion.

All was going extremely well until one day he asked me a question that would change both of our lives dramatically, shifting our relationship into a roller coaster that could never find its way back to the starting point. "Have you ever heard of Islam?" he asked.

"Yes, I have," I said. I knew very little about it, but I'd heard it was a progressive religion. "Why do you ask?"

"I'm studying to be a Muslim," he told me. "I'm going to convert."

"That sounds great," I said. Why wouldn't it be?

"I really believe in it, and it gives me a solid sense of being," he explained, as if needing to justify his decision to me.

"Are Muslims allowed to date non-Muslims?" I wondered, suddenly concerned for our relationship.

"Yes," he assured me. "Nothing to worry about. You don't have to convert or anything like that. This is just for me because it makes me feel good."

That was fine, and our discussion quickly moved on to some other topic. I wondered what made Lew turn away from the Catholic religion of his parents, but as long as he was happy and we continued to spend time together, he could do what he liked as far as I was concerned.

12 My Boyfriend
and His God

I loved spending the night in Kareem's Malibu apartment, in his enormous bed. I was there a lot, and then I would drive into Hollywood early in the morning to work my three jobs. From 8 a.m. to 5 p.m., I was a receptionist at APA. From 5 p.m. to 8 p.m., I had picked up the main receptionist job at American International Pictures (AIP), headed up by Sam Arkoff. And then, after 9 p.m., I spun discs at a popular private club mainly for athletes called the Sports Page in West Hollywood. I'd applied to be a waitress there, but they said I wasn't pretty enough. I think it was my lack of self-confidence. I felt much more comfortable doing the DJ job, where I worked mostly in the dark and no one saw me unless they were deliberately looking.

I kept a glass tip jar to my right and played rhythm and blues artists like Credence Clearwater Revival and disco artists like Donna Summer. I played Chicago, Marvin Gaye, Stevie Wonder, and some white rock like Three Dog Night. When people looked tired and needed a break, I switched to easy listening music until the crowd was ready to rock again. Then I spun Average White Band, Santana, and Tower of Power, one of Kareem's favorite bands. He often visited me at the club, where he danced and people made a huge fuss over him. But it turned out that he wasn't pleased to have me working at a nightclub. A conservative man at heart who was getting more so by the day, he didn't want his girlfriend working.

It was mid-summer when Kareem admitted that although he had tried to avoid it, he was becoming emotionally involved with me. "I see you're getting involved with me, too, but I'm converting pretty soon."

"I thought you said you could date a non-Muslim," I reminded him.

"I can," he said, "but I'm falling in love with you, and I'd like us to get married. I can only marry a woman of the same religion."

"I really can't get married right now," I said. Had he just proposed in a convoluted kind of way? It sounded like it. "We already talked about this. You know I have my heart set on school. You're about to move to Milwaukee. What decent college can I go to there?"

"If we get married, you don't have to get an education. I'll take care of you."

Those five little words "I'll take care of you," which so many women wait their whole lives to hear, did not impress me. In fact, they sent a cold chill up my spine. I knew plenty of women, friends of mine and of my mother's, who were supposedly being "taken care of," until the man divorced them and left them with nothing but a brood of kids and a load of bills. That was generally what women got when they tried to "find" themselves in someone else's life.

My mom had drummed it into me that getting a diploma was the most important insurance policy I could ever have because it led to independence and possibility. School was number one in my eyes, and although I appreciated that Kareem loved me enough to want to marry me and support me financially, I had other priorities.

"I really can't have anyone taking care of me," I said. "That's the master/slave syndrome, and I refuse to ever be oppressed or manipulated." After all, affirmative action was an issue of debate right then.

"Of course not," he said. "I wasn't suggesting that."

"We all know that being educated is the only way to be free in this world," I continued, "the only way a woman can be responsible for herself. Don't forget, not that long ago it was against the law for a slave to have a book on their person. You're a basketball star; you already have an education. I don't."

He looked at me calmly and said, "Let me just give you a book on how to be a Muslim woman. If it speaks to you, we can talk about it."

"Great," I said. "I'd love to read it."

"I think you'll really learn to embrace this religion, Pam," he said hopefully. If we wanted to have children together, that was only possible if we were both Muslims.

"You're going to have to convince me," I said.

I did not indicate in any way that I was ready to jump in. I wasn't, and I didn't believe in pretending. But I was ready to find out what being a Muslim woman entailed. After all, my boyfriend was embracing a religion that made him feel empowered. Since he considered it so valuable, it made sense that he would want the woman in his life to share the same thinking. The least I could do was read about it, so I pored over the book he gave me and I started to study the Koran. But it was all too hard to digest. I barraged him with a load of questions.

"Are you kidding me?" I asked him. "The Koran is oppressive to women. Islam is too strict and dated."

"Not the new Islam. There are lots of different sects. The new Islam embraces everybody and loves everybody."

"Then why is the woman, even in the 'new Islam,' supposed to walk behind the man?" I asked him. "Why can't we walk side by side?"

"That's what Allah wants," he said—an unsatisfying answer that would be repeated over and over again. "The man is the leader. That is how it is written."

"Why can't I walk around without a chaperone?" I challenged him. "Why can't I work?"

"You can," he said.

Right, I thought, imagining the expression on a boss's face when I walked into the office with a head scarf.

Topics like these became the basis for many arguments because

Kareem had no answers, except that Allah wanted it and "That is how it is written." It felt like a parent telling a child, "Because I said so." The truth was that Kareem didn't want me to work or go to school, but if I insisted, he would pay for my school. He really wanted me to just be a good Muslim wife, bear his children, walk behind him, and keep my hair covered with a head scarf.

When I talked to my mom about Islam, she went absolutely ballistic. "This is not a religion for women," she insisted. "Don't do it, Pam. He won't let you work, get an education, or have a life of your own. For women, an education is freedom. I've read all about Islam in *National Geographic*"—it was always on our coffee table—"and I know it isn't right for you."

She was right. I had just learned about certain sects in which women were required to stay in a special home when they were menstruating. It wasn't to make it more comfortable for the woman; rather, women were temporarily isolated because they were considered unclean during that time and they were not allowed contact with men. Particularly confusing for me were the multiple interpretations of the Koran's rules in certain geographical areas and the accompanying laws and traditions. For example, if a woman drove a car in Marina Del Rey, she could be slack about covering her head. By the time she reached Beverly Hills, however, she *better* have her hair covered. And when she was in Malibu, she was forbidden to drive a car at all. But then in Oxnard, about forty miles away, she could drive all she wanted, with or without her head covered.

If that wasn't complicated enough, in Middle Eastern countries such as Iraq and Iran, there were both moderate and conservative practitioners of Islam. A woman had to know the rules concerning where she was at any given time so she didn't make the mistake of sitting on the same bench as a man. In the more conservative areas, this was considered a crime punishable by torture or death. Today, in the strictest Muslim parts of Saudi Arabia, a woman is not allowed to get into a taxi with a man if she has no chaperone. That means that if her child is ill and no one there is considered appropriate to accompany her in the taxi, her child could die. These days, women are trying to get permission to drive taxis in Saudi Arabia so they can take other women with sick children to hospitals, but it's still an uphill battle.

Having been brought up Catholic, I knew that the ancient Christians were prone to hatred and violence. It was becoming easy to understand why many of my current friends followed the teachings of the Buddha, an East Indian seeker who gave up royalty, supreme wealth, and ultimate power to help himself and others end the cycle of human suffering. Peace, meditation, and service to others, the Buddhist way, made a lot more sense to me than what I observed to be the controlling ways of Islam.

I continued to study the book that Kareem gave me, and I met his teacher and a few of his friends who had converted. They seemed nice enough, but I was concerned. What if I converted, married Kareem, had several children, and my mother fell ill? The rules were that if my husband refused to let me go take care of her, I had no recourse. If he divorced me and cut me off financially, I had no recourse. And if he decided to take other wives, once again, I had no recourse. Sure, Kareem promised it would be the first wife's (my) choice to condone other wives or to refuse them, but I knew better. From what I could see, once a woman converted to Islam and got married, she gave up all her individual rights.

While the rest of the world seemed to be making strides in women's rights during this exciting time, it appeared that Islam hadn't changed much since ancient days. Women were still being abused and brutalized, and their lack of education and financial freedom caused them to be stuck forever in a world that considered them of little or no value. I wanted to please my man because I loved him, but nothing could sway me from my belief that the more educated the woman, the more powerful and liberated she could become. Many of the women I knew were innately intelligent, but they often didn't know how to think, how to use their minds to solve problems and make decisions to better themselves.

I didn't know that a small contingent of modern Muslim women was beginning to emerge in more progressive Middle Eastern countries like Jordan. These women were getting educated and had more freedoms, but Kareem never told me about them. Either he didn't know or he didn't want me to know. I can't help but wonder if I'd understood how things were changing if I might have been more open to converting. But the progressive sects were so small and non-traditional that there were no reassurances Kareem would have gone along with them, anyway.

The trouble was that I was falling in love with Kareem. We were closely attached, and yet we were facing a rift that could separate us forever. With our relationship on a virtual precipice, it was clear that he would not leave his newfound religion for me. The dilemma was, Would I leave my world for him and his religion of choice? I had no answers as yet. While being taken care of by a husband might have its upside for some women, for me, it was out of the question. I had to do this on my own, while my mother, my friends, and the burgeoning women's movement applauded and inflamed my dreams and desires.

CHAPTER 13

Me, an Actress?

I stifled a yawn one morning when Hal Gefsky, one of the agents at APA, stood in front of the reception desk where I was working job number one. I wasn't bored. I was too tired to be bored because I was so busy shuttling back and forth between my three jobs in Hollywood and my boyfriend in Malibu.

"Pam," Hal said thoughtfully, "have you ever considered acting?"

I looked at him like he was crazy. "Me, an actress?" I shook my head.

"But have you ever thought about it?" he asked again.

"No," I said, laughing. I preferred being behind the camera, not in front of it. I was much too shy for that.

"Well, I've been working with Roger Corman, and I think you should read for a role in his latest picture."

Roger Corman, the head of New World Pictures, was a prolific American producer of low-budget movies, "B" exploitation films that were notoriously sexy and mediocre and made a great deal of money. Corman was known for hiring hot women, sending them to the Philippines, where it was so much cheaper to make a movie, and marketing these exploitation films into international blockbusters.

Hal continued: "Roger's looking for an actress for a role in his next

97

Philippine location. He hasn't had any luck so far, but you look perfect with your natural afro and no makeup. Do you want to audition for the part?"

"I've never even read a script in my life," I said. As long as I'd been working there, I'd never read the multitude of scripts that crossed my desk because I was instructed not to. I did as I was told back then.

"We can fix that," Hal said. "I have a ton of scripts you can read."

"But I already have three jobs," I reminded him. "I need to save money."

"No better way to learn than to be in a film," he urged. "Besides, you can make five hundred dollars a week for six weeks."

That got my attention. With all of my jobs put together, I brought home a mere hundred and fifty dollars a week. "What's the movie about?" I asked.

"It's about women in a prison in the jungle. Bondage, torture, attempted escape, punishment, drug addiction, machine guns, sex. The usual."

I couldn't imagine myself in a movie like that, and I was about to say so when Hal beat me to the punch. "I know it sounds weird, Pam, but just let me tell Roger about you and see if he wants to see you," he said before I could protest. "What have you got to lose?"

Hal walked out the door and was gone for about a half hour. The next thing I knew, he was back. Together we walked down Sunset Boulevard in the direction of New World Pictures to meet Roger Corman himself and Jack Hill, one of his favorite directors. When we got inside the building, I passed a group of women sitting in the waiting room, practicing lines, about to audition for his latest film, *The Big Doll House*, too. They all had on a ton of pastel blue and green sparkly eye shadow, false eyelashes, and various shades of neon pink to red lipstick. This film was supposed to be about women in prison in the jungles of South America. Where did all that teased-up hair fit in? Where would they find makeup? What movie did they think they were trying out for? They were dressed in bright colors, and yes, I was wearing my white blouse, my black skirt, my sensible shoes, and no makeup. My uniform.

I walked into the audition room shyly and said a quiet "Hello" to Roger, Jack, and a few people who were assisting them. Then I read the words on the page they handed me. I thought I did so-so, but I must have read reasonably well because Roger offered me the role on the spot. It must have been the way I looked, not my talent. He told me that I would be paid five hundred dollars a week for six weeks, just like they had promised. I agreed to do it right then and there—if they assured me that when I returned from location, I could have my job back as receptionist at APA.

Roger looked stunned at the request and so did Hal. "But you're an actress now," said Hal. "Why would you want to go back to your old job as receptionist where you make so little money?"

"Because actresses go from one project to the next and they only get paid when they work. I need steady money coming in. A regular salary. I have goals and I can't be flitting from job to job, not knowing where my next paycheck is coming from."

Amazed at my boldness, Hal Gefsky assured me that if I wanted it, I could have my old job back at the end of this gig.

I was a very good worker and I was focused, but I'd fallen short with my unwillingness and my basic inability to be dishonest in a business that thrived on deception.

"Tell them I'm not here" was one of the most oft-repeated lies that an agent expected from any assistant or receptionist. But I wouldn't agree to do that. "No," I said, "I'm not lying for anybody. I was raised better than that."

When a movie star stood at my desk, demanding to see his or her agent right then, I refused to pretend the agent in question was in Paris at an opening—when he was hiding out in an office just down the hall. And I gave the struggling actors extra parking validations, which I was supposed to hoard. I was not good at policing anyone, and it went against my nature to lie. But I needed to know I had a job when I returned so I would not have to enter the "desperate" category. It was much too risky, since saving money was so crucial for my future.

Assured that I was safe in that regard, I walked out of the audition feeling stunned and anxious. They had offered to get me some coaching and suggested I read books on acting. I agreed to do all of it, but I was far more concerned about how Kareem would take this news than whether I could learn to read my lines.

When I told him about the offer, he looked concerned. "You're going where?" he asked when I said the movie would be shot in the Philippines. He didn't say much else because I failed to mention the exploitative nature of the film. Thank goodness he didn't ask, because he would never have condoned it.

I decided to use this experience as a barometer for our relationship. I made my decision to go. Now I had to see if Kareem could stand me flying off to do a job, making my own money, and coming back home where we could be together again. In the back of my mind, I realized that, soon enough, Kareem would be moving to Milwaukee. What about *my* needs and wants? But then, a Muslim woman had no business worrying about herself. The more I studied the customs of my boyfriend's new religion, the more I was sure I couldn't pull it off. And then, the bottom line was that I really didn't want to.

CHAPTER **14** *The Big Doll House*

I spent the several weeks before I left for the Philippines studying acting when I got home from work at the end of each day. I was drawn to the Constantin Stanislavsky approach in which he says "There are no small roles. Only small actors."

His book *An Actor Prepares* became my bible. I was determined to be the best I could be when I finally boarded the plane and met the other girls with whom I would be working. In the meantime, while I prepared to go to Asia (packing six weeks' worth of clothing and getting various immunizations), I continued the ongoing Q&A with Kareem. I never got any satisfaction.

"Why should I walk behind you on the street?" I asked him for the hundredth time.

"That's how it is written," he said.

"I can't understand why you would want that," I continued.

"It's only when we're outside," he answered over and over. "Out in the world, we have to adhere to the rules. In our home, we can be relaxed and do what we want."

"Isn't that hypocritical?" I asked him as we went round and round.

"I'm willing, so we can be together." He sounded like he was making a huge concession.

"I can't tell if you love me or if marrying me is just part of your religion."

He had failed to convince me that Islam would make me happy, especially since his answers to my questions were always the same as he switched all responsibility to Allah, his new God. So while I knew I would miss Kareem on such a long journey to a distant land, I was also tired of debating him. I looked forward to focusing on acting and making more money for my future than I ever had before.

My mom encouraged me to take the job in the Philippines. Buoyed by her excitement for my latest opportunity, I stepped onto the plane and left my ordinary life behind. After a seventeen-hour flight, three other actresses and I landed in Manila, bleary-eyed, wondering what day it was. We were met by a film coordinator at the airport as the muggy heat overwhelmed us. We gathered our luggage and made our way through the chaos of street vendors just outside the impossibly crowded Manila airport.

Finally, with a layer of perspiration covering our bodies, we were shuttled to the Hyatt, a high-rise luxury hotel on a white sand beach. I'll never forget the tart, smoky scent of burning sugarcane stalks, palm fronds, and other field grasses that filled the air as we drove to our destination. At the hotel, we were treated like royalty. We relaxed in our sumptuous rooms, walked outside in the tropical breezes, and sampled the exotic tastes of the Orient.

After sleeping off our jet lag, we gathered at the production office the next day to start rehearsing. I was playing the part of a tough-talking bisexual prostitute named Grear. Jack Hill, the director, took me under his wing, opening up my cinematic studies to Italian and Swedish directors like Federico Fellini and Ingmar Bergman. I loved our discussions about each director's individual style, and I was fascinated by every aspect of filmmaking, such as sound, timing, and special effects. I learned about period films, how the sound of an airplane overhead was unacceptable because in the 1800s, there were no airplanes. The entire process awakened something in me and stimulated my brain. I got hooked, and I jumped in with both feet. My endless question-and-answer rounds with Kareem took the back burner in my mind, as did studying my Muslim books. The only book I cared about right then was Stanislavsky's *An Actor Prepares*, which I carried everywhere with me.

From the first day on the set, I considered myself an apprentice, not an accomplished actress, and that attitude kept me focused, honest, and humble. Roger had advised me, "Just listen to everyone and watch what the other women are doing. You'll be fine."

I did the best I could. I had plenty of time to think about it because all the other women were asked out by rich Philippine businessmen who wanted to wine and dine the "American actresses." Nobody was hitting on me because of my 'fro (it scared them) and maybe also because I was quite tall and just as shy. Besides, I had a boyfriend. I took on a statuesque demeanor, clean-faced with no makeup, and I gave off an aura of "I'm not here for the regular bullshit." After all, I didn't drink and I wasn't interested in dating because I was in love with Kareem, who was waiting for me back home. I took the opportunity to focus on honing my acting chops.

"An actor prepares." I repeated Stanislavsky's words over and over. I intended to be prepared at all times. For example, when one of the other cast members wanted to go out on the town in a wealthy section of Manila one night, she asked me to join her.

"I can't. We have to work tomorrow," I said. "I need to study my lines."

"This is only a B movie, Pam," she said. "You don't have to work that hard. We can learn our lines in the morning."

I passed, and she took off without me. I had no concept of categories like A, B, or C movies. A movie was a movie, and I intended to deliver an A performance, no matter what anybody else did. I analyzed each of my lines, why I was saying certain things, and I kept my acting goals in mind. I even sang the theme song for the film when they discovered I had a good singing voice. I learned to do my own makeup and hair since the artists who were hired for the job meant well but had no experience with African American coloring and hair textures. I even discovered a brand-new African American cosmetic company that made a luscious foundation to cover zits and my countless mosquito bites.

Kareem and I spoke a few times when we could get around the fourteen-hour time difference, between my work and his practices and games. I was always happy to talk to him, and we discussed the Philippine culture and the filmmaking process. But each time we talked, he always remembered to ask me, "Have you been reading the books?"

"Yes, I'm reading," I said. As soon as we hung up, I went back to my acting studies and abandoned myself to the Philippine experience. I was accustomed to discovering new places from all of our moving around when I was a child, so I didn't feel lonely or intimidated. Quite the opposite. Each morning I woke up, eager to see what this day would bring, and what I would learn about my new craft and my new surroundings. One day, I found a little stray kitten, a gray and black tabby, which I moved into my hotel room. Now I had a friend, someone to talk to and cuddle with at night.

The Philippine film crew couldn't wait to talk with me about the Navy and Subic Bay, the American naval base of which they were so proud. I felt very connected, since my grandfather hailed from this area. The Americans had rescued the Filipinos from the Japanese and given them jobs so they could feed their families, and they all wanted to come to the United States. They were grateful and willing to overlook any differences we might have, and I was eager to do the same.

My hard work paid off when the dailies (the raw footage that we shot each day) came in. Everyone liked my performance very much. My wardrobe for that film consisted of one long T-shirt. Since I was playing a radical black woman, I could draw personally from my own anger and the anti-war rallies I'd observed at UCLA and in Colorado when I lived there. That kind of raw energy was real for me, and I worked hard to make sure none of it looked fake or manufactured.

Jack Hill had told me that I needed to reach into my gut, not my mind, to find the real emotion. I tapped into my intensity, and Roger was thrilled that I could bring so much organic frustration and anger to my performance.

In fact, with the success of the dailies, they were writing another movie, and I was amazed when Roger asked me, "Would you like to stay and do one more?"

How could I refuse? I was already there and I would continue getting five hundred dollars a week for six more weeks, most of which I was saving. Kareem was less than thrilled to hear I was staying, but he didn't protest too much. He knew at this point that he couldn't control me, so he let me do what I wanted because he had no choice. Considering the kinds of movies I was making, I realize now that it was a good thing he never came over to check it out.

In the second film, *Women in Cages*, I played a similar role to the first—an American woman in prison in a foreign country with a sadistic female guard. For this role, my wardrobe was pretty similar to what I wore in the first movie—a long T-shirt, a bra, and a pair of underpants. They sure weren't losing any money on costumes. As we headed out to the location, when our raggedy-ass plane came to a slow roll on top of a mesa in a mountain city called Baguio, we had to jump out onto the ground, where people stood ready to catch us if we fell. I didn't tell my mother I jumped out of a rolling plane, because she'd have had a stroke on the way to the airport to come get me.

Farther north, we shot in the mystical Luzon rice terraces, a veritable network of acres and acres of rice planted in intricate formations, starting at the top of the highest mountains and cascading all the way down to sea level. Described as the eighth wonder of world, these rice paddies are sometimes called "stairways to heaven." But as magnificent as they looked, there was a little bit of hell in there, too, in the form of leeches, protozoa, and parasites that feasted on our naked flesh.

During the course of filming *Women in Cages*, we stayed in areas so remote you could get eaten alive by bugs and lost forever with no hope of rescue. I constantly thought of my grandfather, born and raised in the Philippines, right here, among some of the kindest and most hospitable people in the world. We spent time out in the boon-docks (a Philippine word, by the way) where we filmed in the jungles, watching out for deadly snakes and other predators. Then we returned to the glitzy high-end lifestyle of fancy hotels and the revelry in the nightclubs of Manila.

This country had two societies, rich and poor, but I was surprised to see that even in the Philippines, with its severe class separation, life as we knew it was being shaken to the core by the global women's movement. The Philippines had been occupied by the Spanish for more than a century, and in this extremely Catholic country, women were beginning to fight to get an education and to make their own money. "My wife wants to go to college and get a job," the men com-plained to each other in Makati, the wealthiest business section of Manila.

I made some great friends while I was there, including a young male student with whom I listened to Cat Stevens and Led Zeppelin. He pointed out a group of tall, very dark-skinned indigenous natives with nappy hair, aboriginal types called the Kalingas, who came down from the mountains during the marketing season to replenish their supplies and sell their wares. As I already said, I was not frightened by "different." Rather, I was fascinated, and I couldn't get enough of anything that was new and unusual.

When the second movie was wrapped, I was approached to do a third. As gratified as I was and as much as I still wanted the money, I refused the offer for the time being and said I needed to get back home. I'd been gone for a little over three months, and my mom was having some health problems, and Kareem was getting anxious wait-ing for me. Once I got home and took stock, I could always fly back for a film if they still wanted me.

More than three months after I had arrived, I packed my bags and got ready for the long flight home. As I prepared to depart, the weather looked turbid and dangerous. Monsoons, a steady, pounding rain pattern, were a constant in the Philippines, washing down the city streets, eating up the sidewalks, and turning the ground to mud wherever it was not paved. But the rain that poured relentlessly from the sky the day I was leaving felt biblical, as if only Noah's ark could save me from drowning and get me where I was going. In fact, the film coordinator showed up in an army truck to drive me to the airport because the water was rising so high. In the middle of an Asian monsoon, I felt extraordinarily small and vulnerable.

I actually believed I might die. How on earth could a plane take off in the middle of a monsoon on a half-flooded airfield? I also feared that something terrible was going to happen to the people I was leaving behind. I had made so many good friends who had been so kind and welcoming to all of us. I knew they would suffer in the monsoon and possibly lose everything. It happened there all the time.

Once we managed the takeoff and were in the air, apparently out of immediate danger, I settled in for the marathon flight home. I was sad to leave this home away from home, but I felt full from so much nurturing and so many new experiences. I was familiar with a slice of life that could not be understood by reading a book or studying. I had been somewhere special, I had met fantastic people I would never forget, and I had learned something of substance that I couldn't get in college or anywhere else.

I stared out the airplane window. It always seemed like I got away in the nick of time. I had missed the typhoon, I had finished two films for Roger Corman, and all I could do was wonder what was coming next. I watched the cloud formations, first above us, and then beneath us, as we reached our flying altitude. A cloud warrior with a double-sided spear changed form into a dinosaur, right before my eyes. I started to doze. I had a lot to think about.

CHAPTER **15**   The Paisley
Head Scarf

When I got back home, my first stop was Colorado. I wanted
to check on my mom, and I had so much to tell her. She felt pretty
good, and, as usual, she was eager to drink in every detail of my life as I
described the rice terraces and the women's movement that was emerging in the larger cities over there.

"If you go back and you have time," she said, "you have to go to
Leyte, where Daddy Ray was born, and meet your Philippine relatives. We have a lot of them there, you know."

I did know about them, and I couldn't wait. But once I knew that
Mom was okay, I had to get back to Los Angeles and see where things
stood with Kareem and me. I missed the wonderful, humid, smoky
smell of the rural areas of the Philippines, especially when I landed
back in the smog and the hustle and bustle of Los Angeles. I missed
the fresh fruits: papayas, litchi nuts, mangosteens, guavas, and durians
that fell off the trees. I also missed the coconuts people opened with
machetes, put a straw in, and sold on street corners, where we could
drink the sweet, fresh coconut milk, a potent healing nectar.

I missed a lot, but I also felt better about my life in Los Angeles with eight thousand dollars in the bank, more savings than I'd
ever had. And in Malibu with Kareem, the landscape was beautiful,

the ocean water sparkled, the air was relatively clean, and it was good to be with him again.

I'd been back about three days, which I'd spent getting over my jet lag, when one morning, the doorbell rang. I was cleaning up the dishes after breakfast in Kareem's apartment when he headed to the door. "I invited some of my friends over," he called to me over his shoulder.

It was Saturday, and now that the dishes were clean, I had nothing planned for the day. I had expected to spend it with Kareem, and I was happy he had invited his close friends over. I considered them my friends, too, since I'd always liked them and hadn't seen them for so long. This was the first time we would meet up since they were newly converted, and I couldn't wait to tell them about the Philippines and start asking them questions about their conversion.

"Hi!" I called out, wiping my wet hands on my cutoffs as I leaned in to give one of them a hug.

He moved back, as if I had bad breath or a contagious skin disease. "Nice to see you, Pam," he said. And that was it. Now that they had converted, they could speak to me, but there was no touching allowed. No intimate or personal conversations. In fact, I wasn't supposed to speak to them at all, unless I was answering a specific question. I stood there awkwardly, when Kareem said in a quiet voice, "You're supposed to leave the room now, Pam."

"For how long?" I asked, frowning.

"Until I ask you to come back or my friends leave."

I walked out of the room feeling upset and humiliated. I dragged my feet to the bedroom and stood by the patio door. The hillside was magnificent below Kareem's cliff-hanging apartment with a perfect view of the Pacific Coast Highway and the sparkling ocean beyond. I sat on the bed. What was I supposed to do? Sit here like a dummy until my man came to get me? It was such a beautiful day. Why would I choose to sit in a room instead of being outside?

Suddenly Kareem was standing at the door to the bedroom, grinning. "Can you make us some sandwiches?" he asked.

I was a bit dubious, but I gave Kareem a hug and headed for

the kitchen, feeling a little bit better. I made extra-thick turkey and tomato sandwiches, poured some ice tea, and brought a tray to the kitchen table where the guys were hanging out. They smiled wide and thanked me. I had sat on a chair and was reaching for a sandwich, when Kareem caught my glance. "You have to go now," he said. "You can take a sandwich with you."

Crestfallen, I stood. "Okay," I said, suddenly losing my appetite. "I'm new at this." I left the room. Once I was back in the bedroom, I felt crushed. These were the guys with whom I used to talk and laugh. I had considered them my friends. They said they had considered me a friend. But that was before they converted. Now they were Muslim men and I was a woman, not even a Muslim, who not only would be ignored but was also expected to cook for them and to clean up after them.

I marched defiantly out of the bedroom and stood at the doorway to the room where Kareem and the guys were hanging out. "I have to talk to you," I said to him.

He looked annoyed but got up and accompanied me back to the bedroom. "What is it? I'm busy right now."

"How much longer do you expect me to sit in this room?" I asked him.

"I don't know," he said.

"Are you saying I could end up sitting here all day?"

"I don't know."

"I'm not staying in this room any longer," I told him. "I'm going out for a drive."

"Go ahead," he said in a detached manner. "How long will you be gone?"

I wanted to say, "None of your goddamned business," but instead I said, "I'm not sure."

"Okay," he said. "Don't be gone too long."

What difference did it make to him? Unless he wanted to control me. The day was warm and sunny, so I didn't change my clothes. When I walked through the front room in my cutoff shorts and halter top, I had to keep my eyes averted from the men to get outside. "I'll never be able to remember all these rules," I muttered to myself as I got into my beat-up 1968 metallic blue Firebird with the white vinyl top and a big dent in the fender from when my brother and a tree tried to occupy the same space at the same time. I loved the car anyway because it was the first one I ever purchased for myself so I could get back and forth between work and Malibu. I pulled out a scarf from the glove compartment, something bright in silk paisley that was left over from my hippie days. I took a moment to make the specialized wrap that would keep my head covered like a good Muslim woman should. At least I was trying. Then I started up the engine.

Feeling free and back in control, I punched the accelerator along the winding road that overlooked the Pacific Coast Highway. If Kareem wanted me to cover my head in public, the least I could do was give it a try to please my man. I breathed deeply and savored the feeling of the wind blowing through my hair—but wait. Why was I feeling the wind in my hair? My head was supposed to be covered. It seemed that the special wrap I was still learning to tie had come undone, and the silk suddenly blew across my face, blinding me. I grabbed frantically to get it loose, but it was impossibly tangled. I tried to pull the material away from my eyes, thinking, *I have to STOP*. When I finally managed to stop the car and remove the silk from my eyes, I was two inches from the crest of the mountain that ended in a sheer drop to the Pacific Coast Highway far below.

I can't even tie a head scarf correctly, I chastised myself. I almost died, and if I had, no one would have known I was trying to please my man. But I must have been making a serious error. I simply was not mature enough to do this for Kareem. Breathless, I retired the scarf back to the glove compartment and drove carefully down to the beach. It felt like an omen that my head scarf, meant to be sacred and protective, had nearly killed me.

I walked up and down the sand, my feet wading in the tide pools. I had met "the perfect man," someone whom I respected and was proud to be with. I loved him, he loved me, and now, because of a religion that seemed not to respect women, it was all falling apart.

I ran into a few acquaintances on the beach with whom I stopped to engage in some light conversation. When I headed back home, I felt somewhat better, but I can't say the same for Kareem. It seemed that one of the guys I had just fed had driven down the hill and had seen me on the beach in my halter top, cutoffs, and no head scarf, talking to men. He had called to "tell on me." Kareem was irate when I got back home, and he read me the riot act about disgracing him on the beach. I guess when we met, he considered me young and impressionable enough that he could mold me. But I would show him that I was more than a piece of clay.

"It was hot down there," I argued. "I always wear cutoffs on the beach. According to you, I can't jog, I can't drive, I can't talk to men, and I can't play sports because I might expose my body."

"That's right. You have to be covered. Arms, legs, and head. Only your hands can be seen."

My stomach tightened. "So I can't even wear a bathing suit on the beach anymore, according to you?"

"It's not according to me," he corrected me. "That is how it is written in the Koran."

"But I'm not asking the Koran. I'm asking you," I said.

By the time Kareem left for Milwaukee, I had lost my sunny personality and was depressed a lot of the time. I loved Kareem, but I was not ready to commit to him or to Islam (one and the same), and I didn't go the airport to see him off. It was too painful, because I just couldn't deal with his demands for strict adherence to a set of rules that made no sense to me. When I explained I wasn't clear yet about any of it, all he said was, "You don't really love me, do you?"

"I do love you," I countered. "But you're in love with a religion. You're not thinking of me. I like to fish, drive, take flying lessons, and participate in outdoor sports. I ride horses and motorcycles, and I like to climb mountains. I like adventures, and I like to talk to men friends and look them in the eye. I can't imagine staying isolated in another room, having a chaperone, walking behind a man, and sitting in the backseat when my husband drives."

It was a terrible dilemma to be in love with a man who was in love with a religion that seemed to have no regard for women's freedoms.

It was a quandary for Kareem as well, who kept calling me to come see his apartment in Milwaukee. He was playing for the Bucks, and he told me on the phone that he had an apartment in a high-rise that was beside a beautiful lake. He knew I'd love it. Why didn't I come and see it?

"If I marry you," I said, "what if you decide to take a second and third wife? I don't think I could handle that."

"You'd have to agree first."

"And if I didn't?" I asked.

"Then I wouldn't marry them."

"Or you'd divorce me. Right?"

"That isn't going to happen," he said. "Why are you wasting time with worst-case scenarios when we love each other?"

I wasn't born yesterday. I knew about Muslim laws that were in place right then in the Middle East that proclaimed a man's right to kill his own daughter or wife who was infertile, unattractive, or dishonored the family by talking to a man, riding in a car with a male driver and no chaperone, exposing her hair, or refusing to marry a man chosen for her, no matter his age or circumstances. They called them "honor killings," and they were hideously common. I called them criminal acts and slavery, and I would have no part of that or anything that encouraged or supported it.

"Kareem, I'm reading this book about Muslim women, and I just can't—"

"It'll be different for us. I promise. We'll go to M cca together and make friends there. We can be moderate. Just keep reading and practicing and you'll get better at it."

"What if you decide not to be moderate somewhere along the line?" I argued. "What if you become a lot more conservative? I'll have to do whatever you tell me to do."

I was clear that wasn't going to happen to me. The word *Islam* meant submission and obedience. There was literally no "self" in the religion of Islam, and everyone was guided by Allah, who clearly preferred men over women. I think that, in truth, Kareem knew, deep in his heart, that I could never submit to a religion like Islam, where there was no self. Everything was decided by Allah or rather by how some man interpreted Allah's teachings. I was just beginning to understand what freedom was all about, I was feeling it deep in my soul, and I wasn't about to give it up. "What about my education?" I said.

"I'll put you through school. I told you I'd take care of you."

There it was again. He was offering to take care of me. I knew he loved me, and I knew his parents loved me, especially his mom, Cora, with whom I had a special connection. But Kareem's commitment to his religion above all else was too rigid. I felt he was trying to make me dependent on him, and he was denying it. "You don't trust me enough to marry me," he said.

"It's not that I don't trust *you*. I don't trust that your feelings about me will necessarily stay the same. People change. You could decide you don't like our sex anymore. Then what do I do? A Muslim woman has no rights. Why do you have to get married right away, anyway? What's the big rush?"

"Allah says that Muslim men need to marry."

Back to the beginning. Exhausted from the same old debate with no answers or solutions, I finally agreed to go to Milwaukee to see what life would be like as the submissive, obedient Muslim wife of a huge up-and-coming basketball star.

CHAPTER 16

Lightning, Thunder, and Blood

Milwaukee was magnificently beautiful and dramatic with its lakes, pouring rains, and lightning and thunderstorms. Just like Kareem had promised. I was happy to see him because I had missed our talks, our sex, and sleeping together, and so had he. But just like before, our conversations nearly always deteriorated into my questioning him about Islam and his inability to provide me with satisfying answers.

One night, when we were locked in a particularly tense argument about our favorite topics, submission and slavery, I lost control and stormed out into the night. It was pouring rain, but I was so upset, it didn't register that I was cold and soaked until I got to the edge of the lake. I climbed a huge boulder and sat there for close to an hour, shivering while the freezing rain poured down on me. I stared out into the iridescence of the choppy water. Lightning flashed through the sky, thunder clapped loudly, and I prayed that a wave would wash me away forever and end my pain.

It was a bad cosmic joke that I was with a man who seemingly had everything. I loved him, the world loved him, he loved me, and he promised to marry, protect, and cherish me and take care of our children. But all of that was contingent upon my embracing a religion that

117

was bigger than both of us and our love. I didn't feel the draw. There were too many red flags, and I couldn't fake it because I respected Kareem and myself too much.

The rain continued to pelt the ground as I stood up on shaky legs. I was cold and miserable, and I wanted to get warm, when I lost my footing and slipped down the side of the boulder. I landed hard on my back and hit my knee while the rain poured down like the devil's flood. When I realized after more than an hour that Kareem had not come to look for me, I wished the storm would drag me out to the lake and drown me. Why hadn't my man come to save me? He was probably concerned that if he slipped and fell while he was walking in the rain, it would adversely affect his basketball career. It didn't matter if I hurt myself. I obviously had nothing much to lose in his eyes or he would have come out to find me and take me home.

Trembling from the cold, bleeding from my knee, and hurting badly, I made my way back to the apartment. Kareem had not come to save me. I knew he never would. I walked inside to find him standing over the stove, cooking a lamb curry stew. Without looking at me, he said calmly, "Did you have some time to think?"

When he turned, however, and saw the blood dripping from my knee and how violently I was shivering, he grabbed towels and began to dry me off.

"I need to leave," I said between shivers and sobs. "Right now."

"There are no flights out tonight," he said.

"Then I'm leaving in the morning." He didn't argue and I didn't eat. I went straight to the sofa and spent a sleepless night there, shivering and aching, wishing I'd drowned in the lake. When Kareem drove me to the airport in the morning, he dropped me off and said, "I still hope you'll think about converting. I love you and really want us to marry."

"I'm doing my best," I said, "but you're not giving me enough time. You've been studying this for nearly two years. Maybe three. For me, it's only been four months. You have to be patient."

�֍

When I got back to Los Angeles, a few friends and I pooled our money together and rented a house. I was tired of living in a pool house and wanted a regular, four-walled apartment like any other human being. But I also needed a job. New World Pictures was talking about putting me in some more films, but so far, it was just that—talk. I was adamant about not dipping into my savings for my survival, so I went back to doing some odd jobs. Since my receptionist position at APA was taken, I didn't speak to Roger or Hal about it. I just went out and found some alternative ways to make money.

After about two weeks of working in a pharmacy as a temporary accounting clerk, a call came in for me. I'd never gotten a call at the pharmacy, so I was surprised to find that Hal Gefsky had tracked me down. "What the hell are you doing working at a drugstore, Pam?" he asked.

"They pay me a weekly salary here," I said.

"But you're an actress now," he insisted.

"An out-of-work actress," I reminded him.

"We have some roles for you coming up really soon," he assured me. "Your popularity is really rising around here."

"My popularity?" I echoed, feeling surprised. I had no idea. "Well, when I get hired, I'll quit the drugstore. Until then, you know where to find me."

Working several jobs like before, I contacted Cora, Kareem's mother, and we talked. Kareem was her only child, and she really wanted me to marry him. At the same time, she was a devout Catholic and she understood how I felt about converting to Islam.

I continued to communicate with Kareem after my trip to Milwaukee. For me, a great deal had changed. For him, though, it was business as usual as he asked over and over if I "had been thinking." I'd tell him I had, but I didn't have any answers yet. I was still wounded from the awful night in Milwaukee when I had felt abandoned in the rain.

On my birthday, several months after that fated trip, it all came to a head. I was sitting on the sofa in my house with my roommates, who were having a celebratory birthday drink with me, when the phone rang. It was Kareem. He had kept his place in Milwaukee and had also bought a huge Tudor-style mansion in Washington, DC, which he donated to his Muslim sect. I'd expected him to wish me a happy birthday, so I wasn't surprised to hear from him. But I was not at all ready for what he had to say.

"Happy birthday, Pam," he began. "Are you having a nice day?"

"I am," I said, glad to hear his voice. Our house cat had just had kittens, and they were climbing all over me, licking my fingers with their tiny pink tongues, making me laugh.

"You sound happy," he said. "I'm sorry to have to do this on your birthday, but I need to know if you're planning to convert so we can get married."

"You need to know right now?" I asked him.

"Yes."

"Why?"

He paused a moment and said, "Well...if you don't commit to me today, I'm getting married at 2:00 this afternoon. She's a converted Muslim, and she's been prepared for me."

Prepared for him? Was he talking about a wife? Was I on acid? "Do you know her?" I asked.

"Yes, I know her."

"Have you been dating? I thought we were only seeing each other."

"No, no. It isn't like that. We're just friends. She converted, her Islam name is Fatima, and she's prepared to be my Muslim wife."

It felt as if my heart stopped beating. "How long have you been planning this?" I asked.

"When you left Milwaukee," he told me, "I realized you might not convert. I'm just giving you an opportunity to commit because I want a life with you. If you do, too, I'll cancel the wedding this afternoon. When I get the rest of my name, we'll get your name, too. Then we can get married. That's what I really want."

"And you can marry any other Muslim woman you want as well as me?" I asked.

"Don't think about that. I told you it'll all be up to you, and you don't know how you'll feel a year from now. Once you become a Muslim, you might appreciate another wife. Whatever happens, you'll always be my first wife."

Was that supposed to be alluring to me? Was he suggesting that being the first wife was a huge gift, no matter how many more there were? I gasped for air while my head reeled. I must have dropped to the floor, because suddenly I was on the carpet and my knees were scraped and burning.

"Sorry to hit you with this on your birthday," he repeated. Was he also sorry he had to get married to someone else on my birthday? What about the other 364 days in the year? "My mom wants to talk with you," he said, and he handed the phone to Cora.

She sounded devastated when she said, "Oh, Pam, I really want Lew to marry you. I want you two to be together."

"I want that, too, Cora. I love him. But I have to give up too much of myself," I said through my tears and rage. "I'll end up pretty far down in the hierarchy. I just can't do it."

"I know you can't, Pam," said Cora. "I understand. I love you, and I wish you well." She handed the phone back to her son.

"Hope it all works out for you," I told him.

"Can you send me back the book I lent you? The one on being a Muslim woman?"

What was he afraid of? That I would do something disrespectful to it? I hung up the phone without answering. I spent the rest of my birthday in bed, crying and wishing I were back home with my mother.

CHAPTER **17** Scheherazade

The next day, Cora called to tell me that Kareem had done it. A man of his word, he got married that same afternoon to his "prepared" wife while his own mother was not allowed in the mosque to witness the wedding. After all, she was a Catholic woman. They had tried to keep Kareem's father out because he was Catholic and only Muslims could enter a mosque, but he forced his way in so they let him stay. In the meantime, Cora had been made to wait in the car while her only son got married to someone she barely knew in a religious ceremony that didn't want her there.

"He did it while I sat in the car, Pam. It was a terrible day," she told me. "Are you okay?"

"Yeah, I'm okay," I said. "I really hope you learn to love your new daughter-in-law."

"I'll try," she said.

I was shattered by the breakup, although I must have known it was inevitable. I stopped reading *Ebony* and *Jet* magazines because Kareem had become a superstar and every month his photo was plastered all over those publications. As usual, I turned to work to keep me busy, always entertaining the idea of college as my ultimate goal.

One of my roommates back then, Tamara Dobson of future

Cleopatra Jones fame, became my best friend. David Baumgarten introduced us because he thought we had a lot to share with each other, and he was right. I still remember the day she arrived from New York, a six-foot-two, stunningly beautiful dark-skinned supermodel with six pieces of Louis Vuitton luggage. She breezed in wearing a long fur coat—she was ultra-sophisticated, and she really knew who she was.

My apprenticeship began immediately as she unpacked a ton of makeup and several pairs of stiletto heels that made me want to hide my Timberland hiking boots. In a few minutes, Tamara and I were laughing as I tried on her elegant clothing and high heels. Destined to become my big sister and teach me the tricks of the modeling and beauty trades, she was excited to hear about my experiences with farming, horses, skiing, and ice-skating in the 'hood back in Denver. We were as different as two women could be and just as interested in each other's life and adventures.

Although I kept working my various jobs, it turned out that my days away from the big screen were numbered. My popularity as a Roger Corman film star was rising, and I made several trips to Aspen, which was becoming a smaller version of Hollywood. Stars gathered there, and I had dinner and skied with the likes of Warren Beatty, Jack Nicholson, and Ivana Trump, before she married the Donald. I tried my hand at skiing, and because I had always been athletic, I did a decent job of schussing down the slopes.

Before too long, I returned to the Philippines to do two more Corman movies, *The Big Bird Cage* and *Twilight People*. In *The Big Bird Cage*, another "women in prison" movie, I played the role of Blossom, the machine-gun-toting girlfriend of revolutionary leader Django, played by Sid Haig, as we tried to liberate a women's prison camp. In *Twilight People*, I got a chance to play a strange creature that was part human and part animal, and I found the work exciting and challenging. This was my time, when my popularity and the success of the films were going through the roof. Thousands of people would show up when I was scheduled to appear at theaters, public fund-raisers, and promotions at TV stations. They were hungry for a female action hero, and at this particular moment I fit the bill, but my popularity never ceased to amaze me.

Now that I was tired of group living and could finally afford something on my own, I got myself an apartment in West Hollywood. The best part was that I got an apartment for Tamara in the same building and we remained close friends, living down the hall from each other. She was fascinated by my childhood in the military and that I was a world traveler, while I was drawn to her sophistication. She was hardly the giggly collegiate girlfriend. She wore furs in the middle of the summer, and her makeup was impeccable. One of the first black models ever to appear on the cover of *Vogue* magazine, she received tons of free samples and shared them with me.

I was very impressed with Tamara's ability to mix and match makeup colors for the African American woman, complete with her own personal blending. She was a pioneer in a variety of ways, and when she applied makeup to my face and told me her fantastic international modeling stories, she seemed like Scheherazade herself. I remember her introducing me to the famous weeklong "green beans" diet, to lose weight before a photo shoot. Not that I needed to lose weight back then. I was very thin and twice as active. But everything about Tamara was a source of learning and fascination for me.

It was obvious that David Baumgarten's instinct about Tamara and me helping each other out made a great deal of sense. I needed to understand glamour and how to fix myself up. At the same time, Tamara needed to be more adventurous and take some risks. So while she polished up my rough edges by teaching me to apply makeup, make my hair more sophisticated, and walk like a model, I taught her how to ride a motorcycle for her upcoming film shoot. I also taught her to shoot a gun, which she had never done before. When I told her I could teach her to shoot, she looked at me like I was crazy. "Are you telling me you own a rifle?" she said one evening, when she was showing me how to do a thorough cleansing ritual for the delicate skin under my eyes.

"I got one for hunting when I was young," I said in a matter-of-fact way.

"Did you ever kill anything?" she asked.

"A tree or two," I said. We tried to keep from laughing so we wouldn't crack the green clay facial masks drying on our faces.

Unbeknownst to both of us, we were an integral part of the burgeoning black film movement that became known as "blaxploitation." It's difficult to define something when you're in the center of it, so I really didn't see what was happening while I was living it. But there were a lot of opinions about this genre, as it was being defined by the mainstream, the black leftists, the religious right conservatives, and the lesbian community.

To me, what really stood out in the genre was women of color acting like heroes rather than depicting nannies or maids. We were redefining heroes as schoolteachers, nurses, mothers, and street-smart women who were proud of who they were. They were far more aggressive and progressive than the Hollywood stereotypes. Despite the fact that many men and some women were not supportive of female equality like they are today, the roles all made sense to me. After all, these were the women with whom I grew up. I guess I was ahead of my time, because today, contemporary women are scantily dressed but are still dignified and very intelligent.

At the time, in the early seventies, I was pulled in many directions, and my life was changing drastically as this explosive film genre emerged, targeting the urban black audience with black actors and funk and soul music appropriate to the time. Blaxploitation films generally took place in the 'hood in an atmosphere of crime as they dealt with hit men, drug dealers, and pimps. Black against white, rich against poor were common themes, featuring negative white characters such as corrupt cops, as well as black women of ill repute, easily fooled organized crime members, and corrupt politicians of any and every race.

In the background of each story were hunky pimps and pushers, knockout whores, and crooked police snorting, shooting, and screwing everything in sight. The black characters wore wildly colorful 'hood garb, and the plots nearly always resembled old Warner Bros. melodramas, with dashes of MGM fashion glamour—via the street—thrown in. It was common for the persecuted female character, angry and less conflicted than her male counterpart, to destroy a white-based power structure that had caused pain and harm to herself and her family.

I was emerging as one of the leading women in this genre, as was Tamara. The press continually tried to create competition between the two of us, since she was the sophisticated one and I was more "grassroots." But she and I both hated the controversy the press cooked up. We were so disturbed about them trying to come between our friendship, Tamara wrote the following letter to *Ebony* magazine on November 8, 1973:

Dear Ms. Horton,

I'm writing in reference to an article which appeared in Ebony *magazine, Nov. 1973 issue, titled "The Battle Among the Beauties." I would like to point out that there were several erroneous statements in the article, namely that I have refused to appear in the same celebrity events, let alone the same page, with my good friend, Pam Grier.*

I would like to point out that Miss Grier and myself have been very close friends since 1969. In fact, we are neighbors. I never authorized any persons who represent me in the field of management or agency work to make the aforementioned statements.

I have always had a great respect for Ebony *magazine and the other Johnson publications, however, I feel that under the circumstances, my growing lack of enchantment with the magazine based on this article is understandable.*

I would like to respectfully request that the facts be set straight.

Sincerely, Tamara Dobson

The press was determined to divide and conquer, but Tamara and I would have none of it. I started to create a movie for us, similar to the popular male buddy comedy *I Spy*, starring Bill Cosby and Robert Culp. It would be the first time that two black actresses would star in a buddy picture, but the producers weren't ready to risk the money on women being funny. Maybe they were still attached to story lines where black women were victims who transformed themselves into heroes. They were not interested in what we thought was the logical next step in our careers, even though we felt we were on the right track. After all, comedies were "king"—they were more mainstream and more lucrative at the box office right then. That was where we wanted to go.

Although we could not make that happen, Tamara and I enjoyed our friendship, no matter what the press or the producers said or thought about us. We were thrilled to join the ranks of black women making a splash, including Diahann Carroll, Lena Horne, and Eartha Kitt. Even though I was a private person at heart, I was excited to promote my films in big cities, where they treated me like royalty. And now that I knew Tamara, I was embracing the glamour of Hollywood, and I finally felt pretty and self-confident. That was a big step for me during this historical time of political ascension for African American women.

Society was in a dilemma about what was considered "pretty" among women of color. If we straightened our hair, we were labeled "pretty." If we let it grow out into a natural afro, we were called "ethnic." So far, there were few people in the mainstream who were ready to accept our natural looks as part of our beauty, and that really pissed off both Tamara and me. They convinced us to straighten our hair or to wear a wig for TV and movies. But along with Cicely Tyson, my friend Tamara was one of the first black models to wear an afro. She was demonstrating her sense of self and her nationalism, determined to express her natural beauty and have it be accepted by her audience.

It was different for an actress. The craft itself demands a person to change who she is and how she looks for the duration of a role. But there were issues to consider. How much skin were we willing to show and where? Nude scenes were considered racy in the United States, while they were considered art in Europe. We had to make decisions for ourselves that would affect our careers in the future, but in what way, we couldn't be sure.

While Tamara shot her most famous film, *Cleopatra Jones*, I was hired for a role where I finally made some real money. It was the part of a woman named Coffy in a movie of the same name, which had been originally written for a white woman. She had turned it down, however, because she was not willing to do her own stunts, since stunt work can be so dangerous.

Very few actresses were willing or capable of performing stunts. I didn't blame them, but this was where I got singled out. Unafraid, I was a natural adventurer and stuntperson as I rode horses and motorcycles, and jumped off of buildings into nets. If you needed a woman of color to handle a gun, do a wheelie on a chopper, or fall off a cliff into a rice paddy, I was the one to call. Push me out of a plane, throw me into a fire, I was ready. It all excited me, and I loved the challenge.

When it came time for me to show up in a bra and panties for my role in *Coffy*, I was willing to do that, too. My stay in Europe had opened me up, but there was a debate about what to do when I had a Janet Jackson–style wardrobe malfunction. A strap on my black and white polka-dot dress broke, and I was so into the scene that I was unaware that I had bared my nipple. Since it had occurred on its own, not planned, I was all for leaving it in. Why would people be afraid of a nipple?

The truth was that it was still considered uncouth for a woman to breastfeed in public. But nudity was becoming more prevalent, and men and women alike were taking off their clothes, soaking in coed hot tubs naked, and skinny-dipping in swimming pools. It was post-Woodstock, and we were being told to love our bodies. These days, no one thinks much of nudity. Even Halle Berry allowed her nipples to show in *Monster's Ball*. Back then, people were accustomed to seeing black women mainly play hookers and drug addicts where they wore skimpy clothes and allowed themselves to be exploited.

We left the wardrobe malfunction in the film, and I got a lot of respect because I did it in my own integrity. I viewed the exposure as artistic, not salacious, and I was comfortable walking that edge. The audiences were enthusiastic as I shot one more major film in Europe before I headed out on a big-city tour across the United States to promote *Coffy*, which was my best film and largest role to date.

CHAPTER **18**   Donatello

Cinecittà Studios are located in the heart of Rome, home base to legendary world-renowned Italian film directors like Bernardo Bertolucci and Federico Fellini. Roger Corman had decided to produce a film called *The Arena* through Cinecittà Studios, the Italian version of Universal Studios. It was to be shot in Rome, directed by Steve Carver, and I was cast as the co-lead. I would be working with Margaret Markov, a beautiful, tall, blonde actress who had appeared in Roger Vadim's *Pretty Maids All in a Row*. We previously had worked together on the Corman film *Black Mama, White Mama* in the Philippines, and we had developed a wonderful friendship. Now, not only would I be working with someone I liked, but I was also going to Italy, a dream of mine, to act and to do stunt horseback riding.

They put us up at the Pontevecchio Apartments in Rome, a twelve-story high-rise with a swimming pool, down the road from a number of large mansions and villas. I had a gorgeous apartment there, and the producers wined and dined me in the finest restaurants and took me to the open market. I did my best to learn Italian cooking (tons of garlic), which was flavorful, organic, and very pure.

I jogged in the mornings along the road in front of my building, and I often spotted a gorgeous guy with a colorful scarf speeding by in a red Ferrari. *How Italian can you get?* I thought. I had on my favorite pair of Nikes, jogging along the Via Cassia beside my apartment building, when the Ferrari pulled to a screeching halt beside me. The Italian hottie flashed his deep brown eyes at me and said, "Hey, what are you doing?" At least he spoke English. "Why you running all the time?"

I smiled. I suddenly realized how I must have looked to him as I ran down this dirt road every day, as if someone were chasing me. "It's called jogging," I told him.

"An American thing?" he wanted to know.

"Yes, it is," I said. "We like to stay fit."

"So do we," he said. "But we don't jog. We Italians drink wine and make love."

I broke out into a smile. "My name is Pam."

"I'm Enzo."

"I'm here doing a movie," I said.

"Oh, cinema," he said. "Allow me to take you around Rome and introduce you to my friends."

I brought him to the set that day, and everyone took me aside, informing me that he was a famous playboy and chased all the actresses, and that I needed to be careful. I knew a playboy when I saw one, and Enzo was just that. But it didn't matter to me, because I was not interested in dating him. I just wanted to make friends, and although he tried for more with me, he didn't get very far. He probably assumed I was gay since I didn't want to sleep with him, but I knew exactly what I was doing. I was not interested in creating a sexual bond with a guy whom I'd be leaving in a month or two. Besides, he was far too promiscuous for me as a romantic interest, but he turned out to be a really good friend.

He and a few of his buddies showed me the sights in Rome, like the Coliseum, the Trevi Fountain, and the Sistine Chapel. I rented a little Machina Mini Cooper and drove it all over the place with a woman friend named Lucretia Love, who worked on our film. While the guys showed me the sights, Lucretia showed me where to shop and taught me some rudimentary Italian.

I celebrated my birthday in the Latina Beach area where we shot most of the gladiator fighting in our film. The premise of

The Arena was women slaves fighting their way out of bondage. The film was a period piece, taking place during Roman times, and I was set to ride a black stallion called Donatello. But when I looked at the tack, which was also from that period, I saw immediately that it would give me very little control over the horse. I trusted my riding ability—after all, I'd been riding horses since I was a child and I had taught myself to do stunts—but one look at the tack told me that even if I managed to stay on Donatello's back, I was in for one sore behind, no matter how well I rode or how much experience I had.

Donatello, our lead stunt horse, was as sleek and black as Frodo's famous horse in *The Lord of the Rings*. I fell in love immediately as I trotted him around a few times to see how he moved and how he followed directions. Donatello seemed to like me—he wasn't trying to get away—but he refused to acknowledge my verbal commands. It didn't take me long to see that I had a major spitfire on my hands, and I wondered how he'd get along with the other horses that were tethered nearby. I got the attention of the Italian horse handler and asked him, "Are you sure this horse is trained? He feels really wild, and he's paying no attention to my directions."

The man watched me call out commands that the horse completely ignored. Then he began to laugh and said, "He no speak-a English." He taught me some commands in Italian, to which the horse still barely responded. Now Donatello seemed to know what I was asking him to do, to start and halt on cue, but I guess he wasn't sure he wanted to listen to me. I would have to establish our partnership. While that took time with any horse, I had a special case here with such a high-spirited stallion as Donatello, who was more interested in the mares than putting in a good day's work and minding his manners.

When you work a horse, instead of getting tired, he usually becomes even more excited. For example, if you're taking him on a course with eighteen jumps, by the time he gets to the ninth jump, he's more energetic than when he started and is excited about the next jump and the one after that. It makes sense, then, that of all the skills a professional horse rider needs, keeping a horse calm and collected is first on the list.

I made it my personal mission to work Donatello for fifteen minutes every day in order to burn off his energy and build trust, speaking to him in a firm, comforting voice. We didn't have a lot of time for training, but by the time we were ready to shoot the scene where the horse and I gallop off to war, I felt I had established a pretty solid connection with him. The trouble was that there was so much going on around us during those long days of battles and sword fights, Donatello was getting more fired up from one day to the next. With the smoke rising off the fake fires, we had some trouble, since horses are notoriously afraid of fires and smoke. They tend to make them skittish and unresponsive.

When the time came for the ultimate action shot, I climbed on Donatello's back, speaking gently and quietly to him, keeping him calm and relaxed. I tucked my feet into the tiny stirrups and tried to take control, but the more noise the crew made, the more Donatello got excited, and he began tossing his head from side to side. The fact that I was riding in sandals with a leopard skin wrapped around me, sitting on a small fur piece that was supposed to be a saddle, only added to my difficulty. "I need some time to calm him down," I called out to the director.

"No, we need to do the shot now," he yelled loudly. "Before lunch. Make him listen to you."

Yeah, right. Easy for you to say. "I need a minute," I said, straining on the reins to hold him back. "If he takes off," I warned the director, pulling him up and turning him in circles, "the other horses are going to follow, and you're going to have a big mess on your hands." I could imagine what the Vatican would think when they saw a load of horses galloping unchecked through the middle of the city, led by a tall black woman with a huge 'fro, in leopard fur and Roman sandals.

We decided to give up on the shot and finish it after lunch. That would give me some time to school the horse and get him collected. While everyone else ate, I rode Donatello back and forth calmly, talking gently to him, getting some control back, wearing off some of his energy. And then something unexpected happened. It seemed that a crew member who had been watching me work with the horse was impatient and had decided to help. When he finished lunch, unbeknownst to me, he came up behind the horse and me and popped him on his flank with a towel.

Donatello took off like he'd had a kick from Satan himself, with me on him. Four other horses joined the runaway parade, and while I tried to get him to stop, the crew members became hysterical, screaming curses and commands at Donatello in Italian at the top of their lungs. "Stop screaming," I begged them. "Keep your voices down." Horses are flight animals, and the pop on the flank gave Donatello a message that he was being attacked by a predator.

No one could hear me, and even if they could have, it was too late, as an overzealous crew member rushed in front of us, waving a colored banner at the horse.

"Get out of the way," I yelled. "Stop waving that thing in front of him or he'll kill you."

In the next few minutes, everyone who was trying to help me made every mistake in the book. But even if they had known the right things to do, it probably wouldn't have mattered, because Donatello was fast and young. The only thing I could do was try to stay on him until I wore his energy down. I figured if I ran him at full gallop for about five minutes, he would have to slow down. At the moment, he was in a panic, and the people around us were only making it worse, so I looked around me to see where we could run freely without trampling anyone.

I guided him to an open area at the start of a clearing. Someone jumped in front of us, and Donatello made a quick turn. I held on for dear life as he began charging toward a fifty-foot, two-story backdrop. I jerked at the reins to turn him when a crew member interfered again, scaring him as he ran away from the set this time. Now we were heading for a backdrop of a painting of an ocean liner in the distance where another movie set had been erected.

I feared I was about to die as I held on to the horse beneath me. I tried to breathe deeply, knowing that the more I panicked, the more the horse would panic, too. The distant movie set got closer and closer until we galloped toward a slight-looking man with dark hair, a cowboy hat, and a viewfinder around his neck. He ducked out of the way as the back of the huge ocean liner came into view. We galloped right through his set toward the backdrop. The director's jaw dropped as he watched a nearly naked black woman with an afro, wrapped in a leopard skin, riding a black stallion with a group of wild horses following behind. He gasped, "Oh, *Il mio Dio*, my fantasy has come true." It was Federico Fellini, someone whom I'd always wanted to meet. But not like this.

We were clear of Fellini's set when I could feel Donatello starting to slow down a little. But my girth had slipped, and I had no stirrups and nothing to hang on to. I managed to keep my seat until the horse stopped, and then I held on to his neck and went flying over his head. Thanks to my martial arts training, when I slid off his neck, I knew how to tuck and roll. But I'd never done that in a leopard skin and sandals, no bra, and no padding whatsoever. Ouch! I didn't get badly hurt, but I got the wind knocked out of me.

As I tried to catch my breath, looking up from where I lay with black horse hairs stuck to my legs, Federico Fellini was staring at me. Was I dreaming? He helped me up and said with great enthusiasm in his thick Italian accent, "I love American cinema. We should talk."

The next thing I knew, he had broken for lunch and had escorted me back to the kitchen of Cinecittà Studios. He decided we would have lunch together, and he would teach me to make an authentic Italian red sauce. He wanted me to teach him to make authentic southern fried chicken. I was willing, but there were no chickens, so I used squab instead. A first.

When we sat down to eat lunch together, he said, "You must live in Rome. You must learn Italian. You must do movies here. Broaden your horizons. Don't be just an American. They oppress Americans in America."

Starry-eyed, I returned to my own set for the afternoon, but first I had to have a talk with our crew, who had nearly gotten themselves and me killed. I gathered them together and asked someone to translate for me. "Do any of you know what happens when you touch a horse's flank?" I asked them.

No one said a word.

"That's what I thought," I said. "If he thinks a predator is attacking him, like that pop on the flank"—I glared at the crew member who had done it—"he kicks at the predator and starts to run completely out of control, because horses are flight animals."

I waited while the translator made sure they understood what I was telling them. I went on, "You could have caused several people to be seriously hurt or even die. *Morte, morte,*" I repeated. "Don't you ever do that again. I could have ended up crippled, physically or mentally. I was very lucky, and so are you. If I'd gotten hurt, you would have lost your jobs."

After close to two months of filming, we wrapped the movie and I returned to Hollywood with a great deal more confidence than when I left. I had bonded so deeply with Donatello, I fantasized about bringing him back with me and getting him gelded. It turned out, however, that I couldn't afford such an expensive stunt horse, so I left him behind. Fellini wrote to me occasionally, and I really missed Donatello, but I had my hands full. I was about to go on tour to promote *Coffy*, which was premiering shortly after my return. And then, I would have even less time to myself than usual, as I was about to enter into a relationship with a man I adored and could easily call a great love of my life.

CHAPTER **19**   Freddie
                                 and Me

In the early seventies, there were no satellite interviews that aired a broadcast for millions of people. To properly promote a film back then, an actor had to show up personally in at least thirty cities. To promote *Coffy*, for example, a film rep and I hit a city a day—in some cases, every two to three days—for a couple of months, and it was utterly exhausting. I usually had no idea which city I was in, since I only saw the inside of a few TV studios and a hotel in each place. But Chicago stands out. I'd been booked on the *Irv Kupcinet Show*, and someone in the green room asked me if I'd heard of a burgeoning comedian named Freddie Prinze.

I hadn't, but he was booked on the same show, and when he entered the room, I liked what I saw. A fine-featured Latino a few years younger than I, Freddie had a striking demeanor and a sophisticated polish. He was not muscled, but his skin was smooth and he had adorable freckles on his face. It took only a moment to see that he was a true gentleman who respected women, and he kept everyone around him laughing. When we were introduced, he was complimentary, and apparently he had not only heard about me but had also seen my movies *Black Mama, White Mama* and *Coffy*.

I had never experienced love at first sight until I met Freddie that day in Chicago. Maybe *lust* at first sight is a more accurate description,

139

but when you're young, it's a little hard to tell the difference. I only knew I was as intensely drawn to Freddie as he was to me. He loved my spirit and I loved how he held doors open for me, the way he spoke, his scent, and how he carried himself. We fell hard for each other, and he contacted me the moment we were both back in Los Angeles.

Ever the cautious one, I needed to find out if Freddie was the same person back home that I had met in Chicago. It didn't take me long to find out that he was. He and his roommate, another struggling comedian named Jay Leno, were doing stand-up at the Comedy Club, a popular LA nightclub. And Freddie was about to audition for a possible sitcom called *Chico and the Man*, with Jack Albertson as his co-star.

At Freddie's invitation, I went to the Comedy Club one night to watch his show. During the half hour that I sat in his dressing room before the show, I saw how his magnetism drew crowds of people to him. He was a bright light, fully acknowledging and enjoying the attention that people were lavishing on him. He scanned the notes that he had taken during the day concerning his political and religious observations. Maybe he would insert some of them into his routine that night. He was a lover of old-school vaudeville, especially the Marx Brothers, and he utilized this kind of humor as the foundation for his performances.

I left the dressing room about ten minutes before the show began and took my seat to the side of the stage where he couldn't see me. I didn't want to be a distraction. Suddenly the lights went down and Freddie walked onto the stage, glowing like a lightbulb, wearing a brown silk shirt, a pair of blue jeans, and black dress shoes—his Puerto Rican macho attempt to always look well-dressed for the ladies.

The room was packed that night. He was making everyone howl, and I was stunned to see how popular he really was. Every single joke he told tore the roof off the building, as he was literally blasting into stardom. I laughed through his entire set because he was so damned funny. You could tell that Freddie had been influenced by Richard Pryor, Lenny Bruce, and George Carlin; his jokes were intensely political, edgy, and charming, all at the same time. I wondered if a comedian like Freddie, who was this hysterical onstage at night, was the same man in the morning. He was so accustomed to living the night life, drinking Courvoisier, partying, and eating late, what would he be like when he first opened his eyes the next day? I had yet to find out.

Freddie got off stage and rushed right over to me. When he introduced me to his agent and his manager, who had high hopes for their rising star, I felt the powerful aphrodisiac of dating someone who was about to pop in the entertainment world. Money, lust, and power hung heavy in the air, and everyone wanted to be seen with him and around him. He seemed to be eating it up, and I was getting familiar with the lifestyle of a comedian, someone who lived differently from me and kept very different hours.

In fact, I was getting accolades tantamount to his. I had become one of the most recognizable female stars of the blaxploitation genre. My characters pulled out shotguns and blew away armies of abusive pimps, aggravating johns, corrupt politicians, pushy whores, and anybody else who got in my way. This movement of which I was such a prominent member was shadowing the women's movement, where women were demanding equal rights to men in art, business, family, and all aspects of life. My movies featured women claiming the right to fight back, which previously had been out of the question. My roles were written as vanguard personalities who were the first to defend themselves against violence and prejudice. At the same time, these women were determined to bring peace to a situation rather than engage in the draconian ways of war in the lower income communities.

Freddie's and my fame were rising at the same time, but while I felt I didn't really deserve the accolades and was generally wary, Freddie seemed to be eating them up. I understood, because we were both being exposed to a new kind of life that was hard to turn one's back on. I was being given entire floors of hotels and first-class plane tickets whenever I needed to travel, and so was Freddie. But for me, the ugly racial prejudices were still at play in my world when, for instance, a flight attendant didn't recognize me and questioned why a woman of color should have the right to sit in first class. She was about to escort me to the back of the plane when my film rep stood up for me. Some things never change.

While Freddie and I were enjoying our ascension to stardom and were very attracted to each other, I refused to sleep with him at first. I made it clear that I really liked him, I was very attracted to him, but I was also aware of his reputation. I was not interested in a "booty call" or becoming a notch on his belt. I wanted more than that from a man, and getting pregnant was not an option at the time. I was still determined to keep my goals in sight.

As a result, before we ever got into bed together, I insisted we get to know each other. We went to different restaurants each night and talked about our lives. Freddie was fascinated with skiing, which I loved and he wanted to learn. He loved my stories about the Black West, and he wanted to come to Colorado and meet my family. I found that romantic, and so was going to Catalina Island for dinner one evening.

We sailed there on a tour boat. Freddie played in the arcade, and we checked out the town and ate in a great Italian restaurant for which Catalina was famous. We also walked up and down the marina, where Freddie admired the extravagant yachts. He suddenly took on the persona of a yacht owner, speaking with a British accent, pretending to wear a monocle, and ordering his phantom crew members around with a slight lisp. He made me laugh so hard, I begged him to stop until he beckoned me to join him as the lady of the yacht, the captain's wife. He often took on alternate personalities and created scenarios until it seemed like he was giving me a private stand-up routine, always encouraging me to play the game with him.

We spent a lot of time talking about our dreams, where we had come from, and where we wanted to go. Freddie was part Puerto Rican and Hungarian, and he turned to me to be one of his mentors in life. I took the job willingly, entranced with his romanticism and his passion for life. I loved that Freddie constantly told me how beautiful I was, asked me questions, and actually listened to the answers. He may have been chronologically younger than I was, but he often showed a maturity beyond his years. When we finally became lovers, we were truly in love, deeply affectionate, and eager to support each other in any way we could.

It turned out that Freddie had the best taste in clothes of any man I knew. While I was more rural, he was more urban, and he really knew how to put an outfit together. I showed him how to hold his own in his various business dealings and new projects, and he helped me pick out my clothes and take on the glamorous affect of a movie star, in keeping with the advice I was getting from Tamara, my other mentor.

It was a powerful time for me when feminine activist and editor Gloria Steinem decided to put me on the cover of *Ms.* magazine. I was thrilled, and stunned when I found out that she had to fight her own company to feature me, a woman of color, in her magazine. Her board consisted of a group of old-school publishers who thought a black face would not sell makeup or anything else, no matter how good she looked. Gloria Steinem defied them, and my cover article was a hit, not only for the quality of the photo but also because of Gloria's chutzpah in using me as her lead story.

Another great honor was being offered the job of emcee at the NAACP Awards. This was prestigious because it celebrated my success as a leading actress. I was being honored for determination as a woman of color with no mention of blaxploitation. It was enough to simply be a woman of color.

I asked Freddie to be my escort, and he helped me pick my clothes and rehearse my speech. "You have to wear fur," he told me.

"Why?" I asked him. Wearing fur was a prestige symbol for most movie stars, but I was against it. I was accustomed to seeing *living* fur running in the wild, not dead fur hanging in my closet. I left that to runway models, who seemed as comfortable in fur as the animal who had unwittingly sacrificed its life. I, on the other hand, got queasy wearing suede, so forget about mink or sable. "Don't you feel empathy for the little animals that were killed?" I asked Freddie.

Apparently he didn't, so I bent to Hollywood's customs and agreed to wear fur that night, to please Freddie and the people who wanted me to represent the glamour and glitz. I could only imagine how my dogs would bark at me if they ever saw me wearing one of their cousins on my back.

The night of the awards, Freddie came to pick me up wearing his tuxedo, a shiny pair of black shoes, and an expensive tie. He stood about six feet tall, and I could hardly believe he was my date when I met him at the door, still in my robe. He strode in with a huge smile and helped me with my hair, my makeup, and my speech. I remember him asking me to stand on the couch in my robe, my hair still in rollers, while he had me practice my talk. He was trying to instill confidence in me, and the next thing I knew, he was trying to kiss me and take off my underwear.

I playfully pushed him away. "C'mon, Freddie," I said, giggling, "I really have to get ready."

"Let's be late," he said, trying to unhook my bra.

"No," I moaned. There was no way I would be late for an honor like this. Freddie knew that, and although he was joking, I took a mental note that he was acting frivolous about something very important to me. "Do you want me to get there with nappy hair?" I teased, feeling a little anxious.

"We're not going," he teased back. "I can see the headlines now: 'Pam Grier is a no-show at the NAACP Awards. She and her lover stayed home and fucked each other's brains out.'"

I couldn't help but wonder if he was trying to control me by making me late. My mom had warned about men trying to control me. Would I have to encounter this with every relationship? I had never thought Freddie fit into this category; I didn't think he would even joke about making me late. After all, the show was live. But I paid attention.

He finally let go and helped me do my hair and put the finishing touches on my makeup. I wore a designer dress from Rodeo Drive in Beverly Hills, a cream knit with sequins, and despite my protests, I wore a silver fox fur that he had bought me. My Charles Jourdan gold high heels with straps that wrapped around my ankles and a platform sole were identical to a pair once worn by Tina Turner. But I refused to wear diamonds. I was a political activist, aware of the oppressive diamond industry in South Africa, and I wanted no part of it.

Freddie tried to sway my decision, but I was adamant. "I can't support a diamond industry that's oppressing its people to the point of slavery," I told him.

"But they're mined in Amsterdam," he argued.

"No," I said. "They get processed in Amsterdam, but they come from South Africa."

"That's why I love you," he said. "You really care about other people."

CHAPTER **20** Fame and Relationships

Freddie and I were getting amazingly close, and I considered marrying him—not that he had asked. We had become inseparable when we were in the same city, and he had gained enough trust to really confide in me. He was truthful to a fault, he was punctual, and we shared a professional work ethic. When either of us was working, we supported each other by refusing to be an impediment to the other's dream. Freddie was never jealous of my success, and I was not jealous of his, one of the overwhelming issues present in almost any romantic relationship. We both enjoyed fast cars, great movies, and watching other stand-ups work.

As much as we cared about each other, however, there were some serious obstacles that emerged the longer we dated. No matter how much I was growing to love Freddie, in the back of my mind I couldn't help but wonder about fame and relationships. How could two people stay connected and raise children when we were both so goal and career oriented? We were often on different sides of the country. When you have children, someone needs to be home to see them off to school each day and put them to bed at night. Would one of us have to give up our dreams to raise a family?

The drug culture was another major obstacle. It was on the rise, and many comedians (along with a whole lot of other people) were doing a lot of cocaine as well as LSD and other hallucinogens. Coke was becoming a daily thing for Freddie and the rest of his friends, but I couldn't accept it. The more coke Freddie did, the more he dropped his inhibitions, suddenly acting rude and unrestrained with no filters to his language. He became less prudent when he was high, speaking in stream of consciousness and losing all track of time. His trustworthiness disappeared, and he became capricious and undependable. And he wanted me to indulge, too. But if I did what he did, how would we ever get home without a designated driver? Would we be photographed by the paparazzi, sitting at a bus stop together, all high and raggedy, waiting for a ride home?

When I continued to refuse to do drugs with Freddie, he became paranoid. "Why won't you play with me?" he asked. He jumped into his Groucho persona to lighten up the mood.

"This isn't about you," I told him. "I have to keep my mind clear."

As if he hadn't heard me, he said, "You should go to New York and do Broadway."

I appreciated his confidence in me. He really seemed to have faith in me, and when he was sober, we got along great. But one night, as we got into bed at his place, I asked Freddie, "Where are the condoms?"

"I forgot them," he said.

"C'mon, where are they?" I asked again. I knew there was a drawer full of them. I also knew how much Freddie disliked condoms. Was he being lazy, or was he trying to get me pregnant?

"Don't worry," he said. "I'll pull out."

"Do you know how many 'pull out' babies there are? You and I might be pull-out babies."

A pattern was emerging. He would start wrestling with me, the energy would get sexual, and he would want to have sex without contraception. Each and every time I refused to be with him without a condom, he said, "Don't you want to have my baby, Pam? I thought you loved me."

"Do you see your big head?" I joked with him. "I better be really drunk when I give birth to your Fredito, with a head as big as yours. I'm not ready for no big-headed kid." And we both hollered with laughter. But this condom conversation, a continuing saga in our relationship, was no laughing matter. Did he want to be the man to "knock up" Pam Grier, the star of *Coffy*? I knew Freddie loved me, but he was a man, and he was capable of that kind of ego trip. When I realized he *really* was trying to get me pregnant, I made it very clear that no, I did not want to have a child right now.

One night, when we had finished off a bottle of champagne, I asked him if he had brought a condom. It seemed like the champagne was acting as some sort of truth serum when he admitted, "I *am* trying to get you pregnant. I love you, and I'm afraid you may not marry me. You may want out because I'm not cool enough. Or this or that enough. But if you have my baby, I'll have a connection to you that will never go away."

"You need to be as committed to your work as you are to me," I told him.

He shrugged that off. He was so caught up in the drug culture, he was neglecting his work and going for more fame and fortune. But his misery and pain were surfacing. I was learning that while comedians brought joy and laughter to the people around them, they were often tragic figures with a great deal of sadness in their lives. I saw this playing out when Freddie called me from the set at NBC, pleading with me to take him away from it all. "Pam," he said, "come and get me. I'll give this up right now if we can move to a farm in Colorado, get married, and have kids."

Fifteen minutes later, after he had filled his nose with enough white powder to forget his pain, he called back to say, "Hey, I just made a great deal. They want me for a comedy special."

The roller-coaster ride was on, and as far as I could see, there was no end in sight. How could I bring a child into the world with a parent as unstable as Freddie? I couldn't do it to a child, and I couldn't it to myself. I was also upset because it seemed that the bigger a star Freddie became, the more his reps discounted me. They might have seen me as a threat. I was a woman of color. I was also a threat because I was a positive influence on him, encouraging him to clean up his life, whatever it took. What if I talked Freddie into quitting drugs and taking off?

Between Freddie's management and his denial concerning his drug addiction, I had to step back. I asked him if he understood that what he was doing was illegal. Freddie believed that his fame catapulted him to being above the law, but I tried to explain to him that there are natural laws that cause your body and mind to break down when you neglect your health and well-being.

The day I pushed him away for good was one of the saddest days of my life. When I look back, I can say without a doubt that Freddie truly was one of the great loves of my life. But I really had no choice. "You let yourself become a commodity instead of a human being," I told him. "Now they see you as a product or a brand. I love you too much to continue to watch this."

He knew I was right, but he couldn't muster the inner strength to do anything about it. Everyone was fighting over him while all he could do was withdraw and drug himself even more. There were so many people pulling at Freddie, I finally realized there was no place for me. Freddie insisted I was being dramatic, but I held my ground. When I finally ended it, he was inconsolable.

"We'll still be friends," I told him. "I love you and I'll be here for you. I just can't let you get me pregnant."

"I don't want to be friends," he said. "I have enough friends."

I must have sounded patronizing and condescending to him. No lover wants to hear the words "We can still be friends." It feels like a consolation prize.

As his depression escalated, I distanced myself by filming *Foxy Brown*, an action/adventure film about a sexy black woman who seeks revenge when her government agent boyfriend is shot down by gangsters. Jack Hill, my old friend, was the director, and I understood the role since Foxy Brown was a fighter and so was I. While my role in *Coffy* had reminded me of my mother, a nurse who stood up for herself, Foxy Brown was my aunt Mennon, who had a bad temper and was quick to pick a fight.

When I signed on for *Coffy* and *Foxy Brown*, the leading role in *Sheba, Baby* was the third of a three-part deal. I played a woman named Sheba Shayne who returned to her hometown to find thugs trying to steal the family business from her father. I also did a film called *Friday Foster*, where I worked with the iconic Eartha Kitt. I was also honored to play a role in the blockbuster TV miniseries *Roots*. I had made it. I was a working actress, and I took roles that appealed to me and did the best I could with them.

CHAPTER 21

John and Harry

During the time between my breakup with Freddie and his tragic death, I was true to my word as he and I stopped being lovers and stayed in touch. When he was considering getting married to someone I didn't know, I was the one he called to talk it over. I asked him, "Are you sure this is the right woman for you? Will she be there for you when you need her?"

In the end, he didn't pay much attention to my advice. It was his time of jet-setting, squandering abundance, and moving fast and furiously without thinking things through. The Eagles' lyric "Everything, all the time" from their famous song "Life in the Fast Lane" rang true as the sexual revolution was in full swing.

Women were clamoring for their independence, and for the first time we talked openly about men's penises. We wanted equality in everything: work, friends, and sexuality. It's as if we walked out of the kitchen, took off our aprons, put on our platform shoes, bell bottoms, and halter tops, and we were ready to play like men—and with men. Freedom of expression was the main focus back then. Suddenly whites could listen to James Brown without being called "nigger lovers," and blacks could sing along with the Beatles and the Rolling Stones without being called "Uncle Toms." A new era was unfolding, and the message was "Love your body. Love your breasts. You are beautiful exactly as you are."

Who offered more to this explosive era than the Beatles, and particularly John Lennon? We were all Beatle crazy, and I could not believe my luck when I had the opportunity to meet John Lennon himself through a mutual friend, Jack Haley Jr., who went on to marry Liza Minnelli.

It was 1974, when Victoria Principal, one of the stars of the future hit show *Dallas*, and I had been chosen as Oscar Girls. Our job (considered a great honor) was to dress in long white gowns and guide the stunned stars who had just won an Oscar across the stage to the backstage area, where they would be photographed by the press. That year, Jack Haley was producing the show, Marty Pasetta was directing, Peter Lawford was a presenter, Burt Reynolds was one of the emcees, and we were even graced with the presence of a streaker, a buck naked man who ran behind David Niven when he was introducing an award. For some unknown reason, streaking was all the rage right then, and our award show was definitely one of the main marks for any streaker worth his salt.

We were rehearsing when I heard a rumor that the great John Lennon was in the house, accompanied by his famous musician friend Harry Nilsson. As if seeing John Lennon was not enough! Victoria and I kept pointing him out to each other. There he was, in the flesh, and I was more than stunned when Jack Haley said to me, "Hey, Pam, we're heading over to the Troubadour to catch the Smothers Brothers act. Why don't you come join us?" The "us" he was referring to were John, Harry, and entourage. "We'll come back to finish rehearsing in a couple of hours."

"Yes" was my answer. I gathered my things together quickly. I didn't want to keep John Lennon waiting. I mean, there were stars, and then there was John Lennon.

The Troubadour was a popular nightclub on Santa Monica Boulevard where the hippest musicians performed their acts while large audiences imbibed the latest designer drinks and drugs and danced all night. That particular night, the Smothers Brothers were staging their comeback show, and we all loved their irreverence, their political wit, and their hysterical spoofs.

The place was packed that night in anticipation, and a burly man who was married to a famous porn star met our limo. He maneuvered the crowds to make a space while out of the limo came Jack Haley Jr., Peter Lawford, Marty Pasetta, Harry Nilsson, John Lennon—and moi!

Someone must have called ahead, because the manager led us through the crowded room to an elevated VIP section at the back of the room. We sat and ordered drinks. So far, no one had noticed that John Lennon had just walked in, and I had a few quiet moments to have a conversation with my favorite Beatle.

"Where are you from?" he asked, his intelligent eyes looking through his signature rimless glasses as he threw back his first drink.

"Colorado," I said.

"Where's that?" he wanted to know, in his unmistakable Liverpool accent.

"It's out west," I said. "They have cowboys there."

"There are black cowboys?" he asked.

"Absolutely," I told him.

"Well, I'd really like to see Colorado. I'd like to see black cowboys in that part of America."

It was a well-known fact that one of John's earliest musical inspirations was Little Richard, along with many other R&B artists and African American gospel singers. As John continued to knock back drinks, his eyes got a little glassy, his words got slurry, and he began to discuss his separation from Yoko Ono.

"How do you feel about her now?" I asked.

"I really miss her," he said.

"I bet you do," I said.

"There is this woman now, and I spend a lot of time traveling," he said wistfully.

"But what do you really want?" I asked him. "You were so involved with Yoko, and the two of you built something together. Are you ready to throw it all away? People trade in their mates like cars. I'd love to have what you have with Yoko. But I don't."

"You will," he said.

"Maybe and maybe not," I answered. "I don't know. I think I have to learn more about people. I feel like I'm on the outside watching."

John finished his drink and gestured to the waiter to bring another. "I have to think about what you just said," he told me.

I looked into his eyes, which were unfocused and staring off into the distance. We truly do get haunted by the ghosts of our lovers in this life, and there was no doubt that I was looking into the eyes of a haunted man.

Suddenly, as if someone had tapped him on the shoulder, he turned to Harry and said, "I heard this great song by a woman. Something about, 'I can't stand the rain.'"

I knew that song. It was one of my favorites, so I launched into a chorus immediately. "'I can't stand the rain,'" I sang, "'on my window.' It's by Ann Peebles."

John broke out into a huge smile. "That's it. I love it."

Harry joined us in the next chorus while John started singing and pounding out beats on the table with his hands. As the three of us raised our voices in song, waiting for the Smothers Brothers, people began turning around to see who was singing. When they realized it was John Lennon, Harry Nilsson, and a crazy black woman, the place erupted. All boredom and impatience were gone and everyone joined us in a chorus of "I Can't Stand the Rain." I'd have hated to be the Smothers Brothers that night and have to follow this act!

Now I was feeding John the words, and the rest of the audience was joining in the chorus. People were getting hysterical—they were getting up out of their chairs and calling out for John to come up and sign autographs. The waiters were trying to sit them back down, because if this continued, the Smothers Brothers wouldn't be able to do their act.

"Sing us another song, John," the people called out.

"No, no," John said with false humility. "This isn't my night. I'm just here to catch my friends perform."

There was a stir on the stage and in walked the Smothers Brothers, the main event, but no one was bothering to look at them. Who cared about the Smothers Brothers when John Lennon was in the house?

Someone was offering John a guitar, and they were urging him to get onstage to perform a one-man show.

"No, no," said John. "I don't want to do that. The Smothers Brothers are here."

The lights went down and Tommy and Dick started singing. But the audience would not calm down. They were so excited to be in the presence of one of the Beatles, they refused to take their attention away from him. John, looking pretty tipsy by now, began to sing again, encouraged by the crowds.

Jack Haley tried to quiet him down. "C'mon, John, why don't you be quiet? That's rude."

"I don't give a fuck," John slurred.

He started singing louder and banging on the table again. People were staring, and Harry was trying to reason with John, who was getting antagonistic. "We better get him out of here," Harry said to Jack just as the manager approached our table. "C'mon, man," he said to John. "They wouldn't do this to you."

"Okay, okay," John said. "I'll be quiet."

We should have left right then and there. That was our cue, but John started up again and the manager was back. "This isn't cool, John," he said. "You really need to leave."

John uttered an obscenity, and the next thing I knew, fists were flying. The manager tried to grab John by the arms and shoulders and pull him across Harry and over the railing that was next to our table. Drinks spilled all over us as a war broke out. John was punching indiscriminately, taking people out right and left in a drunken brawl. I was trying to block my face against flying chairs when the police showed up.

In the next moment, John, Harry, and I, along with the rest of our party, were all standing at the curb outside the club. Photos of us were was splashed all over the *LA Times* the next day, and my claim to fame was getting thrown out of the Troubadour with John Lennon and Harry Nilsson. It doesn't get much more notorious than that.

CHAPTER **22**   An Unlikely
Couple

When you consider contributions in the seventies that changed the way people talked about life, comedian Richard Pryor comes to mind. Born and raised in Peoria, Illinois, few were more prone to addiction and self-destruction than Richard, yet another comedian caught up in the glitz and speed of a dangerous game of Russian roulette called "Drugs." A look at his childhood says it all. Richard was raised in his grandmother's brothel in Peoria, where his mother, Gertrude, was a prostitute and his father, LeRoy Buck, was her pimp. On top of that, or maybe because of it, he was sexually molested by both a neighbor and a priest before his mother deserted him at age ten. His grandmother raised him, and it's a miracle he survived as long as he did. But we all have our obstacles to overcome in life.

When Richard was in his prime in the sixties, conservatives and "the establishment" judged his urban comedy as vulgar. But to the youth movement, urban was hip and Richard was the king of hip. His audiences got a charge out of hearing him say the words *dick* and *pussy* in public, and they loved to hear him talk about drugs. "Hey," he famously said, "cocaine ain't addictive. I've been using it since I was thirteen, and I ain't addicted."

Everybody laughed because he was saying what people were

thinking but didn't dare speak out loud. In the spirit of Lenny Bruce, Richard was a champ at dropping the filters, opening his rebellious mouth, and saying whatever came out of his drug-addled mind. And like Lenny Bruce and so many others, his addictions would be his downfall.

I met him when Freddie called me from his new house in the Hollywood Hills and asked me to take a drive with him. It had been a while since Freddie and I had split, and I wondered where he was taking me that morning when he pulled up in his brand-new blue Corvette convertible. He called upstairs, and I looked out the window to see him there, smiling and idling in his car.

"Ready to go?" he asked.

I walked downstairs and stood by his car.

"I need to prove to someone that I know you," Freddie said. "He doesn't believe me."

"Who is it?"

"I'll tell you when we get there," was all he'd say.

Freddie drove me to Northridge, about twenty miles north of Hollywood, where we made our way through a private citrus orchard and pulled up to the security gate of a sprawling Spanish hacienda that was being renovated. Freddie pushed the button and spoke into the intercom. "It's Freddie. Let me in."

The intercom emitted a stream of expletives, like a parrot that was raised by a pirate. "Hey, fuck you, you goddamned motherfucker, motherfucker, motherfucker."

I gave Freddie a tentative look. "I don't know who that is, but I'm getting out of the car right here," I said. "You can go in without me."

"Please, Pam, just wait a second."

The gate swung open, and before I could get the car door open, Freddie drove onto the property and the gate closed behind us. Several men in overalls were standing on tall ladders, painting the house exterior, as I saw a man in a black and white robe and house shoes walking toward us. It was Richard Pryor. Although I'd never seen him in person, I was familiar with his picture, I *loved* his comedy records, and I was well aware of his reputation for having an obscene mouth.

"Great fuckin' wheels," he told Freddie, referring to the blue Corvette that had been a gift from Freddie's studio. He had liked my Corvette and had asked the studio for a blue one, just like mine. At that time, Freddie usually got what he wanted.

While I was still sitting in the car Richard stared at me and turned his gaze toward Freddie. "Motherfucker," he said with wide eyes and a grin, "you *do* know the bitch." Unbeknownst to me, Richard had already "started his day," meaning he was well into his recreational drug ingestion by 11 a.m.

"I won the bet," said Freddie, "but don't feel too bad." He reached into his pocket and took out a vial of what he told me later was pure liquid cocaine.

Richard's face lit up. "C'mon," he said to me. "Get out of the car." I sat there.

"I'm not gonna hurt you," he said. "Come on up and hang out. Let me show you my new pad." He took off on a diatribe, reciting my exact dialogue in one of the hottest scenes of *Foxy Brown*. Clearly, he was a fan of my movie. He had memorized the lines, and I had to laugh. But I was not interested in watching two grown men get stupid on cocaine.

"It was really nice to meet you," I said politely, "but I have to go."

A look of amazement swept over Richard's face. Then he looked offended. I must have been the first woman who had ever refused his offer of checking out his massive pad, doing the best designer drugs, and whatever else was expected to go along with it.

"You have to stay," he told me with a grin. "Please be my guest."

"Sorry," I said. "I have to go." Freddie shrugged his shoulders at Richard, promising to come back as soon as he dropped me off.

I met Richard again in Georgia, in 1976, when Melvin Van Peebles cast me in his new movie, *Greased Lightning*, starring Richard Pryor, Cleavon Little, and Beau Bridges, with music by the Commodores.

Later, Michael Schultz took over as director. I was twenty-six, and I remember showing up for that first day of shooting and seeing Richard face-to-face once again. We stared at each other, speechless. I was in sweats with no makeup, and he held a cup of coffee in his hand, looking bleary-eyed so early in the morning. We both smiled when we realized that neither of us was at all like the characters we emulated for the public, the ones with the big 'fros who went around yelling "motherfucker" all over the place. In fact, after a short conversation before we headed to makeup, he said to me, "Pam Grier, you're just a farmer. A hick."

He was right, but no one ever wanted to see me that way or to acknowledge my real background. They didn't want to know that I'd been raised in a rural town, that I'd been raped several times, that I loved science and medicine, that I was not too squeamish to put a worm on a fishhook, that I had begun to study premed, and that I didn't curse or do drugs. But Richard seemed fascinated by the real parts of me. He wanted to get away from the drug culture, so he said, and maybe he saw me as his way out.

I found Richard to be very personable, but I wondered why he was interested in me. After all, I was focused more on work than play. As for Richard, during the filming of *Greased Lightning*, he was a softer, gentler, humbler personality in the mornings when we arrived for work. But by mid-afternoon, after his friends had spent ample time in his trailer, he emerged like a haughty, outwardly confident macho man, definitely different from earlier in the day. I understood why his personality was so mercurial. He was getting high.

Actually, Richard and I did not begin dating until several months after *Greased Lightning* had wrapped. That was right after he broke up with his most recent girlfriend. A photograph appeared in a gossip magazine of Richard, in a full-length chinchilla coat, having a public argument with her. He was single and lonely, just like me, when we dropped our outer facades and got to know each other as real people instead of constructed film images. I saw a wonderful side of him: the way he loved his family, his pride in his success, and his humility about his career. This was a good sign, since he had power coming to him that was unprecedented in the world of black comedians—or any comedian, for that matter. I wanted to be friends with him, and I thought we might become lovers, but I also feared what power and money would do to his psyche. Would it help or hurt, and where did I fit in? He was part of a world that I didn't really understand. And I had to wonder what it was about comedians that attracted me. Was it a hormone and estrogen cocktail that inexorably drew me to these men?

It didn't take long until Richard and I realized that maybe we were not as unlikely as we first thought. For starters, we had a wonderful and romantic sex life—an *ordinary* one, which was contrary to both of our images. The truth is that he was shy and my military upbringing (as well as my difficult past) had taught me to be cautious. But I was interested in helping him get healthy, which he wanted me to do. He was a great talent, a brilliant man, and I hated that drugs were stopping him from attaining real success. The most profound and naked comment he ever made to me about his drug addiction was, "I'm afraid if I stop doing drugs, I won't be funny."

"But you're naturally funny," I told him. "The drugs just enhance what you already do and say. Maybe they give you courage to say things that you normally wouldn't. When the filter is gone, you can just go for it. But that has nothing to do with whether or not you're funny."

We'd met at a time in Richard's life when his body was starting to rebel against so much abuse. He was having physical symptoms— his skin and his scalp were broken out, he was losing sleep—and he desperately wanted a way out of the drug culture. Something inside of him was telling him that he needed a break, and he hoped I was that break. He hoped (as I did) that he could conquer his addictions and we could be together indefinitely with a deep commitment and dedication to each other and our relationship. He was banking on my strength and will to help him stay away from the wrong people—his so-called friends who claimed to love him and told him how great he was, while they devoured his food, did his drugs and alcohol, and took whatever he offered them. And believe me, he was a generous man.

"The first thing you have to do is find yourself," I said. "You have a good personality so you can attract good people who care about you for *you*, not for what you can give them."

My presence in Richard's life was a positive influence—for a while. First thing in the morning, Richard embarked on a health regime that I helped him fashion. He wanted to get up early like a normal person instead of sleeping in until two in the afternoon as he was accustomed to doing. He wanted to eat a real breakfast, so his cook and I made fresh oatmeal with berries, eggs, bacon, toast, and his favorite—my mom's recipe for pancakes. Whenever I had time, I cooked them for him, added some cinnamon and nutmeg, and he was in seventh heaven.

After breakfast, we met our trainer on the tennis court and lobbed some balls around for a while. Some days, he invited over his friends who were stuntmen, and we all engaged in tennis tournaments. There, he would get inspired with an idea and would run various stories by me. His creative energy seemed to flourish when he was doing sports, and more than once he took on several different personas throughout the tennis game, which he would write about later.

After I'd known him for a while, Richard confided in me that he couldn't read. He learned all of his lines phonetically with the help of a few intimate acquaintances, and more than anything in the world, he wanted me to teach him to read. I found some novels about humor and Western history, and he made great strides in his reading, with me coaching him along the way. It turned out that he loved words, and his dream was to read *War and Peace*. He said, "I heard that *War and Peace* is the hardest motherfuckin' novel to read. I'm gonna read it. If I can't read it, it's so damned big, at least I can kill someone with it. Use it as a weapon."

I loved his four dogs and played with them every chance I got. I also helped remodel his house, the former Wrigley estate. This was my first experience of putting a house together with a man, and it was not easy. We both had eclectic tastes, but Richard was so indecisive, he eventually caused five different contractors to resign because he couldn't make up his mind. Of course, it was always their fault, and

I was seeing another side of Richard—the one where he refused to take responsibility for his own mistakes. I don't know how many times he ordered someone to rip out a brand-new floor or wall because the color he himself had chosen didn't suit him any longer.

I decided to leave most of the remodeling to him, and I taught Richard to swim in his Olympic-size swimming pool. I bought him a bicycle so we could ride places together, and when he said he wanted to ride bikes with his kids from his four relationships, I was very supportive and helped to make it happen. In fact, for his birthday, I invited all of his children and their moms to celebrate with him.

He had only a sixth-grade education, but Richard was witty and bright with common sense and street smarts. When he did drugs and drank, there was no telling what he would do to himself or say to anyone else. But when he was sober, he spoke quietly, he acted humbly, and he was sensitive and quite different from his aggressive, profane image. He was a good athlete and turned one of the buildings on his land into a boxing ring where he could exercise. He also became pretty good at tennis. Actually, in many ways, Richard and I mirrored each other. As horrible as it was, we'd both been raped at six years old, we had suffered the shame and indignity of it, and we understood the pain of silence. Although I was raised Catholic, I was interested in the principles of Buddhism that invited a person to look within, and so was Richard.

We were getting along really well. His skin and scalp were clearing up, and he was eating great food and had lots of energy. And so I wasn't surprised when he asked me to move in. "Pick a room, Pam, and make it yours," he offered. "You can have a whole wing."

"Not now, Richard," I told him. I'd already watched drugs eating away at Freddie, and I wasn't eager to go through that again.

He got frustrated and said, "Most of the women I date want furs and jewels and they can't wait to move in. You're the opposite. Whenever I give you a piece of jewelry, you don't wear it. You're a hard nut to crack, Pam, because you're so fuckin' independent."

"I am," I agreed, "but I can share my independence when I feel safe. The thing is, I don't feel safe living here yet because I don't know who you are."

"You don't love me, do you?" he said.

Echoes of Kareem, who had said exactly the same thing, resounded in my head. "It's not about that," I explained. "I don't know who you are—the kind, loving man who's sober and fun, or the drugged-out person you become when you abuse yourself. I have no idea how long you're going to be the real you. Give me some time."

"I promise I'm really gonna try," he said.

I was well aware of women friends who put up with their husbands' affairs and drug use, and one day woke up beside a stranger. Or they found themselves traded in for a newer model. I refused to allow that to happen to me.

CHAPTER 23 Three Strikes and I'm Outta There!

Richard included me in so much of his life that I found myself falling in love with him. When he was sober, we had a good balance, but I wondered if I would be a strong enough influence to keep him on a sober and healthy path or if he would have to do it all on his own. If he let me help him for even a few hours each day, we might be able to make our relationship work. But the thing was, I had my own life and my own career, which didn't leave a lot of room for taking care of Richard. He was of two minds: He wanted me to have my career, but he also wanted me to drop everything and be there for him.

We had a few good months, but soon enough, Richard started missing his buddies—the way they stroked his ego and complimented him. He was addicted not only to cocaine but to everyone telling him how great he was. He had been sober for about six months when he told me he felt much better. "I miss my friends," he said, "and I'm ready to see them again. I can do it, Pam, and stay straight. I know I can. They want to help me."

"I hope you're right, Richard," I said.

As his friends began trickling back into his life, he introduced me to some of them, and they were sensitive to his situation at first. They got high before they got there and Richard got very busy writing and setting up deals. He had finished shooting the successful action comedy *Stir Crazy*, and A-level producers were hounding him. He was the new kid on the block, he was writing and creating, and all the heavyweights in production wanted to meet with him. But they were aware of his past troubles with alcohol and drugs, since he had made some public scenes and had earned a bad reputation after flaking out on a few important meetings.

I became the go-between. A producer would call me and say, "How's he doing? Do you think he'll show up today?"

"He isn't the same Richard you knew before," I'd assure him. "Just wait until you see him."

But the truth was that Richard was regressing. He was in denial, of course, assuring me his buddies were going to just hang out, eat some food, and play tennis. I looked at them suspiciously. I hated the fact that my relationship with Richard was based on whether or not he was getting high, which, in turn, determined whether or not he showed up for meetings and kept his life together. I feared that renewing his association with his old friends would sabotage what he was building and what we were building together.

He and his friends used to hang out in the kitchen for hours on end. They liked the large dining table there where they could play "bones," the hip name that African Americans had for dominoes. They also liked the close proximity to the refrigerator with a constant supply of beer and food. One afternoon, when I went into the kitchen to ask Richard about a contractor, I saw a pile of cocaine sitting on a mirror next to a razor blade and a rolled-up $100 bill. I stuck my finger into the white powder and tasted it. My tongue went numb, and I made a terrible face. "Ugh," I said, "that tastes like aspirin. Why would anyone want to do it?"

Richard acted like he hadn't been indulging, but I knew better. I saw the signs—his bloodshot eyes, the lines of coke, the half-smoked joints, and the nearly empty bottle of Courvoisier.

I wondered for a moment if I did cocaine, would it make me a genius like Richard? Nah! If I wasn't a genius by now, it probably wasn't going to happen. I left the room, disgusted and discouraged. I wanted to speak up right then and there and call out his friends, but I feared his reprisal. I had a healthy sense of self-preservation, so I waited until the time was right to talk with him. Later that day, I tried to make Richard understand that his friends were taking advantage of his good nature, not to mention his addictive tendencies. "Your friends are staying here way too long," I said. "They're here for days at a time, they're doing drugs in front of you, they're taking everything and giving nothing."

"They don't have as much as I do," he argued. "Besides, I've known them a lot longer than I've known you."

Because it felt like those words had lacerated my heart, I knew I was in love with him. Why else would it hurt so much? Were his words based on his being high, or was he trying to exert his ego over me? Or was it some of both?

"If you want to keep feeding your so-called friends and loaning them money," I said, "that's up to you, but they're using you. Why doesn't anybody call and say, 'Hey, I'll bring some ribs and a roast over or a six-pack or a bottle of wine?' They don't bring anything. You supply it all."

I suggested he get his financial matters in order to help him save some money for himself and his children's future. Richard didn't trust managers, and he refused to give over his power and authority to anyone—except me. He wanted me to take over his finances, but I refused. "I have a career, too," I reminded him. "I need to focus on myself. If you want to stay up on your pedestal and keep taking care of all your friends, go ahead."

"You got no problem with that?" he asked.

"No, I'll be doing my thing. But if you continue to stay high and drink, you know you're destroying any chance of success."

He looked at me suspiciously. "I'm surprised you'd give me my space," he said. "All my other women wanted to be right here, listenin' to everything."

"I'm not like your other women," I said. "But maybe they hovered around because they felt they had to watch over you. Being holed up in a room for three days with your friends is bad for any relationship.

At some point, you have to come out and say hello and see how your woman is doing. If you don't, that's a sick lifestyle."

Richard kept it together, just barely, for another week or so. Then I got to his place from the set at the end of a day of filming the movie *Drum* to hear the phone ringing. I picked it up, and it was a producer that Richard really respected. "He blew me off, Pam," the man said. "Richard didn't show up for the meeting today. I've been calling and calling. There's been no answer."

I got a dull ache in the pit of my stomach. I knew Richard was in trouble, because he had really been looking forward to this meeting. "Listen, I just got home," I said. "Let me see what's going on. He's been doing really well lately," I lied. "I know this meeting meant the world to him."

When I hung up the phone, Richard came sauntering into the kitchen in his terry-cloth bathrobe and with a smug smile on his face. "Hey, babe," he said. "How'd it go today?"

"Why did you miss your meeting?" I said, peering into his blood-shot eyes. "You worked hard to get that meeting."

"Oh," he said, "I'll reschedule it. No problem. I canceled the day to hang out with a buddy from out of town."

"You must really like this friend of yours," I continued, "because you canceled the day, and now the producer is about to cancel *you*. Why are you still in your robe at five in the afternoon? What's going on?"

"Nothing," he said defensively. "I told you, we're just hanging out."

I turned away from him. I couldn't stand seeing him lie to me like a kid lying to his mother. I also hated that I was actually acting like his mother.

That was strike one.

I was a little tired from a lot of work and trying to manage Richard, but I felt healthy enough when I went in for my annual checkup with my gynecologist. After the exam, however, he asked me to step into his office to talk. I was scared because that had never happened before.

I sat opposite him and he said, "Pam, I want to tell you about an epidemic that's prevalent in Beverly Hills right now. It's a buildup of cocaine residue around the cervix and in the vagina. You have it. Are you doing drugs?"

"No," I said, astonished.

"Well, it's really dangerous," he went on. "Is your partner putting cocaine on his penis to sustain his erection?"

"No," I said, "not that I know of. It's not like he has a pile of cocaine next to the bed and he dips his penis in it before we have sex." I had a nauseating flash of one of Richard's famous lines: *Even my dick has a cocaine jones.*

"Are you sure he isn't doing it in the bathroom before he comes to bed?" the doctor asked.

"That's a possibility," I said. "You know, I *am* dating Richard Pryor."

"Oh, my God," he said. "We have a serious problem here. If he's not putting it on his skin directly, then it's worse because the coke is in his seminal fluid. I have to ask you something very personal, Pam, and you need to be one hundred percent honest with me or you're going to have some serious cervical and uterine problems. You can become sterile, and you might have to have a hysterectomy. When you give him oral sex, do your gums and lips get numb?"

It was as if a light went on. "Yes," I said, incredulous. "I couldn't figure it out."

He explained, "Cocaine causes a numbing, like novocaine, and it's very dangerous for you and for him."

"Will it ever go away?" I asked. "Will he have it in his system forever?"

"It'll go away eventually," the doctor said, "if he abstains for long enough. In the meantime, he has to wear a condom or you're going to be a very sick woman."

I left the doctor's office depressed and scared. I knew Richard wasn't going to like this, and I was right. "I have cocaine inside of me," I told him. "It's eating me up, and it could kill me. Have you been putting it on your penis?"

"No. Of course not," he answered quickly. "What are you sayin'?"

"I'm saying that you've been doing cocaine for so long, it's in your seminal fluid." I took a deep breath. "I have to ask you to wear a condom when we have sex."

"What?" was all he said, but I could read between the lines. It was as if he'd said, "Me? Richard Pryor, wear a condom? I don't think so."

"You have to, Richard," I pleaded with him. "Only for a while. I have to get rid of these lesions so I don't get infections."

"No, I won't do it," was his answer.

You'd think I'd asked him to get a vasectomy or be castrated, he put up such a fuss. "But it's about my health," I said.

"I hate condoms. I can't feel anything."

"Will you at least talk to my doctor?"

"No."

I realized in that moment that I was not truly loved by this man. That was strike two.

❈

As much as I cared about Richard, I had to realize that, in the end, we are all responsible for our own decisions, the environments in which we choose to live, and the friendships we decide to nurture, no matter our childhood circumstances. A huge rift had grown between Richard and me, but we carried on as sometime lovers. I made sure to clean myself really well, inside and out, after we made love, because as much as I cared for Richard, love can kill. Wasn't that a refrain from a country and western song? "Love can kill in more ways than one."

The truth was that I loved Richard, there was still affection between us, and then we women always think in the back of our minds that the guy might change, and I was no different. I ran the house and made sure the dogs were taken care of, and I gave instructions to the housekeeper. I was sad about the way our relationship had deteriorated, but I thought maybe, if we waited long enough, things might fall back into place.

Then Ginger, a miniature chestnut horse, arrived at the house. The beautiful sorrel horse was a gift to Richard from producer Burt Sugarman, and I was as delighted as he was. Ginger was small and adorable, Richard loved her, and I was thrilled to have my own little horse to raise and train.

I filled up the feed shack in the stables that had been empty until Ginger arrived. I gave her some hay and put her out in a little meadow beside the house to graze. Even though Richard and I were not being intimate, I was staying there most of the time to look after the house and him. Now I added the horse to my daily duties, giving Richard a stern lecture about never letting the dogs out in a pack around the horse. They would tear her limb from limb, I explained—it was in the nature of pack animals—and Ginger, a miniature, was not large enough to kick them away like a bigger horse would do.

Richard understood and was careful about letting the dogs out one by one. But the housekeeper was not. I explained the characteristics of pack animals to her, but one morning, when the dogs wouldn't stop barking, she threw them all out into the yard together, right where the horse was grazing. The next thing we knew, the dogs were attacking Ginger, growling and biting at her stomach.

I heard the ruckus from a room upstairs and flew outside to find the dogs about to kill the horse. Richard rushed out as I turned a hose on the dogs until they went flying off across the meadow, leaving Ginger at death's door. Richard sobbed as I rushed inside to call the vet. He was backed up with sick animals and couldn't make it to our house, but he could see Ginger at his office as soon as we could get her there.

I glanced around the property. There was no horse trailer or truck. Richard was standing in his robe, screaming and crying, and Ginger was lying on the ground with her intestines coming out. I needed to get her to the vet. "We're putting her in the backseat of my car," I told Richard.

"Pam," he said, "you drive a Jag."

"We're putting her in the backseat of my car," I repeated. "I'll pull her through and you push. She's only about four hundred pounds.

That's about three or four people. I think the springs under the back wheels can handle it."

While Richard continued to cry and mutter under his breath about shooting the dogs, we pushed and pulled Ginger into the backseat of my yellow 1974 Jaguar XJ6 L. "Get in," I called out to Richard as I slid into the driver's seat.

As we tore down the street and onto the 405, I can only imagine how we looked in a brand-new yellow Jaguar with brown stripes, a horse's head and tail sticking out the two back windows, and two black people in the front—a man in a robe sobbing and a wild woman driving.

Richard wailed constantly, "My Ginger. My baby." I looked down at my feet to see that I had on two different shoes. Nothing mattered except getting Ginger to the vet. The back of the car was bouncing and giving off sparks where the metal kept scraping the road. When someone on the freeway recognized Richard Pryor in the front seat (they had no idea about the identity of the wild woman who was driving), we ended up with a long line of cars following us to see where in the hell we were going.

The entire staff was standing outside the vet's office when we pulled into the driveway. They got Ginger out of the car and began treating her immediately while we waited. I have the vet and his assistants to thank that Ginger survived, but I'd had enough of taking care of Richard and his crises. We stayed at the vet for about five hours until Ginger was stitched up, medicated, and out of shock. Then we pushed her into the car again for the trip back.

I drove much more carefully on the way home, completely exhausted from the ordeal. Just as we were pulling into the gates, I said to Richard, "You know what? Ginger hasn't peed since this morning. We better get her out of the car fast. She must have a river of urine in her."

The gate closed behind us, I stopped the car, and just as we started to push Ginger out the door, she let her bladder go. In a moment, there was a gallon of horse piss soaking into the seats and the carpets of my Jag.

"How can such a little horse have so much pee?" Richard asked as the yellow stream flowed like a river out of the car and onto the ground. We both laughed in spite of ourselves, but we were on very shaky ground. When I finally got a chance to take stock, I realized that this incident had been an omen. I'd saved Ginger, but I couldn't save Richard.

That was strike three.

I got no sleep that night. I might have totaled my car, caused an accident, hurt both Richard and me and God knows who else. I realized that in essence, although I was in Richard's house, I was alone. We were hardly lovers anymore, but I was there for him, and if need be, I could keep him safe. Who would keep me safe? Not Richard, who completely fell apart when Ginger had needed him. What if it had been our child? How many more tragedies did I need to convince me that I wasn't capable of supporting my boyfriend? I decided that as talented and powerful as Richard was, I was not strong enough to be there for him in his heavily complicated life.

The next morning, I got up after Richard left the house. I was done. I had given up too much of myself, and although I loved him and I knew he loved me, I couldn't do this anymore. I rented a car and tearfully packed up my clothes. I patted the dogs' heads, cried some more, and left a note saying that I was heading home to Colorado to spend some time with my family. Now, much to my relief, my grief, and my disappointment, I was outta there!

CHAPTER **24** LOSS

I t was 1977, shortly after Richard and I split, when I got a disturbing phone call from Freddie. We hadn't been together for about two years, and he sounded depressed and loaded out of his skull. Still, it surprised me when he said he'd been thinking about taking his life. "I have a gun, Pam," he said, "and I'm thinking about using it."

He wanted me to come and help him since I was staying at a friend's home only a few blocks from the Beverly Westwood Hotel, where he was staying. I thought about Freddie's life and how he had handled it. Did I really want to go and rescue him? I had no professional background to help someone as disturbed as Freddie sounded. If I did show up, what could I do for him? Perhaps the most disturbing part was that he claimed he was broke and asked me for a loan for a couple hundred dollars. He said if I wouldn't come to him, he could send a messenger to pick it up.

"Why do you need money?" I asked. "You just signed a multimillion-dollar contract for *Chico and the Man*."

"I only need it for a little while. I have to pay back some guys." I knew what that meant.

"If you're that broke, how can you afford to pay a messenger?" I asked him.

"I can use the studio messengers." He paused a moment and said, "They all keep screaming at me."

"Who?" I asked.

"My people."

I didn't go rescue him, and I didn't loan him any money. When the call came three days later that he had taken his life, I was heartbroken. For quite a while, I wondered if I could have helped him. I wanted to save his soul, but I knew that only he could help himself, and he hadn't really wanted to. I had loved him, I always would, but some people just don't survive the blitz and chaos of a show-business life, and Freddie was one of them. If only he'd had a larger group of friends who could have helped him.

He was buried in Forest Lawn Cemetery overlooking some of the movie studios, but I didn't go to the funeral. I had loved Freddie so much, I didn't trust myself to keep quiet when I saw some of the people who I wish had helped him. So far, he was the second man I'd dated whom I could have considered marrying or at least having a baby with—if the drugs hadn't gotten in the way.

I went to the cemetery alone the day after they put him in the ground. I laid a bouquet of white stargazer lilies at his grave and sat with him, feeling how much we had cared for each other. Then I threw myself into my work, taking as many roles as I could find.

I was lonely, feeling the effects of the loss of my relationship with Richard and Freddie's death, when the sun came out once again—in the form of meeting renowned musician Minnie Riperton. Originally a member of the group Rotary Connection and a backup singer for the amazing Stevie Wonder, she had sung with the greats: Etta James, Fontella Bass, Ramsey Lewis, Bo Diddley, Chuck Berry, and Muddy Waters, to name a few. Her most famous song, "Lovin' You," had made it to the top of the charts in 1975 in record time, and she was now one of the best-known and best-loved black singers.

I discovered why she was so popular when I met her at a black entertainment awards show in Oakland, California. I was fortunate that they put Minnie, her husband, Richard Rudolph, her daughter, Maya, later of *Saturday Night Live* fame, and her son, Marc, at my table. I was such a fan, and I told Minnie how much I loved her music. She couldn't have been kinder, and her eyes were filled with warmth and joy. There was no competitiveness or jealousy in her. I could tell that immediately. She was a rare kind of woman who embraced other women with compassion, love, and caring.

"I have no interest in ever demeaning another woman," I told her. "We get enough of that in the workplace, and I won't add to it."

She agreed. She was as great a human being as she was a singer. Her daughter and her young son, Marc, loved her, and those of us whom she called her friends considered ourselves lucky. "We'll be friends for life," she told me. And we were. We just had no idea how short a period of time we were talking about, as I watched Minnie design her own clothes and go on tour dates. A true artist in every sense of the word, she dressed beautifully, her makeup was always meticulous, and she shared her knowledge and her experiences as a mother and a wife with me.

At five foot six, Minnie could walk in stilettos like they were ballet slippers. She loved taking me shopping in Beverly Hills, where she showed me all the latest fashions and advised me on what to buy. She suggested rouge colors for my cheeks, I introduced her to yoga, and we experimented with herbal teas and metaphysics. We had stimulating discussions about Buddhism and other religions and cultures. It was so refreshing to be around a woman, a peer, who wasn't envious of me and didn't see me as a threat. She just took me under her wing, taught me what she knew, and I did the same with her.

Minnie was so encouraging, she got me writing music and singing. "You have a great voice," she said. "Don't ever let anyone tell you that you can't sing."

I followed her advice when I went into the studio with Giorgio Moroder. He had produced Donna Summer, and he wanted me to sound like her and kept trying to direct me toward a European disco sound. I, however, wanted to sound like myself, and Minnie agreed with me. "You have a distinct sound and feeling. It's funk. You need to be yourself and sound like yourself. Not like somebody else."

My music career was short-lived, but Minnie and I savored our time together. She gave me great advice about men and dating. She said, "When you meet a man, he puts you in one of two categories—the woman he wants to marry or the woman he wants just for sex. The way you dress will help determine that. If he shows up in a suit and you have tattoos and urban apparel, he'll want to have sex with you. Nothing more. Gentlemen always marry a lady."

I smiled. "I get it," I said. "If the guy dresses urban, you can dress urban. If he dresses preppy, so do you."

"Now you're getting it, girl. Oil and water don't mix."

She was trying to protect me from being a notch on some guy's belt, and I appreciated her advice. I told Minnie everything, as we went to restaurants together and noticed all the guys who were looking at us. When she began categorizing them like they were categorizing us, I laughed my head off. We shared some incredibly intimate tidbits, like, "You know a man really loves you if he likes the smell of your armpits." And "Everyone has baggage. Just make sure you and the guy have compatible baggage. I come from the land of Samsonite." She was talking about compatibility.

I was home in Colorado visiting my mother when Minnie was diagnosed with breast cancer about a year after we met. She was so young, about thirty, and I prayed that she would beat it. I was back in Los Angeles when she went in for surgery. I spent as much time with her as I could, aware that she needed to spend most of her time with her family and I didn't want to impose. But I missed our spontaneous phone calls day or night, to discuss men, our careers, and anything else that popped into our heads. Anytime I called, she used to called me back, but now, since she'd been going through chemotherapy, she was too weak to talk on the phone.

One day when I called and she couldn't come to the phone, I realized that her treatment plan was not working. She was sleeping most of the time, she was in a lot of pain, and she was slipping through my fingers. I called occasionally to check on her, and when she couldn't talk, her sister would let me know how she was doing. I visited her for short periods and sometimes dropped things off for her when she was asleep or couldn't see visitors.

I called one day after her chemo was over, and she picked up the phone. She sounded like the old Minnie when she told me that in a few weeks she was going to record an album with Stevie Wonder. Did I dare hope she had beat the illness? She was very excited to be feeling better, and we made a plan to have lunch the next day.

Whenever we had luncheon plans, she always called me an hour early to discuss what we were planning to wear. When she didn't call that morning, I called her. Her sister answered the phone in a hushed tone. "Yes?" she said quietly.

"Hi, it's Pam," I bubbled. "Minnie and I are having lunch pretty soon, and we haven't talked about what we're wearing."

"Oh, Pam," she said tearfully, "Minnie just passed away." It was July 12, 1979, a day I will never forget.

I dropped onto the couch and sobbed. I hadn't had a chance to say good-bye to Minnie, but she knew that I had been a true friend. I was in a fog a few days later when I picked up some of her family members and drove them to Westwood Cemetery. There, Minnie was interred in good company, as she was laid to rest in the vicinity of the grave of Marilyn Monroe. Minnie and I had shared a love of Chinese culture, and she was buried in a blue Chinese wedding dress. I had one just like it in red that she had given to me. I kept it, and it's still a constant trigger for memories every time I look at it in my closet.

When I think back, I see that Minnie gave me great wisdom and that she was a true friend. She always said that if we could have five good friends in this life, we were truly blessed. Minnie was one of mine, and I always think of her when I explore the meaning of a real friendship, recalling her unconditional presence and encouragement in my life.

CHAPTER 25

The Actor
Prepares

Mom was ill and Krista was battling cancer in the early eighties, so I was making various trips to Colorado to see them both. I had done some TV roles in the miniseries *Roots* and on *Miami Vice* and *Crime Story*, but I hadn't had a good movie role since *Greased Lightning*. I was still passionate about acting, but the movie business had so many difficult twists and turns, I felt I was at a crossroads.

There is a grassy area in West Los Angeles called the Santa Monica Esplanade, where people run up and down San Vicente Boulevard. I was jogging there, deciding if I should quit the business or do some serious theater, when I noticed a pleasant-looking man passing me, running in the opposite direction.

"Aren't you Pam Grier?" he called out to me, doing an about-face so he could run beside me.

"Yeah, I am," I said.

"David Moss. I'm a theatrical agent."

The name was familiar, and I felt easy about him running beside me. I weighed about 117 at the time, soaking wet, and I was a size 4. He obviously liked what he saw, but he was not a bit obnoxious or even flirtatious. He was a perfect gentleman, and he even said, "Oh, my God, you're a great actress."

"Thank you," I said, as we continued running.

"So what are you doing now?" he wanted to know.

"I'm getting involved in theater. I really like it. But in California, there are very few theater productions."

He smiled, understanding what I meant. We ran in silence for a few minutes until he said, "There's this role I'm trying to cast for a movie. If I could swing it, I think they'd see you."

"What is it?" I asked.

"They've seen everybody," he said, "but no one is quite right. It's the role of a psychotic drug-addicted hooker/killer."

I looked down at my running shoes hitting the ground with each stride. What the hell kind of vibe was I giving off today?

"Paul Newman is starring in it," he added.

I stopped running and so did he. Panting and sweating, my hands on my hips, I stared at him. "Paul Newman?"

"The very one."

"Why me?" I wanted to know.

"You have a quiet intensity," David Moss said. "I've seen your work, and no one can see past your beauty. It gets in the way of your greatness. But I can see the real you in there. Give me your number and I'll call you this week."

"Wait just a minute," I said. "Playing a junkie hooker is not a walk in the park. I need time to do some serious preparation. You don't get to that overnight."

"If you're willing to do the preparation, Pam," he said, "I'll get you the audition and some time to prepare. A week at least."

"Is that all? A week? I'd love to work with Paul Newman," I said, "but a week isn't enough."

"It'll have to be," he said. "They'll fly you to New York tomorrow. You can do your preparation there."

Never one to pass up a major opportunity, I tucked my bible, *An Actor Prepares*, under my arm and got on the plane, scared to death. I had a major challenge ahead of me. What if I failed in front of Paul Newman? The stakes were high as I checked into the Wyndham Hotel where David Susskind, the producer, put me up in Midtown

Manhattan. Now that I was there, I had some work to do.

In my estimation, one actress stands out above all the rest in her ability to immerse herself in a role and make an emotional impact on everyone who watches her. I'm talking about Meryl Streep, and no movie better demonstrated her range of talent and emotion than *Sophie's Choice*. After weeping my way through that Oscar-winning performance, I read that Alan Pakula had been looking for a European actress to play Sophie, even though Meryl Streep really wanted the part. As much as Pakula admired her work, he was not interested in casting her. He told her no, but Meryl refused to take no for an answer.

Rather than calling her reps to lobby for the role for her, she took matters into her own hands. She hired a voice tutor to learn to speak with a perfect Polish accent, she studied the Polish culture, and then she literally forced her way into Pakula's office. There, she gave the performance of a lifetime, and when she left, the role was hers. It was all about her superb preparation and her unwillingness to be deterred from her goal. In essence, she did a great deal more than read for the role of Sophie. She became Sophie from the inside out.

Constantin Stanislavsky and Meryl Streep were my teachers as I anticipated my upcoming audition. The movie was called *Fort Apache, the Bronx*, a cop war/crime drama that takes place on the drug-addled streets of New York City. My role was a drug addict named Charlotte—a hooker and a killer. They had literally seen everyone for this role, including my friend Tamara, and now it was my turn.

Wanting to look the part, I went into a sleazy sex shop and got a blonde wig, red stockings, a garter belt, and some seriously high stilettos. Then I cleared my room by stacking all the furniture in the corner and began to study my lines. But when I got to the part where Charlotte shoots up and overdoses, I panicked. How could I portray the life of a drug addict/prostitute when I had never met one? Well, if I had, I didn't know it. What made me think I could I do better than the other actresses who already had read for the role and were passed over?

This is not going to work, I thought. I picked up the phone to cancel the audition. Who was I kidding? As luck would have it, the line was busy, so I hung up and took stock of things. Maybe I should do the audition anyway, so they could at least see my work and keep me in mind for something else. How many times did the opportunity arise to read for Paul Newman?

Hardly ever, was the answer, and I needed to do some on-the-spot research. I walked to Tenth Avenue, and there I was, in the shabbiest 'hood I'd ever seen. A few blocks from the subway, I spotted a street corner where groups of overly made-up, haggard-looking women were standing in high heels and ultra-short skirts, pretending to be alluring. Some men were being serviced right there on the street while others were making deals with the women from inside their cars. One hooker, who was very tall with a red wig, got into my face. "Whachou doin' here?" she demanded in her street voice. "This my corner."

"I don't want your corner," I assured her. "I'm doing research for a film."

Her persona shifted dramatically as she leaned in and said in a normal voice, "I'm a schoolteacher. I have a degree, and I'm trying to put my husband through school and support my son. I make good money here. I once made two grand in one day."

I heard about a porn movie house off of Forty-Second Street where, for the right price, you could watch a film of women performing sexual acts with men and other women. It was a world of sexual gratification above all else, where men were certain to get the kind of sexual release they wanted. They got their manhood validated, and it was exciting for them to get what they desired without putting their marriages and relationships at risk. I could see both sides now that I was having a direct experience of a world I had only heard about in the ugliest of terms.

My head was reeling when I finally got back to my empty room, where I tried sleeping on the floor, unsuccessfully. Charlotte was an addict to such a degree, she would pass out wherever she landed. I wanted to wake up in the morning like a drug addict would—cold and hurting. It was hard as a rock, and I had painful visions floating through my head of women and pimps and johns—a world that, before now, I'd only known about from television.

On the magazine cover:

WHO'S NEWS...

AUGUST/1975 $1.00

Ms.

FILM
PAM GRIER,
super-sass

POLITICS
ELAINE NOBLE,
not just another
gay legislator

FASHION
DIANA VREELAND,
mother of pizzazz

ABORTION
DR. KENNETH
EDELIN,
champion
of choice

MUSIC
CARLA BLEY
and all her

WRITING
MERIDEL LESUEUR

PAM GRIER

Gloria Steinem courageously put me on the cover of *Ms.* magazine. Acclaimed author Jamaica Kincaid wrote the story. I was so honored to have them interested in my past and how it would help me survive my future. Women have so much to share in strength. Numbers win in unity.

Jet magazine photo of Freddie Prinze and me attending the NAACP Awards in Los Angeles.

Cards from John Lennon that came with bouquets of flowers and apologies for the Troubadour fracas.

Sincere
Appologies

John
Lennon

HAHN'S FLOWERS   BEVERLY HILLS, CALIFORNIA

Dear Pam,

I apologize for being so rude and thank you for not hitting me.

                    John Lennon

P.S. Harry Nilsson feels the same way.

Paul Newman and me on the set of *Fort Apache, The Bronx*.

Tough Enough
Wilford Brimley

Me and dear friend Wilford Brimley in Los Angeles,
California (not the set of *Tough Enough*).

Press picture of a wedding scene with Richard in *Greased Lightning* (Warner Bros.).

Richard at his house in Northridge, California, preparing to go for a bike ride with me. The infamous yellow Jaguar is in the foreground.

My sister, Gina, Richard, and me at Mom's house in Denver.

Philip Michael Thomas and I worked on *Miami Vice* together. He had been in Denver on business, and Mom had to see him in the flesh. True to his word, he dropped by to pay Mom, my stepfather, Edward, and my nephew, Gael, a visit, and he stayed for dinner. Mom can cook, and he could not resist her cooking. He is one of the most sincere friends in this world.

Me and Don Johnson on the set of *Miami Vice*, circa 1984.

Me and Eddie Murphy on the set of *Linc's* at Paramount Studios in Los Angeles, California.

Snoop Dogg and me on the set of *Bones*.

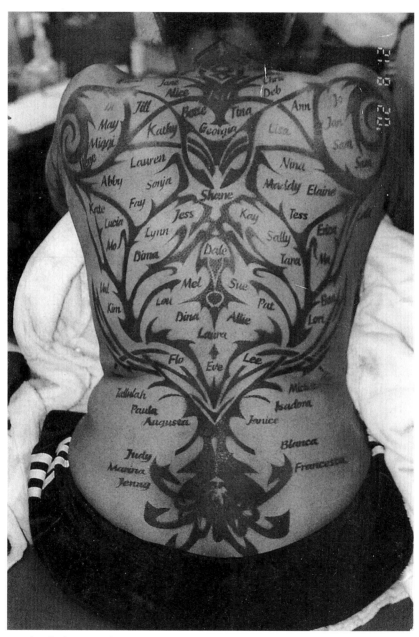

My back for my character, the Captain, in the pilot of *Earthlings*,
later titled *The L Word*. Three hours of tattoo work all for art.

26 # Becoming Charlotte

I spent a great deal of time thinking about who Charlotte really was on the inside. A woman who was dependent upon her pimp, she either had to bring in her quota, even when she got the flu, or risk being beaten. Her addiction to heroin had aged her well beyond her years, robbing her of her beauty and her health. I read some books on junkies, and considering the unhealthy lifestyle and the body deterioration that occurred, I realized that when I went in for the actual audition, I needed to look the opposite of wholesome. I thought back to how the hookers on the street had looked and smelled. I called a makeup artist and asked her how to create dark circles under my eyes in a few days.

"Try eating cherry pie," she said. "A lot of it. And don't eat anything else. The sugar and starch will sap the color from your face and give you dark circles. Alcohol will help, too. Try getting a hangover. That'll make you look really bad."

I kept myself awake for the better part of three nights on caffeine and sugar. I cut up a skirt to make it much too short, and I cinched my stockings to my garter belt. Then I did my walk in front of a mirror and slept on the floor without a pillow. I woke up each morning with a sore back, but what junkie ever complains about body pain, since they sleep wherever they fall down and wake up hungry for the next fix?

The night before the audition, I ate a whole cherry pie and nothing else. I felt like crap as I laid out my outfit for the next morning—the wig, a halter top with a stained gray Mickey Mouse satin jacket—and I lay on the floor to sleep. I had done what I could to prepare. I felt as bad as I could imagine, and now the rest was up to the gods. If they all laughed at me, including Paul Newman, there was nothing I could do about it. If I could just remember my lines with so much fuzziness in my head!

When I woke up, my head ached, my breath tasted like sulfur. I don't remember ever feeling that bad and grungy before. I had not taken a shower, brushed my teeth, or washed my hair for several days, and I put on my costume, wondering what in the hell I thought I was doing. When I finally took a gander at myself in the mirror, I was afraid. I looked so much like a woman of the night, what if the cops arrested me before I ever got to the audition? I was so cheap-looking, I turned *myself* off. I mean, one look in the mirror and we were talking "Hos R Us!"

I called downstairs to the doorman to warn him that the hooker he was about to see in the lobby was actually me.

"We see hookers here all the time," he said with an air of elegance. "You won't be the first."

"Not like this," I said. "I'm about to audition for a film, and I just need you to help me walk through the lobby and out the door so I don't get arrested." I took a deep breath, balanced on my stiletto heels, and got into the elevator. I was alone in there until the elevator stopped one floor down and in walked Carol Burnett, a brilliant actress and comedian whom I admired greatly. I dropped my character for a moment to exclaim, "Ms. Burnett. I absolutely love you!"

She looked at me, frowned, and got off on the next floor. I kept riding down, and the manager at the front desk dropped his jaw when he saw me. "Hurry," he said with his arm around my back. "Keep moving, and don't make eye contact with anyone here in the lobby." When he got me out of the hotel and onto the street, he whispered in my ear, "Great job. You're going to get the part."

I was all Charlotte as I walked outside. *Forget about showtime. It's ho-time*, I thought. My brain was acting crazy due to so much poor eating and sleep deprivation. I teetered down the Avenue of the Americas with men whistling and harassing me. I was building my character for the seven-block walk in broad daylight in my hooker gear. I was ready to turn them on, make them want to fuck me, shake me, pick me up, and drag me around. I needed to make them think I belonged in a mental hospital. I needed to make them react to Charlotte, not to Pam.

Increasing catcalls showed me that my red garter belt was working its magic. I hobbled and stumbled, making myself believe I was too loaded to walk in a straight line. In a few minutes, a blue and white cop car pulled up and began to slowly roll along beside me as I walked. "Ma'am," a cop said, "where do you think you're headed?"

"Hey, baby," I said, sounding just like a drug addict. "I'm goin' to audition for Paul Newman. What do you think?"

"You got my vote," his partner said. "What are you doing later?" They drove away laughing.

I arrived a bit early at the Minskoff Theatre on Broadway, where the audition was being held. I walked into the production office, and the secretary looked me over suspiciously when I said in my rummy voice, "Could you tell them that Pam Grier is here to see Paul Newman and David Susskind?" Then I leaned against the wall to hold myself up. If I looked half as bad as I felt, I had achieved my goal.

"You don't look like Pam Grier," she said.

"Will you please let me get on the damned elevator?" I said.

I was irritable while she looked at me oddly. What did she expect? Did she think Coffy or Foxy Brown would be showing up for this audition? Or how about the way I looked on the cover of *Ebony* magazine? She caught a whiff of me and pointed to the elevators. I got in and rode up. When I knocked on the door of David Susskind's office, the scriptwriter, Heywood Gould, opened the door and jumped backward. First impressions were what it was all about, and I was definitely making one. Pam had done the preparation, but it was Charlotte, a drug-addicted killer, who walked in the door.

"Hey, Pam," said Heywood, "how ya doin'?"

"Hey, motherfucker," I slurred in my Charlotte voice. "Wassup?"

I gazed around the room and saw Paul Newman sitting on a sofa. Charlotte didn't give a fuck about anything or anybody. She would just as soon have seen them all dead! I was Charlotte.

"How was your flight, Pam?" David Susskind asked.

I frowned. "Motherfucker, I don't need to talk no motherfuckin' shit about airplanes," I said. "Let's just do this motherfuckin' scene and do the work, dammit!"

Heywood grabbed a script and said, "Okay, let's read together."

I spontaneously grabbed his crotch like a hooker would, and his script went flying into the air. The room went silent as Heywood stooped to retrieve his papers. I squatted over him, grinding my body against his crotch.

Flustered, he dropped his script again. "Give me a second," he said. "I lost my place. Just hold on."

"Hold on?" said Charlotte, looking slightly amused. "This is my motherfuckin' life. We ain't doin' no holdin' on, motherfucker." I started doing the rest of the scene without Heywood at all. Then I walked around the room until I shot up, collapsed against the wall, slid to the floor, and died. Nobody said a word.

Someone got up and applauded. I looked up from where I lay on the floor and saw Paul Newman clapping his hands and smiling. "That was a great performance," he said. "The role is yours, Charlotte."

I broke out into a grin and sat up. Suddenly I was Pammy from Colorado who couldn't believe I just landed a job in a Paul Newman movie. "Can I call my mom?" I said.

Everybody laughed. "You can call anybody you like," said Paul Newman. "Just get some sleep. Okay?"

Although earning the role of Charlotte was a great triumph, I had no time to celebrate. I took a long shower, I brushed my teeth, ate a decent meal, and slept on and off for the next two days. Then we started work almost immediately, and between costume fittings, makeup, hair, and rehearsals, I was busy every minute of the day. On any occasion that I wasn't occupied or in the current scene, I made it my business to watch the master, Paul Newman, perform his craft. I learned a great deal about how he approached his work, and I got even clearer about what I wanted to accomplish as an actor.

I wanted the scenes to really work by creating a character who was so frightening and ominous that she would make the other actors feel uncomfortable just being in her presence. I worked hard to come off as heinous, vicious, cunning, and repugnant. At the same time, Charlotte had to be hot enough that the cops would think, "Hey, maybe we can get a piece here." An aging hooker who watched the younger girls steal the johns out from under her, she had a subtext going that said, "Danger. Keep away." If I didn't feed my fellow actors that kind of energy to work off of, there would be no way to make the scene come alive.

An actor named Miguel Piñero had been hired for the drug dealer role, and it was pretty obvious he knew his way around the streets. "Miguel," I said to him shortly after we had met, "I need you to show me where the junkies hang out. I have to see them up close."

"I can do that," he said. "I'll take you wherever you want to go, girl, but you better get a letter from the production office. Then, if they cut us up and throw us in a ditch, they'll know where they can send the pieces."

"Thanks for that," I said. If he was trying to give me a heart attack, he was doing a great job.

"Well," Miguel said, "you have to see the real thing."

"I know how to shoot a gun," I offered. "I've gone hunting, and I even ate the animals we killed."

"Oh, you a tough one, girl," he said. "Not at all phony and Holly-wo-o-o-od. I'll pick you up in half an hour."

We headed for Avenue A, which today has been converted into condos. There, Miguel led me inside a large, dilapidated structure that served as the local crack house. Filthy mattresses were laid across the floor of a long room, and all kinds of people, including business-men in suits carrying briefcases, lounged around in different stages of taking drugs. Some were coming back from passing out, and others' eyes were rolling toward the backs of their heads. Here, there was no difference between rich and poor. I carefully stepped over used hypodermic needles that lay strewn on the floor.

A wall menu, handwritten in a scrawling black marker, offered all kinds of paraphernalia, such as pipes, lighters, and papers. For hardcore heroin users, there were syringes for sale for $1.50, and the small print under the menu said, "See Manager."

"I should never have brought you here," Miguel said as we stepped over people who were lying back in a trance, nodding out. Unfortunately, it was a sign of the times: Miguel also took me to parties of the wealthy where large glass bowls filled with cocaine stood in the entry hall for anyone who wanted it. I even visited Studio 54, an infamous nightclub in New York, where the rich gathered and did drugs. Rich or poor, addiction was a huge problem and seemed to be ruining people's lives, even though they often considered their drug use as "casual."

For my character Charlotte, however, nothing was casual anymore. At twenty-nine, she was trying to get away from her abusive pimp because she was too drugged to please men anymore. I had studied the way people high on drugs moved their bodies—in a sort of rhythm that was all about finding balance on unsteady legs—while they were walking, dancing, or just talking. Charlotte was making her way around, but she had become an ineffective and inefficient hooker. Her personal hygiene had gone south, and she had no interest in taking care of herself any longer. All she wanted was to kill the johns who had made her life miserable, and deep inside she harbored thoughts of suicide. She wanted a way out of her perpetual agony, and she couldn't find one. All that was left was to take it out on other people.

I got so well informed about druggies, I could tell the difference between someone on coke or heroin at a glance. I understood Charlotte's motivation when she tried to kill the men who hired her. She knew she was repugnant, and she knew that they knew. She hated them for lying to her when they said she was beautiful, which triggered her schizophrenia. As far as she could see, her only way out was drugs and murder.

Among my nightmares and recurring dreams of things I had seen in the crack house, I often awoke in the night sweating and frightened. One morning, I was anticipating a tough scene in which I had to hide a razor blade in my mouth and eventually slit the neck of the john who was lusting after me. It reminded me of the girl gangs in Denver when I was growing up who walked around with single-edge razor blades in their mouths. I approached the scene with fear and respect. I rehearsed the moves with my partner in the scene with intense mental preparation, having trouble coming to terms with the fact that I was about to do something so ugly and heinous. Sure, it was only a movie, but the actor in the scene better believe it's real or no one else will.

I finished the rehearsal with a sour stomach. It was horrific to cut up another human being in the scene. We did take one, take two, and when it was done, I rushed off the set and threw up. It was a good thing they got what they needed, because there was no way I could repeat the performance. Sick and green for the rest of the day, I took comfort in the fact that it was over and that it had worked. I watched the scene once to see how it had come out, and I never watched it again. I knew it wasn't real, I knew the blood on my victim's neck was just a red rubber application, but to this day, I feel ill just thinking about it.

Paul Newman's children sometimes showed up on the set to watch him. They were as enamored with his work as the rest of us, and his relationship with them was down-to-earth and playful. He treated everyone beautifully, and he was interested in getting to know his fellow actors. One morning he approached me and said, "Hey, Pam, I'd love to take you to lunch today. How about it?"

I had to inhale deeply. Paul Newman, the icon, had just asked me to lunch. "I'm sorry," I said. "Thank you so much, Mr. Newman, but not today."

When he looked surprised, I said, "The thing is, I'm supposed to kill someone in a scene right after lunch. I need to stay in character, and if we laugh and have a great time at lunch, I'll lose my preparation. Can we do it later?"

"You're saying no?" he said, still looking surprised.

"I am," I said with a clarity that amazed me. "You hired me for this role, and it's really frightening to play Charlotte. I don't want to disappoint you, and I need to keep up my continuity and consistency."

"Okay," he said, sounding impressed this time. "When we finish."

Like clockwork, on the day that I shot my last scene, he approached me. "Are you finished now?" he asked with a smile.

"Yes, I am," I said, smiling back. "As soon as I take off the wig, the makeup, and the stilettos, I'd love to have lunch with you."

We went to a restaurant on City Island in the Bronx, a favorite eatery of his, with his lovely daughter. We all had a great time there, laughing and sharing stories. He was a loving and devoted father who adored being a dad, and he opened up about the horror of his son having committed suicide. That was part of his motivation for doing this movie, he told me. He wanted to put out a message to young people on drugs that there was help for them.

I had no idea if this movie would advance my career. I felt good about my performance, but the role of Charlotte had very little dialogue and she did not engage in much character interplay. She was mostly weaving, tripping over herself, speaking slowly with a slurred voice, and killing people. Rachel Ticotin, who played Isabella, Paul Newman's love interest, did a fabulous job, but I can't help wondering if her role might have gotten me more notice. I did the meatier role of Charlotte, but I often considered what might have happened if I had been asked to audition for the role of Paul Newman's love interest. It would have looked great on my resume, but what's done is done.

Incidentally, before the release of the film, I woke up one day to find an original copy of the script of *Sophie's Choice* on my doorstep. There was no card, so I never knew who left it. I supposed it was someone from *Fort Apache* who knew how much I loved this movie. I was thrilled to have such a valuable treasure. As much money as it might have brought, I never sold it or auctioned it off. It symbolized my ability to recognize fine writing and fine acting, and it has remained an inspiration to me.

CHAPTER 27 Mingling with the Stars

Now that I had made a name for myself, I started getting some very interesting invitations. For example, I was at a charity event where I was seated next to Altovise Davis, the wife of legendary performer Sammy Davis Jr. A former dancer, she was a beautiful African American woman with a reputation for taking excellent care of her famous husband and their children.

We hit it off right away when I recognized that we shared a love of dance and fashion. When the evening was about to end, she leaned over toward me and said, "I'd like to invite you to Sammy's birthday celebration. It's this weekend at our home. I really hope you can make it. It'll be a lovely event."

I accepted immediately, but when I got home, I wondered if I was in over my head. What would I wear, and what should I bring? I chose an Armani suit, and since I'd been taught it was bad manners to arrive at a party empty-handed, I settled on a bottle of red wine and a bouquet of spring flowers. When I arrived at the door of this massive estate, I gave my raggedy Jeep to the valet, who welcomed me and drove my car down the street to park it. When I saw the Rolls-Royces, Excaliburs, and Lamborghinis parked in the Davises' driveway, I understood why they were hiding my junk heap as far away as possible.

I clutched my flowers and wine and wandered the property. No one else was holding anything except drinks, and the entire length of the spacious backyard had been tented. My jaw dropped as I looked at the elegant tables and hundreds of people who, I learned later, were giving Sammy gifts like diamond watches and cashmere sweaters. I handed my little presents to a secretary, happy to be rid of them, and checked out the other guests.

When I say that everyone who was anyone was gathered there, I'm talking about the likes of Liza Minnelli and her husband, Jack Haley Jr., whom I already knew from our night at the Troubadour with John Lennon. Then I spotted Elizabeth Taylor. All the women were wearing such luxurious gowns and jewels that I felt grossly underdressed. But when I ran into Altovise, who greeted me warmly, she didn't flinch at what I was wearing to her million-dollar birthday party. Ever the lady, she thanked me for coming and introduced me to Sammy. When I went to shake his hand, my fingers were trembling. How could I not be in awe of this legendary performer who took a moment to shake my hand and welcome me to his home? And he didn't even know me. I thought I could die happy after this night.

When it was time for dinner, gloved waiters served us lobster, filet mignon, and bottle after bottle of the finest champagne. Altovise was kind enough to seat me near her because I didn't know many people, and she promised to take me out shopping with her and the girls. Was she talking about Liza and Barbra? Did they shop anywhere besides Armani and Chanel?

I spent the early part of the evening watching people and sharing little bits of myself with anyone who was interested. People there were interested when I described my country life, where I fished and hunted in Wyoming and skied in Aspen. They must have thought that a "sistah" who was so outdoorsy was intriguing.

When I decided it was time to leave, I found Altovise to thank her for a gorgeous evening. I told her how impeccable her taste was, and the next thing I knew, she said, "Would you like to come over next weekend? I'm having a few people over for dinner and a movie. It'll be more intimate, a small party, so we'll have a chance to talk."

"Small?" I said smiling. "Are we talking about a hundred of your closest friends?"

She laughed. "No, no. It'll be ten or twelve people in the dining room."

"What should I wear?"

"It'll just be casual," she said.

"Casual?" I teased. "Like going from tails to a tux?"

"I'll be wearing slacks and a sweater," she said. "How does that sound?"

"I'd love to come," I said. "Should I bring a casserole? Or I could bake a lemon meringue pie."

"You don't have to do that," she said. "The food will be prepared. Just come and enjoy yourself."

When I arrived back at the estate the next week, Altovise was wearing slacks and a sweater, just like she had promised, and about a dozen people were gathered. What a group it was! Liz Taylor had on a lovely casual dress. Sammy was dressed in slacks and a shirt. The house, now much emptier, contained his amazing history in diaries of his life. He had been embraced by Frank Sinatra and Dean Martin, who supported one another and never allowed Sammy to be forced through a back door because he was black. They were his best friends, and he appreciated their constant support.

I sat down to dinner with a table full of A-list producers, directors, and actors. I just sat back and listened to all the gossip, wondering how I got so lucky to be where I was. When we were through eating, Sammy stood to indicate that we were shifting into the movie portion of the evening. He had a large screening room, and he loved getting his friends together to watch first-run movies, partly because they couldn't go into movie theaters without being swarmed for autographs.

I had gotten up to follow the crowd out when Sammy suddenly grabbed my hand. "Are you having a good time?" he asked me.

"I am, Mr. Davis," I said. "It was so kind of you to invite me. I can't wait to see the movie."

"I'd like to show you something first," he said.

"Sure," I said.

He exerted some pressure on my arm and kept holding on to me while I stood beside him. Then he got his face much too close to mine when he said, "Follow me."

Feeling somewhat overpowered, I prayed for Altovise to come and rescue me. Before tonight, I would have jumped at the chance to be shown around by Sammy Davis Jr., but his manner was invasive, and it felt like he was coming on to me. I stopped short and searched desperately for options. There was a luxurious couch and on it were sitting Liza Minnelli and Elizabeth Taylor. I put him off for a moment, searching for Altovise. I couldn't find her, so I sat on the sofa between Liza and Liz and said quietly, "Excuse me, but I need to ask you something. Is Sammy always like this with women? In front of his wife?"

Liz laughed and said, "Oh, yes, it's nothing,"

"Don't take it seriously," said Liza.

"Well," I said, "when do I tell him no? And when do I get kicked out of the house? Or do I just ignore it and he'll stop?"

"He'll stop," said Liza, "when—" She was interrupted as Sammy came over and grabbed onto my arm. "There you are," he said, "I said I wanted to show you something."

"I'm in the middle of a conversation," I said. "I'd like to stay here."

"No," he said in an angry tone.

"Okay," I said, afraid he would go off on me in front of everyone. I got up. "Where's Altovise?" I added. "Can she come with us?"

She was nowhere to be found, and Sammy insisted on showing me some photographs hanging in a living room so large my whole apartment could have fit in it. He pointed out his various awards, including one from the queen. It was mesmerizing, but I couldn't relax because Sammy was getting more and more touchy-feely. When he started to walk me farther into the house, I pulled back. "I'd really like to go watch the movie," I said.

"I'm not going to do anything to you," he said, sounding very irritable. "I just want to show you my—"

"I'm sorry," I said. "I have to go to the ladies' room."

I felt his eyes ogling my butt as I walked into the safety of the powder room. I stared into the mirror and tried to get my thoughts together. I could imagine the headline news at eleven:

ACTRESS PAM GRIER KNOCKS OUT SAMMY DAVIS JR'S OTHER EYE.

I wondered about Altovise. I'd already seen Sammy's flirtation escalate several notches during the night, and she was right there in the same room. Did she allow it? Did it hurt her feelings? Did she *have* to allow it? I didn't know their boundaries or agreements. I may have been the new kid in the crowd, but I was not about to be the new *meat*.

I was wondering how long I could get away with hiding in the restroom when Altovise walked in. I was so relieved to see her, I spoke up. "Altovise," I said, "I really want to apologize."

She looked confused.

I went on, "Sammy is making me feel really uncomfortable. I don't know if he's hitting on me, but he's being very intimate. I don't know what to do. I think I have to leave, but I don't want to hurt his feelings. Does he do this with everyone?"

"Yeah, he does," she said. "That's just Sammy."

"Well, you know what?" I continued. "I think that's very disrespectful to you. I have to go, because I don't like how he's acting with me in front of you."

One look at this wonderful woman told me everything. It was clear she and her husband had an arrangement. Maybe that was a negotiation that she had to make. But in her eyes, I saw how much she appreciated what I had said and how much she valued the respect.

"How can I get out of here without Sammy seeing me?" I said.

While we were figuring out how to distract Sammy so I could get away, Liza Minnelli came into the ladies' room. She heard us talking and said conspiratorially, "Jack and I are about to leave. If you take Sammy to another part of the house, Altovise, we can drive Pam to her car."

That was the plan. Altovise left the powder room to find Sammy standing there, waiting for me to come back out. She guided Sammy to the kitchen while I ran outside with Liza. When Jack pulled up front in their Silver Shadow Rolls-Royce, I jumped into the back and lay down across the seat. Liza threw her full-length sable coat over me in case Sammy saw us leaving, and they drove me to my car.

It turned out that I never saw Sammy again, but I continued to get together with Altovise until recently—she passed away on March 14, 2009. I had been looking forward to contacting her just before she died. I imagined reading this chapter to her, and I could see her eyes light up with laughter. It didn't happen; she passed away when I least expected it, but I dedicate this chapter to her. I hope she knows how much I still love her and how much I always respected her as a woman, a wife, a mother, a dancer, and an all-around human being.

28 # Haunting

The eighties was a peak decade for my career. Among the many opportunities I was given, I played the Dust Witch in the 1983 film of the Ray Bradbury classic *Something Wicked This Way Comes*, starring Jason Robards, Diane Ladd, and Jonathan Pryce.

I also performed in the Sam Shepard play *Fool for Love* at the newly opened Los Angeles Theatre Center in downtown Los Angeles. The run lasted close to nine months, and the show ran for ninety minutes with no intermission. The work was so physically demanding, I lost three pounds each night, I broke two fingers, and one evening, when Richard Lawson's character pushed my head against the spurs that hung from his belt, my face was punctured in five places. I had to rush offstage, but since the play demanded that the curtain never be lowered for the sake of momentum, I continued to say my lines offstage while the stage manager cleaned and bandaged my face. When I got back onstage, still bleeding, the audience was impressed with what they thought were special effects.

And then there was the night when I pulled a gun on my co-star and he smacked me so hard I hit the floor and bounced. My jaw swelled up so much I couldn't talk, but I managed to make it through the scene. When we got offstage, he tearfully apologized again and again, but I really didn't mind. It was all in a night's work. In fact, I worked so hard in that role, I won the NAACP Image Award for best actress in a play.

I kept the announcement they sent, because I was so proud to receive the award.

JANUARY 9, 1987
PAM GRIER
FOOL FOR LOVE

CONGRATULATIONS! YOU ARE THE RECIPIENT OF THE 19th ANNUAL NAACP IMAGE AWARD

On December 14, 1986, the BEVERLY HILLS/HOLLYWOOD NAACP announced the recipients of the 19th ANNUAL IMAGE AWARDS.

The IMAGE AWARD is made annually to individuals who have contributed to projecting positive images of Black People in their respective areas of endeavor. It is our way of paying tribute to and giving recognition of outstanding and/or meritorious performances.

Your trophy will be delivered under separate cover in approximately thirty days. Attached you will find a souvenir program for the event.

The NBC television network will air the 19th ANNUAL IMAGE AWARDS on Saturday, January 17, 1987, in a 90-minute star-studded special at 11:30 PM.

Again, congratulations and continued success.

It was signed by Willis Edwards, President, and Marva J. Smith, Chairperson.

I couldn't have been more proud. I won the award but it was later stolen from my home.

Then, in 1986, I got a role in *Above the Law,* a film starring Steven Seagal that shot in Chicago. Following that, I did *Rocket Gibraltar* in 1987, with film icon Burt Lancaster. This one shot in Westhampton Beach, New York, and was directed by Dan Petrie, who had directed me in *Fort Apache, the Bronx*. My scenes in *Rocket Gibraltar* ended up on the cutting room floor due to the alleged controversy of the interracial love story. I remember when Dan Petrie and his wife invited me to dinner and he told me that my scenes would be cut because he feared repercussions from the interracial love scenes. I was very disappointed. It wasn't every day I got to work with a great actor like Burt Lancaster. I had liked Burt and his wife so much, I had loved working with him, but there was nothing I could do about it. I took it in stride, since I had met a young actor named Macaulay Culkin in that movie, and Kevin Spacey, who was hot and a brilliant conversationalist. In the end, although I was hardly in the movie at all, I got a great deal out of it, anyway. In fact, all was moving along relatively well, and my life had never looked more promising, it seemed, until I got a call that rocked my world.

My adopted sister, Krista, had had a bout with breast cancer in the early eighties. Married with a child and working as a flight attendant, she'd been forced to undergo a mastectomy, which had saved her life. But her husband had devastated her when he told her that since she had lost a breast, he no longer found her attractive. Back then, the doctors did not do instant reconstruction like they do today when they remove a breast. Now Krista not only had to fight to stay alive, but she also had to face the fact that her selfish husband no longer desired her as a woman.

Her husband didn't leave her or throw her out right then, but a huge emotional separation occurred, and they were never the same again. They eventually divorced after her cancer had gone into remission, and Krista was elated to find a new man who was quite religious and didn't care that she was missing a breast. He simply adored her, and she told me over and over how happy she was to have met a wonderful man who not only accepted her as she was but also got her children to church every Sunday. "I'm learning about God," she told me, "and so is my boy. We do things as a family, and I feel more human than ever before."

She was as happy as I'd ever seen her when her cancer suddenly returned, years after the first bout. As upsetting as the diagnosis was, at least she was with a man who loved her. But it seemed that her new husband's church, which she had joined, was an offshoot of Christian Science, and they did not allow any drugs or medical attention whatsoever. Prayer was what they touted. If you were ill, it was God's will, and prayer was the only method of healing that was tolerated. If you didn't heal, that was God's will, too.

Krista had come to a terrible crossroads. Her husband, whom she'd previously adored, was adamant that she follow the ways of the church. But what about her boy? Shouldn't she do everything within her power to stay alive for her son? At the same time, my mom, her adopted mom, was suffering nerve damage from a previous surgery, and she had excruciating pain in both wrists. Krista, who had always been more devoted to my mom than to her own mother, Mennon, was no longer able to take care of her since they were both in bad shape. It felt like my family was falling apart, and there was little that anyone could do.

I was in rehearsal in San Diego for a Terrence McNally play, *Frankie and Johnny in the Clair de Lune*, when Krista got really sick. Because she had refused treatment, her cancer had metastasized to the bone and she was in constant pain. With more than one hundred fifty tumors, she told me she felt as if someone were sticking an ice pick into her chest and twisting it all day and night. All the while, her husband, the supposed love of her life, refused to get her any pain medications.

Krista had been looking forward to coming to San Diego for my opening. She knew that I had agreed to gain some weight for the part and that I had a scene where I fell out of bed, nude, with only a sheet covering my body. It was risqué, and I visited Krista just before the rehearsals started. She wanted to know everything, and she assured me she'd be there for the opening, whatever it took. As I watched her determination and courage in the midst of her pain, my love and admiration for her only grew stronger. She was my confidante, my mentor, my sister, and my friend, and I couldn't imagine life without her. Who would I tell my secrets to? Who would give me advice on men and relationships?

During the course of her illness, my mom and I fought to get control of her from her husband. We tried to sneak pain medications to her, but he made sure to cut off access. Now all we could do was talk on the phone, and pretty soon he started telling us Krista was asleep whenever we called. One time, Krista called me, sobbing that she had made a huge mistake. She had refused treatment and now she was dying a hard, painful death with no pain meds. "If I'd known how painful this was going to be," she wailed, "I'd have divorced my husband and left the church as soon as the cancer returned."

Now it was too late. One day Krista called me and Mom in tears, pleading with us to come and help her. When we drove over there, her husband met us at the door.

"What are you doing here?" he asked suspiciously, wary that we were bringing her the forbidden drugs that might ease her pain.

"Krista called us," I said. "She asked us to come by."

"She didn't call you," he said. "She's asleep."

"She did call us," Mom said. "Can we just come in and visit for a few minutes?"

"No, she didn't call you," he repeated. "She's asleep. Please go away." He closed the door.

Mom and I sat in the car for a while and sobbed. Since there were no cell phones back then, I drove Mom to a pay phone where we tried to call Krista. Of course, there was no answer. The religious man who previously had adored his wife now refused to allow anyone to see her. One day, my cousin headed over there and tried to rip the door off the hinges. He didn't get very far before someone told Krista's husband what was going on. He rushed back home from church to stop the crime. We were all at our wit's end, starting to commit criminal acts to see our beloved Krista.

Terrified and enraged, I had to return to San Diego to rehearse. I tried to throw myself into my work to drown out the sorrow, but it came and got me anyway. I was onstage in the middle of rehearsal when Krista's son, fifteen, disgusted and horrified to watch his mother suffer with no relief, got hold of a gun and mortally shot himself. His note to his mother read, "I'll meet you in heaven."

When I got the call that he had died, I collapsed onstage during rehearsal. I had seen him and spoken with him a few days earlier, and he'd been very quiet. The boy thought we were all supporting his stepfather in denying his mother pain meds, and I was worried about him. When word came that he had taken his life, I was saddened, not shocked, and worried about what it would do to Krista.

The crew gathered around to help me, and although we were only two weeks away from the opening of this play with a two-character cast, the director and producer allowed me to leave for a week to attend my nephew's funeral in Colorado. They were fearful that the expensive, sold-out production with its cast of two would close if I couldn't recover fast enough, but they gave me the time anyway. I flew to Colorado in the midst of the loss of a nephew, the impending loss of my sister, and the fear of losing my job as a cast member of one of the greatest contemporary plays of our time.

When I arrived at the funeral service, I joined Gina, Rod, and Mom. Krista had to be carried into the crowded room, she was so frail and brokenhearted. From her seat in the front row, she called me over and handed me a piece of paper on which she had handwritten a letter. She was so weak from her grief and wasted from the cancer eating her bones, she could barely speak. "Pammy," she whispered, "you need to read this out loud for me. It's a prayer for my boy."

I looked at the congregation gathered in my mom's church, including family, friends, the mayor of Denver, and a load of my deceased nephew's classmates and teammates. Then I looked at Krista's thin hands, the veins visible, thin as a skeleton. She had been such a strong, powerful being—my best friend and sister on whom I could lean whenever I needed help. Now she had lost eighty pounds, she was nothing but skin and bones, and she had a final request for me, a simple one, so it seemed. She wanted me to grant her last wish and read aloud her final letter to her son. I was ready to do anything for her—until I scanned what she wanted me to read.

My legs buckled as I realized that this note contained a valid account of what her husband and the church had done to her, her son, and her family. She had also included an angry message to her ex-husband and a snipe at whoever else followed the cruel church rules that would leave a mother screaming out in pain in the night. I fell to my knees as I continued to read silently. She had left no one out of her letter of revenge, as she criticized the church, her husband, and anyone else who had denied her the right to ease her pain and that of her son.

Our eyes met—hers were stony and determined—and I began to cry. I rested my head on Krista's hand, which was on the partition between pews. "Please don't ask me to read this," I pleaded with her. "It's going to anger and hurt so many people."

She continued to stare at me, her gaze direct and penetrating. "Pammy," she said, "you have to fight for me. Please. I can't do it for myself anymore. Just read it."

I was trembling and sobbing when my mom came over to ask what was wrong with me. Hundreds of eyes were on me as I prayed to God to let me pass out. *How does a person cause herself to faint?* I wondered. Everyone in the church knew something was going on when I pulled myself up onto shaky legs. My body was trembling, I could barely breathe, and I knew the extreme and long-lasting pain this note would cause a lot of people. I could picture the fights that would break out over the honest and raw words that Krista wanted everyone to hear.

I cleared my throat and started to read the first part of the letter. But I quickly stopped reading. I remembered a Chinese proverb about revenge that said in essence, "When someone dies, you dig one grave. When you seek revenge, you dig two."

The words in her letter were so vindictive and full of rage and revenge, I knew they would start religious and family wars. True, they were Krista's words, not mine, but I was the messenger who would suffer the rage and criticism long after Krista was gone. I couldn't open so many wounds and deal with the aftermath. When I handed the letter back to Krista, the air went out of her body as she slumped down in her seat in disappointment, bewilderment, and rejection. I refused to be the one to read the letter and stir the pot—a decision I regret to this day.

As I began to walk away from Krista, I looked back at her face with an expression that asked her for forgiveness. I will never forget how she looked back at me, betrayed and distraught, as her one chance for redemption had been taken from her. Our relationship suffered greatly after that, and although we spoke from time to time, she really didn't care to connect with me at an intimate level anymore. I explained myself, and she said she understood, but in her heart of hearts, she never forgave me for backing down from her last fight.

Needless to say, Krista never made it to San Diego to see my play. When she died months later, I was devastated that I had let my beloved sister go to her grave knowing that I didn't stand up for her and grant her last request. It haunts me to this day as one of the things in life that I would do over, if only I were given the chance—even though all hell would have broken loose in that church if I had granted Krista's request.

I suffered two close deaths during that play. First it was Krista's son, and then it was Krista herself. And still, as the first black Frankie that was ever cast, I felt a responsibility to be great in my role. It's an act of courage to get onstage when you're torn apart inside. Actors have to work when they're grieving from a loss or sick from the flu. Whether we lose a child, a mate, or get a divorce, we have to show up each day, putting our personal feelings to the side and remembering songs, lines, and stage directions—even when our hearts are breaking. No curling up in a ball for several days and crying our eyes out. We have to strengthen our hearts and souls enough to get out there and do the work, no matter how we feel.

There were moments during rehearsals when I lost control and I wept. My fellow actors and the director picked me up, helped me brush myself off, and got me back into the swing, red puffy eyes and all. I did the best I could with the help of a little wine that loosened me up and relaxed my nervous system. And still, the stress was indescribable, with no relief for a long time. I expect that the work saved my life, as I was required to take breaks from the constant grief and loss that were plaguing me. I was gratified to finish out the run, even performing one night when I had a 104-degree fever. The show must go on, and so it did.

To this day, I carry the weight of my sister's death and that of her son on my shoulders. This constant haunting does not diminish with time, like people told me it would. But it does make me respect life and love so much more than before.

ACT THREE Finding the Balance

1990–The Present

CHAPTER **29**   The C Word

I had just finished shooting *Above the Law*, starring Steven Seagal and directed by Andrew Davis, an old friend, when I met Philip in New York at a charity function. It was 1987, and we were attracted to each other immediately. When I look back now, I realize that the signs revealed the truth about him. But in the infatuation stage of any relationship, the truth has an insidious way of hiding behind gratification, sex, projections, sex, denial, sex, romance, sex, euphoria, sex, picnics on the beach, and more sex.

Tall and friendly, a successful architect with his own New York firm, Philip had reddish-brown skin and keen golden hazel eyes. A magnificent specimen of a self-made man, with little to no college education, he managed about one hundred fifty employees. A genius who could sketch and draw skillfully, Philip had great taste in home furnishings, and I loved visiting his apartment in the city and his second home in the Hamptons. I appreciated the calming influence he had on me in general, since I had a tendency to get overly excited about life.

I remember one night, however, when we switched roles. Philip's firm had taken on a massive job, fitting out several floors of a Dutch bank with chairs, tables, desks, and a load of state-of-the-art office equipment. Philip was responsible for designing the lamps, the cubicles, the carpeting, and the window coverings, which he thought were all well handled—until a disturbing phone call came late in the evening from the bank president.

Philip's beautiful skin turned pale as his client cursed him out on the phone while he remained silent. It seemed that someone (most likely Philip himself) had miscalculated the design and size of hundreds of chairs that would not fit under the desks. When Philip hung up, he said, "Oh, Pam, I have to go to the site right now. I need to open hundreds of boxes, find the chairs, and send them all back. My career is on the line."

"I'm going with you," I said.

"You don't need to do that," he told me. "It'll take all night."

"It'll take half the time with two of us. C'mon. Let's go."

Assuming the role he usually played, I kept him calm as we taxied to the building site where we spent the entire night opening cardboard crates and sorting out what needed to be shipped and what could stay. The sun was starting to rise when we finally headed back to his apartment, exhausted. But that's what people do for each other when they're in love. Or so I thought before that concept was tested.

If I had been looking for red flags, I should have seen them waving wildly when Philip took me to meet his mom in Georgia, where we would stay for a week. I was thrilled that he considered me special enough to want his mother to meet me, but I was saddened when we got there and saw her lifestyle. A professional domestic, Philip's mother had worked hard all her life cleaning other people's homes. From the lifelong fruits of her labor, she had managed to set aside a little money and purchase a small home on stilts that was so unsteady it listed to one side. The living room was tiny, the sofa blocked the front door, and you could only enter from the back. Unstable and too small for much furniture, the house was lit with one naked lightbulb screwed into the ceiling that this poor woman unscrewed and carried from room to room so she could use it where she needed it.

We stayed with her for seven days, during which time she gave up her bedroom and slept on the sofa. One evening, Philip and I were chatting at the kitchen table when his mom came in and unscrewed the lightbulb to use in the bathroom. I opened the refrigerator door to shed some blue light in the room, and we sat there in silence. Times were tough those days, and Philip's mom couldn't work as much as she used to, so she needed to get the most out of everything she bought.

It was stunning to me that while Philip was a self-made millionaire, his mother was living like a pauper, although clean, orderly, and neat, since she took great pride in the little that she had. Could the red flags have been any more obvious? When she and I sat in the living room after she screwed back in the lightbulb one evening, she told me about a yellow brick house she had cleaned weekly for several years, her dream house. It was filled with light, had central heating, and was up for sale for $125,000, so she would continue to dream about it.

"Why don't you help her more?" I asked Philip. "Buy her that house she wants. You can afford it."

"I tried to buy her a color TV once, but she wouldn't take it. She's too full of pride," he said with a look of disgust on his face.

Where would she have put a television? Besides, she needed other amenities a lot more than a color TV. I made it my mission to talk Philip into buying her that dream house before we left. If we broke up, I figured he would never follow through. When Philip left for a day to visit other relatives, I bought his mom several dozen lightbulbs and other basic supplies to make her life easier. By the time he agreed to purchase the house, I was thrilled for his mother, but I had lost some respect and affection for my boyfriend, who was showing me who he was. And still, I refused to see the whole truth about him.

We'd been dating for less than a year when I went to Los Angeles for auditions and to appear on some TV shows. I had been cast in several roles lately as the older woman dating the younger man, something we call a "cougar" today, and I'd become the "it" girl for that type of role.

In the midst of everything, it occurred to me that it was time for my yearly pap smear and mammogram.

I took a break from my packed schedule, went in for the checkup, and headed back home, relieved to have it over with. Actually, I'd forgotten about it when the call came the next morning from the gynecologist's nurse. "We need you to come back in right away," she said.

"Why?" I wanted to know.

"You need to have a biopsy."

"What's wrong?" I felt my stomach drop.

"We have to see you tomorrow at the latest," she said, avoiding answering my question. That made me really afraid, and I called my mom to comfort me. When I told her what was happening, my voice must have sounded awful.

"Oh, Pammy," she said reassuringly, "it's probably nothing. You go back and get that biopsy. I've seen this a million times in my nursing career. You just need to make sure."

Back at the clinic, after the biopsy, I found myself sitting opposite the doctor, who told me, "You have cervical dysplasia. That's a pre-cancerous condition, but we caught it in time. We need to do surgery to remove the infected tissue, and you should be just fine."

I thought back to when I was dating Richard Pryor and the doctor reported a problem with a buildup of cocaine in my cervix. He'd said that I could end up being a very sick girl. Was that the cause of this? I didn't waste much time trying to figure it out, though. I just picked up the phone and called my mom. "They want to do surgery," I told her in a shaky voice.

The moment we hung up, she called in sick at work and made a plane reservation to come be with me in Los Angeles. I called Philip in New York to tell him what was going on, but I wasn't prepared for his response.

"How does this kind of thing happen?" he said in an almost accusing tone. "Is it something you catch?"

I was deeply offended by his reaction. Did he think cancer was a sexually transmitted disease like AIDS? I tried to give him the benefit of the doubt, reminding myself that no one knows what to do when you say the *C* word. "It comes from the HPV virus," I said patiently. But everyone knew that cancer was not contagious.

Philip halfheartedly offered to come to Los Angeles and be with me. Whether it was his lack of enthusiasm or my desire to spare him the stress, I declined. I thanked him for the offer, but since Mom was already on her way, I told him it wasn't necessary. We would keep close tabs via the phone, and it was most likely nothing, anyway. Philip sounded relieved and slightly distant when we hung up. I didn't attach much to it, but I wondered if I'd wounded his male ego when I said I didn't need him. I *did* promise to get to New York, though, as soon as I could travel again.

I had the procedure with my mom at my side. I'd chosen to stay in California so I could be close to work, and Mom stayed at my place, caring for me. She was prepared to stay for up to a week, as long as I would conceivably need her, but we were both in for a shock. The same afternoon they did the surgery, after they tested my blood and some additional tissue samples, my gynecologist called. "We need you back here first thing tomorrow morning," he said.

"Why?" I wanted to know.

"We'll discuss it tomorrow," was the answer.

After a sleepless night, Mom and I went to the doctor to hear what he had to say.

"We ran some additional tests," he said, "and we found an area where the cancer cells have reached stage four." I felt Mom's grip tighten on my arm as he went on. "We need to do another surgery to remove more tissue. I wish we could do it right away, but we have to wait six weeks until you heal from the last one." The tremors I felt in my mom's body were making me terrified. This was not the way I had envisioned things going.

Devastated, I said, "How did this happen? I don't smoke or drink. I jog on the beach almost every day. I ride my bike to the gym, and I eat right. I should be ridiculously healthy. I've had no symptoms at all. How did it happen?"

The doctor had no answers for me. "I wish I knew. We can be successful, but you'll have to listen to me and do everything I tell you." He handed me a large manila envelope. "These are your introductory materials for the cancer clinic at Cedars-Sinai. You won't be able to have surgery right now, but you need to go over there immediately and register. There are various tests you need, and I want you to take all of them. Do you understand?" He gave me the name of an oncologist, Dr. Leucter, whom he liked working with.

When he looked at Mom's and my blank faces, he said, "I hate to be blunt, but you both need to understand something. If you don't follow every single guideline and instruction you're given, you have eighteen months to live."

"That's a year and a half," I said. "I'm thirty-nine."

He nodded. "I want you to take care of your will and your estate right away. You have to prepare for the fight of your life. Now, would you like to harvest your eggs?"

I looked at him, confused.

"There could be damage to your ovaries, and if you want to have children, I'd suggest you harvest some eggs in case you can't conceive later," he explained.

By the time I agreed to harvest some of my eggs, Mom's face had turned a scary shade of yellow, and I could see that she was trying to compose herself. I felt as if I had lifted up and out of my body, the thing that had cancer, and I was staring down at myself from a surreal world or a strange dream from which I couldn't wake up.

Mom drove the rental car as we headed over to Cedars-Sinai Cancer Clinic. Silent and in shock, neither of us said a word as we pulled into the parking structure. I don't remember where we parked or how far we walked to get to the elevator. I only knew that this clinic was reputed to be one of the best cancer centers in the world, and the waiting room was filled with people of every nationality and from every walk of life.

I walked past babies that were black, Asian, and Caucasian, several elderly couples, and everything in between as we stepped up to the reception desk. My voice cracked when I told them my name, my attending doctor, and anything else they asked. Then I broke out in hives as they handed me a clipboard with a load of papers and a plastic hospital bracelet that contained all my pertinent information. They snapped the bracelet around my wrist. Now I was a statistic, one of hundreds of thousands of women who had cancer. Not only was my ability to have children in jeopardy, but my very life had become eerily uncertain. Gilda Radner from *Saturday Night Live* and my dear friend Minnie Riperton had both died from cancer when they were younger than I was.

I sat down to begin the paperwork that would dominate a great deal of the coming year. I had filled in my name, address, and contact numbers when a long, eerie wail issued from one of the cubicles where doctors were consulting privately with patients. I found out later that the moaner was a twenty-two-year-old newlywed who was just getting her cancer diagnosis and was unable to control the terrible sounds she was uttering.

When my paperwork was done, I got up to take it to the reception desk when a nurse stopped me. "Oh, my God," she said much too loudly, "is that you? Pam Grier? Foxy Brown?"

I cringed. Being recognized was the last thing I wanted right then, but I didn't have a say in the matter. I smiled weakly at her, and she shoved a piece of paper at me.

"Can I have your autograph?" she practically sang. I wanted to give her a lecture that celebrities were people, too, and I didn't want to speak to her right then, but I scribbled my name on the paper and handed it back to her.

"So what are you doing here?" the breathless woman wanted to know.

"Just having some treatments," I said. She wandered away, clutching the paper to her chest, never noticing that I was wearing a medical bracelet. Surely celebrities didn't get sick, did they? I was relieved in the next moment when a coordinator escorted my mom and me out of the main lobby and into an area called the Physicians Hall. Trailing in and out of the various offices were people in different stages of therapy, some bald with IV tubes and medications attached to them like an extra appendage. *I better get used to seeing this,* I told myself. This would be home for at least the next six weeks and possibly for months afterward.

When I sat in the doctor's office, he handed me a list of the numerous tests they would be running on me before my surgery—including

CAT scans, brain scans, and MRIs—and explained that I would need to donate six to eight pints of my own blood, which I might need during surgery. Following the doctor's stern talk, I did everything that was asked of me. I was lucky to have good insurance coverage through the Screen Actors Guild, which would take care of most of it, but there was an additional $55,000 that I would have to pay out of pocket. I didn't think twice. They could have every penny I earned if they could just save my life, which the doctors said was highly probable.

Throughout that preparation period, it seemed like I was constantly lying on yet another test table in a cold room, where they injected various dyes into my spinal cord for different scans. I remember having a blue dye injected that was so hot I fainted right there on the table. Another time, I was told to fast for three days before a particular test, and I had to drink the contents of a kit full of liquids that would clean me out like a colonic.

It was all unpleasant, and a lot of it was painful and uncomfortable, but I did it all, and I got my estate in order, naming my mom as power of attorney. I was preparing for my surgery with the same due diligence that I prepared for a film role. "The actor prepares," said Stanislavsky. *So does the human being*, I added. But this was no role. This time it was real life, and I was doing everything I could to hold on to mine.

CHAPTER 30

Separating
the Men from
the Boys

W hen three weeks of tests and checkups had passed, I saw the doctor for an evaluation. There were still three weeks left before my second surgery was scheduled, but I was surprised to hear about a change of plans. "The good news," said the oncologist, "is that you're healing much faster than we expected. It's been three weeks, but you were so healthy to start with, your body has already recovered from the surgery."

I was terrified that my next surgery was being scheduled right away, but I was also relieved to be getting it over with. Waiting was making me crazy, and I was more than ready the night before the actual procedure. I had called Philip and told him that I *did* need him now. He agreed to get on a plane to California as soon as he could, but the concern in his voice was bordering on morbidity.

"Philip," I told him, "it means a lot to me that you want to be here. I really want you here, but when you come, I need strength from you. I need easy conversation and lightness. Most of all, I really don't want to have to take care of anyone else. They keep stressing that in my therapy. Do you understand?"

"Yes," he said, sounding like he was preparing to attend my funeral.

My cancer counselors had taught me that when you first tell people about an illness, you have to figure out who can handle it. Who could support me without needing anything in return? Who had developed their spiritual side enough to be able to process their own feelings without interfering in my healing process? I hoped Philip could do that, but he sounded so negative and somber. "C'mon, Phil," I said, taking care of him one more time. "I'm just having surgery to remove some bad tissue. I'm going to be fine, and we can have a good life and some fun again."

Satisfied that he would be there for me, I asked Mom to rent him a hotel room and a car, which she did. I knew he wouldn't be arriving before the surgery. There wasn't enough time. But he promised to be the first sight I saw when I came out of the anesthesia. That was good enough for me.

Since I was not allowed to eat the evening before surgery, I was hungry, wired, and sleepless that night as I grabbed the TV remote control and started flipping channels. Whether it was divine providence or mere coincidence, I have no idea, but I found a medical documentary called *Bill Moyers' Journal: Mind Over Matter*. The timing could not have been better, since my spirit and my resolve were being so heavily tested right then.

Bill Moyers, a well-respected and brilliant journalist, was visiting medicine men and shamans all over the world, exploring the most primitive to the most technologically advanced healing cultures. This particular show had been filmed in China, and at the start of the show, he introduced a Chinese woman with a malignant tumor the size of an orange growing out of her back. Mr. Moyers explained that if a patient needed surgery, the Chinese doctors would do it. But in general, they were prone to less cutting and more herbal remedies whenever possible, allowing the natural principles of yin (the female energy) and yang (the male energy) to swing back into balance. This was all new to me, but it made a great deal of sense. When you considered the fact that these Chinese healing methods dated back thousands of years, they must know what they're talking about.

I watched this woman drink herbal teas, receive acupuncture and acupressure, and work with her own mind to visualize the tumor shrinking. As the doctors balanced the meridians of her body to strengthen them and remove all energetic obstructions, the woman's tumor began to shrink. Each day they filmed, you could see the tumor literally getting smaller and smaller. In five weeks, it was completely gone, and the woman had avoided chemotherapy and radiation.

I suddenly sat up in the bed with a shot of hope. How can I get to China and save myself? I wouldn't be going to China, and I had to have surgery, there was no doubt. But from what I just saw, there were other ways to work with my body afterward to become healthier and stronger. Bill Moyers had saved my life by renewing my spirit with hope and new possibilities. He had reminded me that cancer was not necessarily a death sentence. I vowed that night that when I was well again, I would find a way to thank him, so here I am, doing just that. Thanks to Bill Moyers's powerful show, when they wheeled me into surgery and the anesthesiologist began to administer the sleeping medication, instead of shaking with fear, I was visualizing the cancer cells being scraped away so completely that they would be gone forever.

The surgery, although extensive and lasting many hours, went well. Several hours later, I was in the recovery room, looking up at my mom's concerned face. "Is Philip here?" I asked, groggy and confused.

"Not yet, Pammy," she said gently.

"Did he call?"

"Not yet."

I fell back into a sedated sleep, waking up every now and then to ask Mom, "Is Philip here?"

"No, honey," she said.

"Hope he didn't get lost," I slurred before I passed out again.

The next time I woke up, Mom was sitting in the chair beside my bed in a hospital room. She smiled at me. "The surgery went really well, and a lot of people called to check on you," she told me.

"How did they know I was here?" I asked. "I didn't tell anyone."

"Someone announced it on the radio."

"That I had surgery?"

"Seems so. A ton of people called."

"But not Philip?" I asked.

"No, not Philip."

That day went by and so did the next without a word from Philip. A few close friends visited me on the third day, and I was distraught, certain that Philip had gotten into a car accident because no one had seen or heard from him. Mom had left a ton of messages on his answering machine, and so had I, but it seemed like he had disappeared into thin air. I even called his office a few times, but it went straight to voice mail. "I just don't understand, Mom," I said. "He promised to be here. I can't imagine what happened."

Gratefully, my medications kept knocking me out. It was stressful to be worrying about Philip, but in the meantime, other friends were showing up and bringing me flowers, books, and various treats. I was touched to receive three dozen roses from the now late Gregory Hines, with whom I danced in his video. Actor Steven Seagal, whom I'd acted with in *Above the Law*, showed up, and we had an intimate conversation about health.

I also got a visit from my dear friend Peter Douglas, producer of the film *Something Wicked This Way Comes*, a film I starred in, written and co-produced by science fiction luminary Ray Bradbury. Peter, brother of Michael Douglas, brought in a blender, and he and my mom got totally loaded on margaritas and kept me laughing, in spite of myself. I also had a visit from an old skiing pal, Alfred Sapse, who later became my entertainment attorney. He came to provide deep wisdom, since he had studied healing from a very young age.

On the fourth day postsurgery, my mom called Philip and left the following message: "The surgery went well, and now Pam has some therapy to get through. We still have your hotel room, and we're wondering if you're coming. Please let us know."

She knew there were people who couldn't handle illness. During her extensive nursing career, she'd seen them walk out on children, wives, and siblings all the time. But I still had hope—until the doctor himself sat on my bed. "He isn't coming," my physician informed me. "I called him myself. But I need you to focus. I need you to get well. This journey is critical to your survival, and I need you to concentrate on you. Can you do that for yourself?"

I made a decision in that moment. No one would rob me of my healing energy. A few days later, still unable to walk steadily, I literally crawled to the bathroom with all my drainage tubes sticking out everywhere. I was in agony, not only from the incisions but also internally, wherever they had cut out tissue. I had so many stitches, I actually fainted from the pain, but I managed to get my head in the shower to wash my hair. Then I got back into bed and did what I could do to exorcise Philip from my mind. He wasn't worth it. No one was.

Friends who visit you in your hospital room are often people whom you didn't expect to show up. These are your real friends, and I was thrilled and overwhelmingly surprised to see Fritz, my songwriting mentor; Carl Gottlieb, my screenwriting mentor; and Tammy Hoffs, my directing mentor from Women in Film. Andy Davis, director of *Above the Law*, sent his sister, a nurse at Cedars, to check up on me, and Lani Groves, my spiritual advisor, also showed up.

When the doctor was doing his rounds a few days later, he stopped to talk to me. "Don't tell anyone what I'm about to say, because I'm a Harvard-trained physician and this would not be good for my reputation. I want you to go to Chinatown."

I burst into a smile. I had just watched the miracles of Chinese healing on TV, and I was enthusiastic to start taking advantage of it. He continued, "People would call me a quack if they knew I was telling my patients about yin and yang energies. Are you familiar with that?"

"A little bit," I said.

"Well, the Chinese are absolutely on target. I've done all I can with Western medicine. Now you need Eastern medicine to create a balance."

Balance was the name of game as I was discharged from the hospital on the third of July. On July 5, I went to a pharmacy in Chinatown run by a renowned Chinese herbalist who checked my tongue and my eyes, took my pulse, and prescribed herbs. Over the next few months, I took the herbs, I got acupuncture and acupressure (the therapeutic massages were nothing short of nirvana), and I started practicing yoga to quiet my mind and learn to be still. In a bookstore in Chinatown, I picked up information on the meridians and how Chinese medicine can help to balance the body. The point was to be able to sense—in other words, to feel and hear—any medical issues in my body and mind.

When I look back at my healing experience, I would have to say that I saved my life by keeping my mind wide open. There is a spiritual term, *agape*, pronounced *a-ga-pay*, which literally means "love and wide open." I stayed agape to treatments, philosophies, and other cultures, focusing on and attacking my illness as if it were an acting role. I used each procedure as an affirmation of life, and I never missed a treatment. I leaned on friends for strength and support, and I avoided self-pity. I set my sights on five years ahead, when I could say to all who cared, "I had cancer, and now I'm in remission." That was my goal and my motivator as I reviewed my life one more time to see where I had come from and where I might end up.

CHAPTER **31**

On the Move Again

Surviving cancer, as miraculous as it is, can also be a shaky proposition, as it demands a complete change of lifestyle and attitude. I'd been given a second chance, and to make the most of it, I needed a clean, healthy, low-stress environment in which to heal. I thought about Minnie and Krista, who both had died from cancer. There was no way to know why they were gone and why I had been saved. I tried to avoid survivor's guilt, since I knew that cancer was random. But I felt I owed it to these amazing women as well as to myself to get strong and become functional once again.

For starters, I had to figure out where to live. My oncologist told me in no uncertain terms that living permanently in the pollution and smog of a big city like Los Angeles was not smart. I also needed to eliminate preservatives and hormones that were often found in commercial chicken and other meats.

When you've been through the terror of facing your death, you find yourself questioning your priorities. Although I would need to be in LA once a month for the next year to get tested, I would have to go back to Colorado to heal, which made me think hard about my career. How much did I still want a career in film? How important was it to me? Would I be willing to commute if need be? Since the radiation

and other treatments, my memory was a little shaky from not working and not exercising my brain. Would I still be able to remember
lines?

I had a lot to consider when I arrived in Denver and temporarily moved in with my sister, Gina, who was eager to take care of
me. I was hoping to find peace and quiet there as opposed to the
stress of Los Angeles, but life has a way of turning things upside
down. I'd been in Denver for only a day when I realized that Papa
Sam's Alzheimer's disease was getting much worse. His dementia
had escalated to the point where he had trouble recognizing people.
This frustration led him into sudden acts of violence, and my mom
felt like she was in danger, afraid to be alone with him. My plans to
heal quietly and recover in a peaceful environment were shot when
I found myself sleeping on the floor outside my mom's bedroom
several nights in a row, in case her husband became dangerous
when they were sleeping. All we could do was bide our time until
he moved up the waiting list for another nursing home.

I had returned to Colorado to be with my dogs and to focus on
myself, but there I was, chasing after my stepdad in the wee hours
of the night and searching for him when he once took the car for a
drive. This would not work, I realized, so when I had time to myself, I
started driving out into the country, looking for a small parcel of land
to purchase. An old abandoned farmhouse was what I had in mind, in
the area south of Denver.

The farmlands were compelling with their clapboard houses and
brick ranch homes. This was the land where we went on hayrides
when I was a little girl, places that got covered with snow so quickly
and completely, they looked like Hallmark Christmas cards. The acre-
age prices were low, and I kept looking, certain that I would be guided
to the right spot. In all the healing books I read, the common wisdom
was to find a quiet, stress-free, unpolluted environment, a sanctuary of
sorts, where you could sleep, meditate, and become better acquainted
with nature. This was what constituted a place to heal.

My family, with their rural sensibilities, had taught me that before
you buy any property, try to live on the land and see how the wind

blows and where the sun rises and sets. Is there adequate water? What about access during bad weather? Could I survive a snowstorm there? Was the place built next to a lake or river that could result in flooding or landslides? With these questions in mind, I kept returning to an area south of Denver toward New Mexico, where the wind was gentle and the land was teeming with healthy trees and abundant vegetation. My plan was to lease the land first and purchase it after I'd lived there for a while.

I moved out of my sister's house after a week or two to give Gina her privacy (and to get some for myself), and I checked into a hotel just down the street from where Mom lived. Still, I slept on Mom's sofa sometimes, until I got a call to do a guest-starring role on the TV show *The Fresh Prince of Bel-Air.* In this show, which launched Will Smith's career, Smith's character was a street-smart teenager from West Philadelphia who was sent to live with his wealthy relatives in a huge Bel Air mansion. One of the first successful African American sitcoms, it was a perfect vehicle for me to reenter the acting world. I took the job since it was a role that would not challenge me too much and I could film the whole thing in one week.

I guess I was also ready to get out of Denver for a respite, since the drama around my family kept escalating. We finally got our step-dad admitted into a nursing home for milder cases of Alzheimer's. But he'd wandered out in the night, and they found him lying down in a field in the snow, slowly freezing to death. He was too far gone, even for this facility. We saved him, but he had to move back in with Mom and stay on meds, and we had to make sure he was never alone until we found another place to put him that dealt with more advanced cases of Alzheimer's.

At this point, I was ready to get away, so the job in LA was the perfect distraction. I loved being back at work and was relieved to find that I could remember my lines well enough. When I returned to Colorado after the shoot, I felt more alive and encouraged that I could commute for work. Some of the producers of *Fresh Prince* and other LA productions lived near Denver in order to get more house for less money, and they commuted every week. If they could do it, I told myself, so could I. True, it might be tough to fly during the periodic snowstorm, but mostly it would work out just fine.

During this period, I appeared in a variety of shows, including *Frank's Place*, *The Cosby Show*, *Martin*, *Fresh Prince*, *The Wayan Bros.*, *The Sinbad Show*, and a sitcom called *The Preston Episodes*, starring David Alan Grier. There were more black series and talk shows popping up than ever before, and I was trying to balance work and family. But that balance veered out of control when one night my stepdad didn't recognize my brother and came at him with an axe. It took five people to restrain his suddenly extraordinary strength. This was my mom's hero, her great love, and it broke all of our hearts that he was taken away in an ambulance, sedated, restrained, and then confined. He had never forgotten a birthday, anniversary, or holiday. Now he couldn't remember the faces of the members of his own family when he was checked into the final nursing home.

As if enough devastation weren't already going on, I was in Denver one day when I had to take one of my dogs to the vet. It was my cocker spaniel, Magic Johnson, whom I named because I thought the dog and the basketball star had similar-looking kind and warm eyes. Magic was the cutest dog in the world, and I took him everywhere with me when I was sick. He always slept on my bed with the rest of my dogs, cuddling me if I was cold and soothing me when I was afraid. Now my poor little Magic was facing a health crisis of his own when the vet found a cancerous lump in his rib cage.

"Most people just put the dog to sleep in a situation like this," the vet told me, "mainly because they can't afford to fight it."

"Well, I can," I said. "I want to give him all the treatments he needs: chemo, surgery, acupuncture. The works." If it was good enough for me, it was good enough for Magic Johnson. I was encouraged by the results of his acupuncture when his blood cell count started changing for the better. But it was too late for my Magic. By the time I'd learned about his cancer, the lump had grown too big. Once again, a loved one was slipping away, when a phone call took me completely by surprise.

"Is this Pam Grier?" a female voice asked.

"Yes," I answered. "Who's this?"

"I'm Tim Burton's assistant," she said.

I inhaled sharply. Tim Burton had directed such blockbuster hits as *Beetlejuice*, *Batman*, and *Edward Scissorhands*, to name a few. "Why is he calling me?" I asked.

"Tim is doing a new film, and he'd like you to read for a role." She was talking about *Mars Attacks*, which would boast an all-star cast. "Where are you now?" she asked me.

"In Colorado," I said. "I live here. I've been taking care of my family. I come to LA to work when I can."

"Can you come out tomorrow to audition for this movie?" she wanted to know.

I'd been a big comic book fan, so I knew *Mars Attacks*. Right up my alley. And what actor didn't want to work with Tim Burton? But I couldn't leave my ailing best friend. "I'm so sorry," I said. "I can't come and audition, but please tell Tim thank you, and give him my congratulations for the success of *Beetlejuice*. His work is amazing. I really think Michael Keaton should have won the Oscar for *Beetlejuice*."

We hung up and I hugged Magic. I couldn't believe I had just turned down Tim Burton, but I couldn't abandon my dog while he was sick. He hadn't abandoned me, and I had to do the same for him, since he seemed to be stabilizing. He was getting a little bit better, and I was encouraged, until a week later, when his health took a bad turn and began to deteriorate.

In the midst of it all, Tim Burton's assistant called back. "Could you just put something on tape for us? Then you wouldn't have to come out. Tim really wants to see your work. It's a comedy. Could you tape something funny?"

There was no way I could be funny while my dog was fighting cancer. I explained that to Tim's assistant. "I'm sorry to disappoint Tim, but my heart is broken right now over my dog, and I don't want to give Tim a terrible performance."

When we hung up, I was sure I'd heard the last from them. I kept repeating the names Jack Nicholson, Glenn Close, and Jim Brown.

They were the stars of the movie for which I had just turned down an audition. I forced myself to forget about it, so no one was more stunned than I when the phone rang four days later and I was talking to the legendary director himself.

"Pam. Sorry to bother you," a warm, highly animated male voice said, reminiscent of some of the characters in his avant-garde movies. "This is Tim Burton. I'm so sorry about your dog, but I really want you in my movie."

"Why?" I asked. I couldn't understand why he kept coming back instead of getting offended that I had refused him.

"The role is a woman who won't leave her children, no matter what. This is exactly how you are with your dog. The mom and the kids in the film are being attacked by Martians, and she won't leave them. She'd die first. That's the role, and your refusal to leave your dog was your audition. I need a woman with your character. The role is yours."

"But I won't leave my dog while he's still alive," I reminded him. "What about your shooting schedule?"

"We'll shoot around you until you're ready. When you are, let us know and we'll fly you out to LA. We'll take really good care of you here. I promise."

I began to sob from his warmth and kindness.

About two weeks later, when Magic was finally ready to go, he gave me a look that was all-knowing. He rested his paw on my chest, as if he were saying, "It's time for me to go and for you to go, too." And he closed his eyes. As he slipped away to heaven, I tearfully gave thanks for having had so much time with him. Then I headed out to Los Angeles to work.

Tim's people took great care of me while I grieved the loss of my sweet Magic, turning to work once again to lose myself. And what great work it was! This was my first film with a budget like this—a cool $90 million. On the smaller films to which I was accustomed, the limited budget allowed for a limited amount of creativity. With this film, however, since the budget was sky-high, the sky was the limit. Gathered together were some of the finest actors in the business, making a movie about big-headed green-and-purple Martians in gold lamé capes. You had only to walk on the set to see the wonder of a studio supporting an artist with everything he needed to make his vision tangible. And I got to participate.

Although one would expect such a daunting endeavor with so many locations and special effects to be chaotic and crazy, it was just the opposite. We didn't need to do a multitude of takes, because they had spent so much time and money on preparation, and the actors were all pros. Everything was organized and sketched out. The mechanics were programmed to perfection, including the lighting, sound, and direction. The actors were focused and determined, with no time to screw around, because they all had other projects coming up right after this one. If we went overtime, we might lose a crucial cast member to their next commitment. It takes intelligence, experience, and preparation to work with such high-caliber people and pull off a film like this, and it felt great to be an essential element of the machinery that would make this film a huge success.

Tim Burton and I became such good friends, he gave me an original painting he did—a framed oil of me as a Martian. When I finished the film, I leased and eventually bought that property in Colorado, and I display the painting proudly in my living room there. Since my mountain home is surrounded by a forest of trees, in case of lightning or a forest fire, I know exactly what I'd save—myself, my rescued horses, my dogs, and Tim Burton's original painting of me as a green-and-purple Martian.

CHAPTER **32** Ghosts of
Boyfriends Past

I t was early in 1992 when I got a call from burgeoning movie director Spike Lee. He was shooting a semiautobiographical film called
Crooklyn that he co-wrote and would be directing in Brooklyn, New
York. The focus was on a young girl and her rowdy brothers all growing
up in the 'hood. He wanted me to play Alfre Woodard's character's best
friend, and I jumped at the chance to work with him and Alfre, one of
God's gifts to cinema.

Close to five years after my initial cancer diagnosis, I managed
to pass the physical that is always required before a film shoot. After
I assured Spike that I wouldn't be dropping dead on his movie set, I
flew to New York, where they put me up at a small boutique hotel in
Midtown called the Paramount. I was eating as healthily as I could and
staying away from smoky rooms. I also went to Chinatown in New York
and got the herbs and foods that were a part of my new regimen.

I was feeling strong and healthy when I got off the elevator in my
hotel on a day off and stepped into the lobby. The doorman, Wayne,
asked, "Shall I call you a cab, Ms. Grier?"

It was the kind of New York weather that encouraged people to
be outdoors as much as possible. "Not today," I told him. "It's so beautiful outside, I want to walk around."

Ever since my life had been in jeopardy with cancer, special moments had become vividly precious in my mind. Much of what I'd previously considered important had been stripped away. Now little things like the smells and the pulse of the city mattered to me. I looked to my right and then to my left. "Which direction should I go?" I asked Wayne.

He pointed off to the left. "That way will be more interesting," he said. "There are some nice shops and cafés there."

"Thank you," I said and began to walk down the street in the direction he had pointed. But in less than ten steps, my attention was drawn to a handsome man with reddish-brown skin wearing an expensive suit. He looked vaguely familiar as I watched him cross the street. Did I know him? I caught my breath. He was damned familiar. He looked exactly like Philip, the disappearing man, the ghost of boyfriends past, who had run from my illness like it was contagious.

My feet went numb and my knees wobbled as he began walking toward me. He hadn't recognized me yet, and maybe he wouldn't. But suddenly he stopped and stared. He glanced to his right and left, as if looking for a clean escape. There wasn't one. I tried to take a step forward and teetered, when Wayne, the doorman, came running over to hold me up. He must have seen me stop in my tracks, and he held my back as I struggled to breathe.

I hadn't seen Philip since my diagnosis years prior. In the last call I made to him, I'd said, "I'm okay. I thought you might like to know. The treatments are relatively easy to get through, and I'm taking Chinese herbs. Do you know anything about acupuncture and acupressure? You can use it on yourself and your mom. I'd like you to call, but if you don't, I understand."

He never responded, and I had put him out of my mind. Now here he was again. Out of eight million people in the city of New York, what were the odds of my bumping into this one man? I saw him take a deep inhale, as if resigning himself to the inevitable. Then he walked up to me and said, "Well, hello there. You're looking very well."

A gust of wind blew his jacket open, and there were the telltale suspenders that Philip always wore. This was no Demerol flashback.

It was Philip, holding a small box in one hand. It was *his* voice, *his* suspenders, and *his* attitude, I realized, as I felt the contents of my stomach starting to rumble. I imagined chasing him into the street and watching him get run over by a car. I know that's a terrible vision, but I couldn't help it.

With Wayne still holding on to me, I told Philip, "You better keep walking, or I'll throw up on your shoes." I was just getting warmed up as I continued, "You didn't care whether I lived or died. You didn't call me just to say, 'I'm glad you're okay.' Or 'Will you be okay?' Or 'Here's why I didn't come.' Something. Anything. Or were you angry at me because I shamed you into buying your mom a home?"

"Well," he said, "I guess I do owe you an explanation."

"No, you don't," I retorted. "I don't want to hear it. I have to go inside now."

"Can I help you?" he asked.

"Just leave me alone."

"I'll take it from here," the doorman said to Phil. "Why don't you go away?"

While the doorman took my arm and helped me walk back toward the hotel, Philip rushed over to take my other arm. I wanted to scream. I could feel everyone's eyes on me as these two men helped me into the building. I hated looking like a sick lady who needed help. I never wanted Philip to see me that way, and I jerked away from his arm.

The doorman went to call the elevator, but there was no way I could step into a moving structure without my breakfast landing on the floor beneath me. I dropped onto a sofa, and Philip took a chair beside me. My head ached. Quietly clutching his little box, he looked sad, as if he wanted to be anywhere else. Maybe he had remorse or guilt. I really don't know, because he said so little, but his silence spoke volumes.

He looked small and pathetic when I said, "I was having cancer surgery to save my life. You said you'd come and you didn't. We rented you a car and a hotel room. I called you, my mom called you, even the doctor called you. You never called any of us back. That was how you wanted to leave it, and I had to live with it. But I'm okay now, and you can go. Please."

He sat where he was, fiddling with the box in his hands.

"What's in there?" I asked.

He looked down and after an uncomfortably long pause said, "I just picked up my fiancée's wedding ring. I'm getting married next week."

My head throbbed harder. "Good luck," I said. "I hope she never gets sick."

My ears were ringing, my head was pounding, and my mind was fuzzy when I got up and motioned to the doorman that I was ready to ride the elevator. Once I was back in the safety of my room, I fell onto the bed and dropped off to sleep in my clothes.

CHAPTER 33   Meeting Jackie Brown

Besides the occasional film, I focused on theater for a while. There was an honesty and immediacy about it that appealed to me, since I was in such a vulnerable stage of my life. A black Renaissance was occurring in live theater as well as in film, and I loved the simple stories, the energy, and the feeling of being right there with your audience. I liked the idea that you had one take to get it right, which was so different from film, where we did take after take until everyone was satisfied.

One of my favorite roles was playing Grace in *The Piano Lesson* at the Denver Center for the Performing Arts, written by talented playwright August Wilson. This play is the story of a brother and sister who argue about whether to sell the family piano that has carvings of relatives dating back to the days of slavery. My co-star was Roger Robinson, a great black actor recently nominated for a Tony Award, and we were sold out for every performance. I was also the understudy for the leading role of Berniece, which I actually performed one time.

Next, I was hired to do a play called *Telltale Hearts* at the Crossroads Theatre in New Jersey on the campus of Rutgers University. It was deep winter and very cold when I worked with the group called the Negro Ensemble. Yes, *the* Negro Ensemble, which was very popular at the time. This group was part of the burgeoning

African American theater. Founded in 1967, the ensemble was prestigious, as it integrated the past with the present. The play was a comedy, and they put me up in an apartment about twenty minutes from
the theater. I was happy walking back and forth; I liked the exercise.
When two and a half feet of snow fell one night, however, I thought I
better call a cab in the morning. But the cabs were running so late, if
at all, I was afraid I'd miss my call.

Being a Colorado girl, to me, a little snow was no excuse for being
late for work. I put my script and some extra clothing in a backpack,
zipped on my skiing gear, and jogged from the apartment, across the
campus, to the theater where we were rehearsing. I was the first cast
member to arrive, and the director said, "Wow, your cab must have
picked you up early. Everybody else is running late. The roads are
completely blocked."

"I didn't take a cab," I said. "I jogged here. It's not very far."

He looked at me like I was crazy. Meticulously dressed New
Yorkers didn't get their clothes wet and dirty, but I didn't care. It was
a fifteen-minute jog on level ground, much easier than when I jogged
for an hour, mostly uphill, in the mountains of Colorado. I was used to
the exercise, and the main thing was that I was on time, doing a play
that was hilarious, having a ball. Despite my illness, which had set me
back for quite a while, I felt that my craft was up to that of the rest of
the cast. I was enjoying my work, and I believed that a well-rounded
actor needed both film and theater.

Now I was spending more time in New York than in Los Angeles,
and I liked the balance of work and social life. I dated some men
here and there, but I chose not to get serious about anyone. My body
was still healing, and I had no room to cater to anyone else. But I did
date Warrington Hudlin, a Yale graduate and producing partner with
his brother, Reginald Hudlin, a Harvard graduate. Warrington had
a beautiful loft in the hip Meatpacking District in Manhattan, and I
found him to be an intelligent man who shared my love of the martial
arts. He introduced me to Chinese herbalist and Grand Martial Arts
Master Doo Wai, who guided me in taking herbs, and watched over
my diet, making sure my cancer did not return. Warrington also taught

me a lot about film production. One day, when Warrington and I were both in Los Angeles, I was driving him to the Valley when we crossed Highland Avenue. There, as we idled in stalled traffic, I spotted a strange-looking man in shorts on the edge of the sidewalk. His long brown hair was unruly, he wore old sneakers, and he was talking to a gorgeous starlet-type young woman, all the while gesturing wildly.

Warrington recognized this man as Quentin Tarantino, director and writer extraordinaire, fresh off his great success, *Pulp Fiction*. I was in awe just seeing him, until he looked straight at me. I saw the recognition in his eyes, and suddenly he was walking into the middle of traffic, heading toward my car. "Pam Grier," he said, staring at me through my open window.

I was stunned that he knew my name. "Yes. Mr. Tarantino. What a pleasure," I cooed and introduced him to Warrington, a big fan. Quentin knew who the Hudlin brothers were, since they had produced *Boomerang* with Eddie Murphy and *House Party*.

"I'm writing a movie for you," he said. "It's based on *Rum Punch*, the Elmore Leonard book."

"Well, that sounds amazing," I said. I didn't believe him.

"It's my version of *Foxy Brown*," he went on.

The traffic suddenly started moving. Quentin waved and weaved his way back to the sidewalk. I had started to drive when Warrington said, "Can you believe that?"

"No, I can't," I answered. "Don't believe everything a Hollywood director tells you."

Warrington was surprised at my reaction. But I'd been around the Hollywood scene long enough to know that without a script in hand, it was all idle talk. In fact, I forgot about it, and when I stopped seeing Warrington, I had no one to remind me. That was just as well, since waiting for a promised role can be deadly. But about six months later, a notice arrived from the post office that they were holding a package for me.

It took me a few days to find the time to claim my package, on which there was 44 cents due for postage. I paid and they handed me a manila envelope. Quentin's return address was scribbled on the left-hand corner in what I assumed was his own handwriting, and inside was a script entitled *Jackie Brown*. He had sent it weeks ago, but they had been unable to deliver it because there was money due.

What do you know? He wasn't kidding. Once I was home, I sat in a comfortable chair with a cup of herbal tea and started to read. The story was about a flight attendant, Jackie Brown, who was coerced by an ATF agent to help bring down an arms smuggler and his accomplices. Robert De Niro, Samuel Jackson, and Michael Keaton had already been cast. As I read on, I figured I could do the role of Melanie, a good-time girl who was one of the accomplices.

I placed a call to Quentin's office, and he got on the line immediately. "Jesus, Pam," he said. "I sent the script to you weeks ago. I thought you were passing on it."

"I just got it today," I said. "They were holding it 'cause you didn't pay enough postage."

"Oh," he said. "Well, anyway, how'd you like it?" he asked.

"It was great. I'd really like to audition for the role of Melanie. I think I could do a great job."

Quentin laughed. "Bridget Fonda is playing Melanie," he said. "You're Jackie Brown, Pam. I told you I was writing a script for you. I loved Foxy Brown, and I wrote this in your honor."

It was true. Quentin Tarantino really had written a script for me, and it had cost me 44 cents to obtain my greatest role to date.

CHAPTER **34** Working with Quentin

F ive years after my cancer diagnosis, I headed to Chinatown in Los Angeles to thank some important doctors and herbalists in my life. They say that having clean MRIs for five years is remission, but I didn't look at it like that. I still don't. There was no actual moment when I stepped back and said, "I'm cured." I knew better after seeing Krista, who had been cancer-free for years when she was fatally stricken again. Life isn't black-and-white like that. But I did have something to celebrate, and I felt grateful to my guides along the way.

The Chinese herbalists were glad to see me, and I was thrilled to report my good health. But Dr. Morgan, the surgeon who had sent me to Chinatown in the first place, reminded me, "Don't get cocky, Pam. I don't want to burst your bubble, but it can come back at any time. You have to keep eating fresh foods with no hormones or preservatives. After all, you lost a third of your lymph glands in your groin area, and you only have two-thirds left to fight infection—in your armpits and your neck. But you can start having MRIs every six months instead of every month."

He was making sure I stayed on my program, and I was on board with him. I had no intention of going back to the way things were. I was healed for the moment, and I was fortunate and filled with gratitude to still be here. "Thank you, God, for giving me another day," I would pray each morning when I woke up. *Namaste*. And now, as I anticipated a great film role, I had also met a wonderful man, a record producer named Caleb. I was determined to stay healthy enough to enjoy it all.

I met Caleb at a restaurant in my hotel in Los Angeles, and I liked the fact that he was from Denver, just like me, and he was unassuming, not at all aggressive. I was surprised that I fell hard and fast for him, but that was a symptom of the way my life was moving at that time. Talk about life in the fast lane! People had been fascinated and marginally excited about me as an actor from my past films—after all, I'd been one of the primary blaxploitation queens and had a built-in audience. But now that I was starring in a Tarantino movie, with famed Lawrence Bender as producer, I felt the full weight of being involved with a group of A-list players and brilliant producers—Bob and Harvey Weinstein.

A powerful aphrodisiac, this kind of fame and celebrity stimulated people beyond belief. I was getting the best tables at restaurants, and people were dropping my name right and left now that I was connected to Quentin, rushing me for autographs wherever I went. While I tried to stay focused on my work, people were hoisting me on a pedestal so high I feared the inevitable drop would kill me. I tried to stay grounded and live as normally as possible, but now that my fame was speeding out of control, my new man, Caleb, was infected, and he was taking a leap off the deep end.

Divorced with three young children (one was an infant), whom he saw on weekends (sometimes), Caleb had been perfectly happy just to hang out with me at first. But when my star began to rise higher than ever before, Caleb wanted the high life and everything that was part of it. "You need to spend more money, Pam, and be the star that you are." He gestured to my red Suburban truck that was getting me around town just fine. "You need to get rid of that thing and get a hot whip [car] and show off a little."

I ignored his advice, and I was reluctant when he decided he needed all new furniture in his 7,000-square-foot Hollywood Hills home. Trying to be supportive, I spent my days off shopping—and fighting with him over furniture I didn't like or care about. "Did you measure the square footage?" I asked him when we were looking at a ridiculously expensive modern Italian sofa that Caleb absolutely had to have. "I think it's too long for the space," I said, stunned at the over-the-moon price tag.

"I don't need to measure it," he stated arrogantly. "I can tell by just looking. It's perfect."

I lost count of how many chairs, tables, and couches got hauled up many levels of stairs that we had to send back down when they didn't fit. Anyone who thinks that money doesn't change people obviously never met Caleb. So why did I stay with him? I was in love, but not with him. I was in love with the idea of getting married and having kids. Caleb already had three of his own, which gave me an instant family, and I could see myself in a Vera Wang wedding dress, saying "I do," and living in a lovely little town like Laguna Beach, overlooking the ocean and raising a bunch of kids together.

Of course, it was all fantasy, since Caleb was falling in love with the "good life," not with me. While his own career was growing by leaps and bounds, I showed up on set each day, ready to shoot with Quentin. He was a wonderful director to work with, as he kept the cast and crew alive and excited. One afternoon, he declared that we would have "skirt day." In the morning, all the men in his crew (the usual suspects with whom he always worked) showed up wearing kilts and skirts, and we laughed all day long.

The way to a happy crew is through their stomachs, and Quentin provided good food and great music for all of us as we worked long and tedious hours. A meticulous director, he encouraged lots of rehearsal before we shot a scene. That saved a lot of shooting time, which was crucial, since time was a rare commodity. The stars in this film had a set amount of time they were available, with their next projects waiting in the wings. Going overtime was out of the question, and I felt so humbled around my co-stars, I made sure to prepare well so I didn't drop a line and ruin an otherwise perfect take.

Quentin sometimes shot scenes that were ten minutes long with no breaks, a challenge to any actor. He liked his director of photography to turn on the handheld camera and catch the action in a continuous movement and flow with no cuts. This was where the expertise of the cast was obvious. It took a lot of adrenaline to work that way, and I had to make sure I stayed on the beat, as if the other actors were my dance partners.

Samuel Jackson, who played Ordell Robbie, an arms smuggler, was a superior performer and was always on point. He knew every word, he never dropped a line, and he looked directly into my eyes when we worked. We were moving along so well, in fact, that a day came when we were ahead of schedule, which was almost unheard of. Quentin wanted to take advantage of the extra time by shooting a scene between Sam and me that was not on the schedule. But Sam said he wasn't ready. He had not prepared, and he didn't want to shoot it cold. I was amazed that Sam had said no to Quentin. If the director wanted to shoot a certain scene, I would simply do it. But Sam felt differently.

As if we were his teenage kids, Quentin proceeded to pit us against each other. A master manipulator, he told Sam, "I just talked to Pam. She's ready. Why aren't you?"

"I don't want to do it," he said simply.

I understood Sam's position. He was the ultimate professional and knew whether he was ready. The truth is that most actors don't like performing a scene in a half-prepared, halfhearted way. We like time to get into the character, the costume, and the setting. We like to figure out the character's frame of mind and be familiar with the lines that hopefully we have already memorized until we know them backward and forward. Since an actor is only as popular as his or her last picture, we don't savor shooting a scene on the spur of the moment. The risks are generally too high to flub a scene. But spur-of-the-moment was what Quentin, the master ringleader, was determined for us to do.

"Pam is waiting for you," he urged Sam, poking subtly at his ego. "She's all ready," he repeated.

His method worked perfectly, as Sam took the bait. "I guess I can do it, then," he said.

Quentin came running over to me and said with a sparkle in his eye, "He's gonna do it—once he knew *you* would."

I became suspicious. "Is he going to take it out on me?" I asked. "What did you say to him? Are you getting me in trouble here?"

"No, no," said Quentin. "It's not like that."

I was prepared to go forward, so was Sam, but not without a rehearsal or two. Since every actor has his or her own timing and speech pattern or timbre, a co-star has to get used to it. For example, Jack Nicholson's delivery is so slow, you wonder if he's still on the other end of the phone call. But he can go from slow to ballistic in a few seconds. Samuel Jackson, on the other hand, has a fast timbre in his speaking patterns. Unlike someone from the South, who might speak as slowly as molasses in January, Sam talked so fast he could exhaust you just keeping up with him. Pulling off a great scene with Sam required total attention to his every word and movement.

The scene ended up working because Quentin was such a gifted director. A real maestro, when he set up a shot, he would talk to the actors and go through the action himself as if he were in the scene. That gave you a clear idea of what he wanted, but he was not rigid. If he did something that didn't make sense to you, you simply didn't copy it, and he was usually okay with that. He gave us leeway and he was patient, but sometimes I think he could have done better at interpreting the emotional qualities of women, which are totally different from those of a man.

He was dating actress Mira Sorvino, a kind and gracious woman who was on the set occasionally. They looked madly in love, and I loved my chats with her. I felt that she was good for Quentin, but I sometimes wondered about his ability to understand what a woman needed.

For example, there was a scene in *Jackie Brown* when my character was in the kitchen, talking to Robert Forster's character, a bail bondsman named Max Cherry. Jackie was frustrated and afraid, which she was trying to hide, and when I did the take, tears spontaneously came out of my eyes. I wasn't sobbing or moaning. I was just crying quietly, because that was what happened naturally, and it surprised me as much as anyone else. The tears showed my internal struggle, as I tried to muster the strength to get through a tough experience.

When we finished the take, there was not a dry eye among the crew members (usually a very tough audience), so I knew I had nailed it. They applauded, and I said, "That was it. That was the performance, right?" I looked to Quentin for validation, but he wasn't satisfied.

"You got another one in you?" he asked.

"Yeah," I said, stunned, "I can do it again. But why?"

"I'd like you to try it one more time without the tears," he said. "I need you to look stronger."

Why do men see crying as a weakness? Jackie was in a very vulnerable state, unsure if she was about to be arrested or killed. I wanted to explain that to Quentin and tell him that my performance had been pure. But he was the director, and we ended up using the second take, the tearless one, which he liked, but in my opinion, it was less effective.

For the most part, however, I agreed with how Quentin envisioned the action. I tried to knock every shot out of the park by being as real and raw as possible. A perfect example was an interrogation scene I did with Michael Keaton's character, Ray Nicolette, a government agent. I wanted it to feel like a real interrogation room where they shined a glaring light on you and didn't allow you to leave the room to go the bathroom.

I sat on a hard chair for eight hours to shoot that scene, and I took no bathroom breaks. I wanted to feel trapped and scared because the agent was supposed to be pressuring me. "I'm cornered," I said to myself as my bladder was slowly filling up. The hours went by, and I had to go to the bathroom so badly my eyes hurt. I thought I might let it go right there in my seat. Finally, when I couldn't have been any more tired or cranky with my bladder so full I could scream, I had a spontaneous angry outburst that defined the agony of the moment, particularly because Jackie was generally a calm person who spoke directly and clearly.

Scenes like these are amazing opportunities for an actor, and I did my best to take full advantage. When the ten-week shoot was over, I felt good about my performance and the amount of effort I'd put into it. I was excited to see how it would come out in the editing room, since that is where so many performances are won or lost. I felt secure that Quentin would be good to me during postproduction. I trusted his judgment, we both wanted the film to be great, and I admired his integrity around his work.

CHAPTER **35**   Caleb

*J*ackie Brown was finished, edited, and promoted. I especially enjoyed being interviewed by my friend Michael Keaton for *Interview* magazine in January 1998.

Among many other questions, he said, "It seems to me you have an amazing perspective on what's important to you. You're someone who's really able to detach from the career part of her life, but in the healthiest way. Do you think you've always had that in you, or did it come because you went through some really tough years, when you lost your sister and faced cancer yourself?"

I answered, "I was brought up to be self-sufficient and to accept that as a member of the human race, there are certain things you have to go through. I always thought that not living here in Hollywood was a way of showing that I'm not afraid of losing my career. I'm afraid of losing me."

Once the PR was over, I took some time off to see what Caleb was really like—without my celebrity calling the shots. I'd traveled extensively through Asia and Europe to promote the film, and everywhere I went, the character of Jackie Brown struck a chord with women. They loved the idea of a woman with no power learning to gather her forces to scam the drug dealers who were trying to scam her.

When we got to New York, they put me up at the luxurious Trump

Tower. I was working with a genius publicist, Kelly Bush, when the phone rang in my hotel room early one morning. It was still dark when I reached over to grab it. "Hello?" I mumbled.

"Pam!" Kelly practically shouted, "You're nominated for a Golden Globe Award."

I sat up. What would I wear? The Golden Globe Awards, with its dinner club atmosphere, is considered one of the most elite award shows, with the winners chosen by the foreign press. It was exciting and humbling to be in the race with such great actresses as Helen Hunt, Julia Roberts, and Jennifer Lopez. I realized that win or lose, this was going to be a rare moment for me, a woman of color, and I was not disappointed when Helen Hunt took away the honors for her role in *As Good as It Gets*. That year, I was up against Helen for every conceivable award, and I lost them all.

I was also nominated for the SAG Awards, and I could hardly believe how these nominations triggered so many people coming out of the woodwork, claiming to suddenly be my best friend. I did so many magazine covers, interviews, and TV appearances that I was happy when it was over and I could go back to my normal life.

But Caleb seemed to enjoy the success of the film more than me and started spending money like it was going out of style. He was also trying to get me to spend mine, luring me with frivolous items like earrings and bracelets he thought I simply had to have. I only hoped that when I got back home, his rush of spending and consuming would be over. It was a very unreal way to live. What if the movie flopped and everything went south? Would Caleb still hang in there with me? I needed enough time to find out if Caleb was really into me. I also needed a clear picture of his intentions.

When I first met him, along with his three kids, Caleb had a ten-year-old car, a modest rented house in LA, and an apartment in New York. But as I became more widely known in the world of celebrity, none of that seemed good enough for him anymore. His own music producing career was taking off, too, and his bank account was getting fatter.

One night after I had just turned forty-seven, he invited me and a couple of his friends to dinner. We were having a nice meal, when suddenly Caleb got down on one knee and handed me a velvet box. Inside was a 2.5 carat diamond ring. He wanted us to get engaged. I tried on the sparkler. What harm would it do to say yes and keep on watching his behavior? It didn't matter that there were no bells or whistles. I was looking for a good man I could trust. That would be the right foundation on which to build a marriage, and once we were engaged, I would see who he really was.

I called my mom to tell her. "Mom, I'm engaged. We're going to get married."

"Really?" she said. "Good. I know you, and you'll pick him apart. You won't get married unless it's right."

Who knew me better than Mom? I was attracted to Caleb's calm demeanor and his familiar midwestern Colorado attitude, but it seemed that he didn't have any particularly close friends. I paid attention to that as I started to get new movie roles. Caleb and I weren't living together—I still called Colorado my home—but I did stay with him when I was in Los Angeles, and I was concerned. I didn't forget the stern directive from my doctor *not* to live in Los Angeles, but what would that do to my relationship with Caleb?

I asked him all about his children, and he said he wanted to spend more time with them. That was important to me, now that we were engaged. I spent the next several months teaching the kids to swim, having a ball, and fantasizing about raising them to become wonderful adults. But I had to remind Caleb that in a few weeks I was starting a new film and I wouldn't be around. "The offers are pouring in right now. I expect to be doing two to three movies a year," I explained.

"But after we get married, you'll slow way down, right?" he said.

"No," I said adamantly. "I have to take care of my mom who isn't well. And I have a nephew about to go to college."

"We can handle it," he tried to assure me, but I didn't feel reassured. Gratefully, I had a respite when I got a role in *Holy Smoke* in 1998, a film that was shooting in Australia.

I headed down under to shoot this film about a young woman, played by Kate Winslet, who fell under the influence of a guru while she was in India. When her parents hired a deprogrammer, Harvey

Keitel, who played my husband, to set her straight, a powerful struggle occurred between the young woman and the man her parents had hired to save her. We were shooting in the outback, where I stayed in a unit in a motel that was next door to Kate's unit. She had her trainer with her, and she exercised hard in the freezing cold each day. I admired her commitment to her craft, and she was warm and personable to me. Off the set, I loved visiting the aboriginals in town. I also loved working with genius director Jane Campion, and Harvey Keitel, a fabulous actor and consummate professional.

I arrived back in Los Angeles and headed over to Caleb's place, hoping for a happy reunion—until he proudly showed me three exotic cars in the garage: a two-seater Porsche, a Bentley, and a Lotus. My beat-up GMC Suburban truck, I noticed, had been relegated to the street.

I looked from the cars to Caleb and back to the cars again as he explained. "I got some money in from royalties, and I—"

"Where are the children's car seats?" I interrupted. "I don't see any."

"We can use your truck," he said.

"That's fine when it's here," I told him, "but I'll be driving the truck back to Colorado pretty soon. It's too big for LA. How will you get the kids around? Why didn't you get an SUV for them?"

"These cars are all on loan," he said.

"Sure they are," I retorted.

"I'm just test-driving them."

"What if something goes wrong with one of them? You'll be responsible."

"So I'll buy it," he said. Another red flag started waving so hard it nearly hit me in the head.

I was about to head to New York for some work, when I realized that I no longer trusted him.

My career was moving too fast to risk my downfall. I had booked three movies simultaneously: one in New York, one in Luxembourg, and I would return to LA for the last one. I did my best, shooting the first two movies. I spoke to Caleb occasionally, but I felt pretty disconnected from him.

When I headed back to Los Angeles, I tried to pretend everything was fine, but Caleb could feel how emotionally removed I was. "Is everything okay with you, Pam?" he asked. "You're not yourself. What's up?"

"Nothing," I lied. "I'm just tired. I've been working really hard."

While he spent his days at the studio, I was slowly moving a few things out of the house each day, pleading headaches to avoid sex, and leaving enough clothes hanging in the closet to keep up the charade. One afternoon, while I was looking through some boxes in the garage, Caleb came roaring up the road in a blue Ferrari. He skidded into the garage and turned off the engine.

"Oh," I said flatly.

He ignored me and said, "This one, I'm keeping. There's a red one just like it in the dealership. I put it on hold for you. You'll look really hot driving it around town. You'll look like a star."

"Oh, really? A red Ferrari will make me look like a star?"

This red flag wrapped around my neck and tightened. All I could think about was the patio furniture. I had bought it, and I wanted to take it with me. How would I get it out of the house? I didn't let on what I was planning, and I had to pretend the next morning when Caleb woke up, turned to me, and suddenly said, "Let's get married. Today."

When he saw the shock on my face, he said, "You're afraid to get married."

"What makes you say that?" I asked.

"Because you won't jump up and marry me in Las Vegas right now. Don't you love me?"

When I refused to answer him, I saw that his radar was on alert. While he went to pick someone up at the airport, I wandered around the property and found a rusted, hidden back gate that led into an ivy-covered walkway, ending at the street. I called an acquaintance who sent some men to carry the patio furniture out the back gate and into my truck. Then I grabbed the last of my clothing that I'd left in the closet for show, and I drove away into a new chapter of my life.

CHAPTER **36** New
Beginnings

A few months later, I pulled the thin blue blanket over my head
to shut out the light in the cabin. I was on a plane from New York to
Denver in the year 2000, sitting in a first-class window seat, still recovering from my breakup with Caleb. "No more heartbreak" was my mantra,
as I saw a tall, handsome Caucasian man slide into the aisle seat beside
me and fasten his seat belt.

I continued to doze. I'd been in New York to tape some voice-
overs for a film I did for Showtime and to work with some friends to
feed the homeless. The trip had gone well, but for me, a breakup is a
sure path to insomnia. I hadn't slept much the night before, and I was
ready to catch up during the flight, now that my work was over. But it
appeared there was no rest for the weary. A flight attendant hovered
by my seat. She and several other attendants had seen my name on
the passenger roster and were excited to be serving me.

I felt a light tap on my shoulder and struggled to open my eyes.
"Miss Grier," she practically sang, "we're so happy to have you on this
flight. I absolutely loved *Jackie Brown*."

I was hardly awake. My brain was fuzzy, and I realized that I needed
to sound somewhat coherent. "Thank you very much," I managed to

say. I was proud to have done a film that empowered women, and I did my best to be gracious.

"Sorry to bother you, but will you be dining with us?" she asked.

"I don't think so," I said. The first-class cabin was filled with wealthy businessmen like the striking, impeccably dressed man sitting beside me. I had hoped my seatmate might be someone fun to talk to, but although this man gave off a sense of quiet strength, he felt rigid and unapproachable. That was fine, since I planned to sleep the flight away. I dozed again.

When some time had passed, I felt another light tap on my arm. This time it was the man next to me. "Are you sure you don't want to dine with the rest of us?" he said jokingly, as if the airline only served the finest cuisine. "It's a long flight," he added.

When I checked in with my growling stomach, I realized I hadn't eaten all day and was starving. I smiled at him. "Maybe I'll have a salad," I said.

"My name is Lance," my neighbor told me.

"I'm Pam," I said. "Nice to meet you." Lance had a briefcase filled with papers by his feet, and I had to go to the restroom. "Will you just excuse me a moment?" I said. "I'd like to go to the restroom before you pull out your papers and get settled."

Having just completed a film with Danny Glover, I had blonde extensions down to my waist and I was wearing a pair of low-rise Prada slacks. When I leaned over to put on my shoes, I was aware that Lance had spotted my hand-size tattoo of a Japanese chrysanthemum that sits just above my tailbone.

While I was going through my radiation treatments for cancer, I saw a picture of the magnificent flower in a *National Geographic* magazine and fell in love with the mythology surrounding this beautiful pink blossom. Japanese folklore says that long, long ago, a volcano erupted and leveled an entire town. Everything was covered with ten feet of lava and volcanic ash, and when it cooled much later, a lone chrysanthemum had sprouted. (It might have grown in manure from some animal, but I'm hoping the truth is a little more romantic than that.) In any event, the little chrysanthemum pod found a reservoir of water and nutrients and grew up out of the ashes. Out of the pain and agony of explosions, eruptions, and death came a delicate flower, and I felt it was parallel to my life at that time.

"It's going to hurt," my friends said when I told them I'd decided to get a tattoo.

"It can't hurt more than what I've already been through," I answered.

It did hurt, by the way, so much that I had to get the tattoo over two separate sessions. It was pink when I first got it, but it faded over the years, and it always reminds me that the worst parts of life can be transformed into beauty. In 1999, when I co-starred in *Linc's*, a sitcom for Showtime, I played a woman named Eleanor, a conservative lawyer on Capitol Hill in DC. When my character started to sow her wild oats and have sex with younger men, we wrote in a segment about her getting a tattoo (my real tattoo), and it freaked everyone out since it was so out of character for Eleanor.

When I returned from the restroom and sat back down, I chatted lightly with Lance. His voice sounded Ivy League and refined, he had a calm and sensitive manner, and he was very easy on the eyes. After a few minutes, I was impressed that he seemed unaffected by the color of my skin. I was also impressed by his manners—how he placed his napkin on his lap and spoke like a man of culture. "Are you headed to Denver on business?" he asked me.

"No. I'm going home," I said.

"You live in Denver?"

"A few hours south. I live on a farm in a rural area," I said.

I saw his eyes widen. Was he really sitting beside a black woman with blonde extensions and a tattoo, living on a farm? "Are you in a witness protection program?" he asked.

We both laughed. "No, no," I said. "I actually live in Colorado. My family comes from there and from Wyoming before the emancipation."

"That's fascinating," he said.

We continued to chat during the flight, and I found Lance to be an interesting man with some great stories. When we were about to land in Denver, he turned to me and said, "When you come to New York the next time, call me and I'll show you around." He handed me his card and I gave him mine, but I figured if I called, he'd never remember who I was.

When we parted company, I headed for the outskirts. The next morning I was up at six, out in the barn and greeting my rescued horses and dogs while the sun was rising. I breathed a sigh of relief as the horses nuzzled me and I fed them carrots. My home, as isolated and rustic as it is, has always felt like paradise to me. But when Snoop Dogg came out to visit me one time, the place was so tiny he drove past it. He thought I lived in a huge mansion and was surprised when I came out the front door of my humble rustic abode to greet him. I headed back to the kitchen and put on some tea while Mom and I cooked up a big breakfast for Snoop and his entourage of twelve.

It was wonderful not to be living out of a suitcase for a change. I was sick and tired of airports, flight cabins, and restaurants.

"Where's Pam?" a friend would ask.

"At the airport," was the usual answer.

Now I was ready for a good, long stint at home, drinking fresh well water with no chemicals and eating garden vegetables, when the phone rang. I was stunned to hear Jerry Offsay, the president of Showtime, on the other end of the line. I'd met him when I was shooting *Linc's* and I knew him to be a man of high ideals. "Jerry," I said, "what an honor."

"Hey, Pam," he said, "you're having dinner with me next week, right?"

I cringed. Had I made a dinner date with the president of Showtime and completely forgotten about it? There was nothing to do but tell the truth. "Let me be brutally frank here, Jerry," I said, "'cause I have no memory of the dinner date. When was it and what time? I must be getting old. Or maybe I had a mental breakdown and can't remember anything."

Jerry laughed. "It's not your memory, Pam," he said. "You're going to be doing a series with us. That's why we're going to have dinner."

"O...ka-a-a-ay," I said. Out the window flew my long, lazy days at the ranch, riding over the land, mucking out stalls, feeding the horses, and enjoying neighborhood gatherings. But I wasn't heading off to New York or Los Angeles. The new show was shooting in Vancouver, and I was already cast as Jennifer Beals's half sister in a show about lesbians originally called *Earthlings* and later changed to *The L Word*.

There were no readings or auditions. It seemed that Jerry Offsay, Ilene Chaiken, and Jennifer Beals were enthusiastic about hiring me for the series. If I wanted it, I would be playing the part of Kit, a straight woman with a tarnished past. They had written her character as a leather-butch documentarian whose body was covered in tattoos depicting various love entanglements. When the series was finally picked up, they changed Kit's character to a straight, sexually curious, and nonjudgmental recovering alcoholic. She was to be her half sister Bette's shattered rock.

I was being offered a role in this new show, no questions asked, and I wanted to ask Jerry if this was some kind of a joke. I thought back to running into Quentin Tarantino in the street when he told me he was writing a screenplay for me. Along with plenty of tragedy, my life has had some magnificent twists and turns that came and swept me up when I was off doing something else.

Jerry Offsay was dead serious about his offer, and he began to break down the show for me. "It's about the lives and loves of a group of lesbian friends living in West Hollywood. It's all about women— straight, gay, and whatever else."

I was delighted. How courageous of Jerry, I thought, to broach such a controversial topic. "Is it a drama or a comedy?" I asked him.

"A little bit of everything," he answered. "My people will call you to make the arrangements."

I hung up the phone, stunned and excited. I was about to take a leap into an edgy new TV series with no audition. I needed to start sorting through my clothing for life in Vancouver. As surprised and reluctant as I felt about leaving home again, I also felt elated that I was about to take part in a project that could potentially become a milestone, both historically and politically.

CHAPTER **37**   *The L Word*

I knew very little about the lesbian community, so when I began to work on this new series, I kept my eyes open. I refused to separate the women into categories, and I learned quickly that just like there are different kinds of heterosexual relationships, the same is true in the lesbian world. These amazing women were far more specific and dynamic than one might have imagined. I respected them as a community, with their various images and ideologies, not so different from being part of my own minorities.

Over time, I did my research and learned the different social types and classifications. For example, there were lipstick femmes—women who wore makeup and looked very feminine. There were also femmes who didn't wear much makeup but had prominent feminine characteristics. On the polar opposite side, there were the butches, who exhibited the stronger male characteristics, among them those who wore leather and studs. I also learned about bisexuals and transsexuals (trannies), who were changing their sexuality, either male to female or female to male.

It's not as if I went up to each woman and said, "Hi there, my name is Pam. What kind of a lesbian are you?" Instead, I looked at them all as human beings. Then, when we got to know each other and they felt they could trust me, they slowly revealed their identities. I

257

was surprised to find out how changeable they were. A woman could act out the male dominant role in one relationship, and in the next, she might be with someone who was dominant over her. The bottom line was that everyone shifted and changed and no one was generic. That understanding gave me an opportunity to look at each person as an individual, no matter her sexual preference.

I swiftly became more connected to the women I was working with than I expected. Like most other minority groups, these women were being denied their rights to marriage and inheritance because they were different. Some of them didn't care because they didn't want marriage. But for those who considered the marriage ceremony to be sacred, it was disappointing to be denied the right to validate that commitment in front of God and their friends and family. In some cases, it was dangerous to come out at all. They might lose their jobs or be ostracized by people who were prejudiced against them.

It was sad to see fabulous, talented women being forced to live secret lives. There were plenty of gay men doing the same thing—staying in the closet, getting married to women, and having children for appearance's sake. It's one thing to be black because you can't hide your race—everyone knows it the minute they see you. But hiding your sexual preference is another story altogether. From what I saw, being gay was a biological distinction, and women had the right to be with anyone they chose. There are cases, I learned, when women who had been abused by men chose to be with women out of fear. But mostly it seemed to be something innate that attracted women to each other.

Lance, the man from the plane, actually called me, and we started to date casually. The first time we saw each other again was in Denver, and he barely recognized me without my blonde hair extensions. He must have been satisfied with the "real" me, because he came with me to Vancouver when we shot the pilot for *The L Word*. He loved the concept of the show and the openness of the discussions. I was impressed by his support for a show that was so daring and groundbreaking.

A senior executive at his company for close to twenty years, Lance had a charming way about him, and everyone who met him liked him immediately. He was complementary to me, clearly pleased that I was not a flashy star with a huge ego who threw money around. I'd had enough of that with other boyfriends, and from what I could see, Lance was their opposite, smart and unobtrusive. Together, we were calm and peaceful, which created a perfect balance for my life, which was generally chaotic and very demanding. I remember one of our very early conversations when he told me he had a passion for women of color.

"Well, I need to know if you can see me as your partner," I told him. "We can be great companions and lovers, but I need to know up front if you see me as your potential wife. I want us to take care of one another. Do you see me that way, or am I just a sexual fetish? Either way it's okay, but I need to know."

He assured me about his intentions, and his love letters certainly reflected that. They were richer and fuller than any I'd ever gotten from a man, and I was falling in love with him. But there was something else I needed to know. I'd noticed that men generally treated their women like their fathers treated their mothers. I needed to look into Lance's family dynamics, because I didn't want my feelings crushed. I was tired of having to slap guys upside the head (just a metaphor!) when they acted disrespectfully toward me. So far, Lance was making a terrific impression, and I looked forward to meeting his family.

I only hoped they were as inclusive as Lance was. He seemed so open to the stories I told him about my family. One day, he was stunned to find out that my family and I had camped out all through my childhood.

"I never knew you liked to camp," he said.

"I'll send you a picture of my family camping in pitched tents by a river with our dogs, our mountain bikes, and a canoe."

He believed in inclusion and was interested in educating others who did not. I had finally met a partner with the potential for a long, fruitful relationship.

Ilene Chaiken, a true pioneer, had spent years trying to get the series on the air. Showtime had already created a successful series called *Queer as Folk*, about the male homosexual community. It was now time for the distaff side of the homosexual world to express themselves in a series as a contemporary group of women living in West Hollywood who were relatable to the current general public. Talk show hosts Rosie and Ellen were preparing the way, and now the political voice of gay women was making itself heard.

As one of the straight women in the cast, I saw an opportunity to bridge a sociopolitical gap between women's gay and straight worlds. I felt that women's rights could be better recognized if all women, straight and gay, united in their common issues, such as raising their children, women's protections, corporate glass ceilings, and demanding equal pay. So far, we had been divided, and as a result we were losing ground socially. I wanted to be an influence to further the unification that already had begun.

There's nothing better than working with a great TV ensemble, with a group of actors who are all taking care of each other. I had great support from the other cast members, particularly while my grandmother was dying. When I had to fly back and forth from Vancouver to Denver, the other women helped me by picking me up emotionally. When they had issues, I became keeper of their secrets, as they would come to me for advice, both emotionally and financially. We turned to each other to make sure we looked right, and we always told each other the truth.

"Do you like the way they did my hair today?"

"Mmm, not really."

We could be that honest with one another. We checked our egos at the door and we all pulled our own weight. That was so necessary because shooting an entire show on location in a different country was stressful. We needed to make the new place feel like home while we maintained our permanent residences in the United States. We also had to find a way to stay true to our life philosophies and our integrity as we struggled against the isolation of working in a foreign country.

In all of these things we turned to each other. We took care of each other's dogs when we were away, and we protected each other when the show got more popular and started attracting stalkers and paparazzi who did not have our best interests at heart. There was an extreme fascination about the cast. People traveled from all over the world to see lesbians in real life, and the more well known the women became, the more security we needed. We understood the importance of avoiding dangerous situations, because if one cast member had an accident or got ill, the entire production could shut down.

As I studied the character of Kit, my role in the show, I was amazed at how art was imitating life. Refusing to give up her life to a man as her mother had done before her (so did mine), she had pursued her singing career and lost her husband and child in the process. She turned to her sister, Bette, who helped her get sober and start out on a new path. Kit built herself a better life and was supported by her sister's friends, a group of wonderful, creative, caring women who loved women.

Each day we arrived at the set as early as 5:30 a.m. I had my own large motor home with two bathrooms, a king-size bed, a TV, and places to lounge around in between shoots. I spent most off time in my trailer, rarely watching TV, but rather rehearsing Kit's dialogue, doing yoga, and working on my own screenplays.

When we shot at Kit's café, called the Planet, we used one hundred and fifty extras—called "atmosphere"—and tons of air-conditioning to deal with so much body heat. These extras made our job much easier because they were pros and knew how to support the principal actors, never getting in our way and giving us energy to work off of. On many occasions I went over to the extras' tent, called the holding tent, and thanked them for showing up no matter the weather, keeping their attitudes positive, and doing their own hair, makeup, and wardrobe with no complaints.

During the first season, Kit wore a handmade wig we called the Beast. Created by my Denver hairstylist, Carma Davis, and Vancouver stylist Paul Edwards, it was a long, curly afro with blonde streaks and a mind of its own. I had two of them made originally so that if other people's hair took longer to get ready, I could throw on the Beast and have it camera-ready in five minutes, as opposed to sitting in a chair for at least a half hour. And everyone loved trying on the Beast and having their photographs taken. Some of us even put the damn wig on our dogs, because the Beast was legendary.

As far as my character, I related to the bohemian side of Kit, a rock-and-roller, AA enthusiast returning from the ashes of her past. When I was working on my wardrobe, I chose to use a local Vancouver designer, Cynthia Summers. When the show began, our wardrobe was simple and low-key. But the more popular we became, the more the designers wanted to work with us. While I joined forces with Cynthia to create a wardrobe for Kit, I began to enjoy fashion in a whole new way. She was a genius at accessorizing an outfit, and I became meticulous about my accessories and choosing the right jewelry. I also worked with Joanne Fowler, a brilliant makeup artist who found the perfect makeup to enhance my skin tone and the clothing that would best complement my figure. As I studied the designs of Chanel and Valentino, I saw the perfect blends of science and art. I salivated over Louboutin, Prada, and Balenciaga, whose classic footwear and clothing transcended time.

The more I studied the various designers, the more I began to view wardrobe and clothing in general as a celebration of beauty. It felt tribal as we did our hair and dressed in the latest colors and decorations, and we attended various award shows and luncheons in a dress code that spoke of elegance and refinement.

Of all the social gatherings I attended, none represented women better than Oprah Winfrey's Legends Luncheon, where she honored and celebrated women of color the world over. Cynthia Summers had dressed me in a green Escada pantsuit with Gucci shoes, a color that complemented Oprah's and Maya Angleou's outfits. I couldn't take my eyes off the celebratory clothing of the likes of Tina Turner, Chaka Khan, Beverly Johnson, Diana Ross, Halle Berry, and Leontyne Price, an African American soprano who broke through the white ceiling in the world of opera. I left the luncheon grateful that I was a part of the significant changes that were swiftly occurring in the world at large.

CHAPTER **38**

How I Became a Scandal

Between seeing Lance on my breaks and shooting season after season of *The L Word*, my life was making sense. I felt a balance for the first time, and I was encouraged that I could have it all—a family, a career, and a continuing curiosity about life that was matched and sparked by a worthy partner. It was so comforting, it was almost too good to be true. But wasn't it my turn for my dreams to come to fruition?

The work continued to motivate me as I recognized the similarities in the challenges that African American women and lesbians faced on a daily basis. I felt inspired to stand up for them, and they really appreciated it. After all, we were a strange and unusual family, and Jennifer Beals told me I was the sister she never had. Laurel Holloman's mom was a nurse just like mine, and so was Leisha Hailey's. Many of us shared common backgrounds, dreams, and goals, mainly because we were all women.

We got so close that we knew who was on their period, who was partying, who could cook, who could shop, and who could put clothes together. It was our private world, and I got to spend time with everyone and find out about their diverse lives and special interests and abilities. Mia Kirshner, who played Jenny, went to Malawi during one of our hiatuses and wrote a book about the abject poverty there. I suspect she was an influence in my decision to write this book, because she took so much care and pride in hers, and the information added a lot to all of our lives. And then Jennifer Beals implored me, short of twisting my arm and wrestling me to the ground, to write my book.

During the six years we worked together, I encouraged Leisha Hailey, who played Alice, to beef up her musical chops. I supported her by attending her concerts, and she was so talented, she came up with a little video of all the girls as they worked hand puppets. We did these kinds of creative games to keep each other's energy up during long shoots over many years. We knew that we had to focus our energies on the work in front of us, and everyone cooperated beautifully. We avoided creating trouble and left the drama to the scriptwriters. We were all in agreement that we didn't need the added strain of bad behavior.

One of our best shows occurred when actor Alan Cumming did a guest role with us. His character was an entrepreneur who offered Kit suggestions for her café, and he was hilarious and had impeccable timing. Another amazing coup was when Gloria Steinem did a cameo as the lover of the man who played Bette and Kit's father, Ossie Davis. Gloria was funny, intelligent, and playful, and we all made sure she had a great time. After all, who had fought more for womanhood in general than Gloria Steinem? I would be remiss not to also mention guest appearances from Anne Archer, Rosanna Arquette, Kelly McGillis, the B52s, Goldfrapp, Elizabeth Berkley, Camryn Manheim, Paris Hilton, Eric Roberts, Eric Handler, Charles Dutton, Snoop Dogg, and Kelly Lynch.

In fact, I thought our regular cast were some of the more talented actresses I'd ever worked with. And still, the show got absolutely no nominations during its run, besides mentions from the NAACP and the GLAAD awards. Could it be that the press did us no favors, since some of the women should have been recognized for their work? In the end, many great performances were overlooked, but the impact of the show speaks for itself.

I have to say, I have never worked so hard for such an extended period of years. I was disciplined, so I didn't get sleep deprived, but I was exhausted a lot of the time. I learned to take power naps on the set, and on my days off I rode horses to unwind and stay fit, both mentally and physically. I often got up at 4:30 a.m. so I could get in a workout. Then I headed to the set for breakfast with the cast and crew. This was a welcome ritual where we women and the production staff reveled in a sense of family and enjoyed the camaraderie and support of one another.

Then it was time for hair and makeup as I rehearsed my lines for the day. I had fewer lines than some of the other women, but I didn't mind, because several episodes were dedicated to my character. I simply loved the work, and I also loved the breaks with Lance. He had a home in the country that felt like a different world altogether when he took me there. Lance's home had a garage that had been a barn for horses, and there were three bedrooms, hardwood floors, and a wood-burning fireplace.

The best part was that Lance was not at all an ostentatious man. I remember how proud he was of me when we first began dating, and his friends and family wanted to know who was making him so happy. But after he took me to my first dinner with his family, it seemed there was trouble in paradise. The intimate dinner at the club was uncomfortable and I did not feel welcome.

Lance was upset. He did not talk with me about it, but I knew something was bothering him, and I pulled the information out of him. Now I began to wonder—was our relationship going to work?

When *The L Word* went on hiatus over Thanksgiving and Christmas, I asked Lance if I could give a Thanksgiving dinner for his family at his country house. He thought that was a great idea and said he would invite his father, from whom he had been estranged for many years. When I asked him what the problem was, he told me that after his mother had passed away when he was young, his relationship with his dad had never been the same.

"Are you ready to see your dad?" I asked him.

"I really would like to," he said.

I figured he knew what he was doing, so while Lance and I cleaned the house and got out his finest dishes, I ordered the turkey and began to prepare the trimmings. I'd never seen Lance so excited. He wanted this dinner with his dad and his siblings more than anything, and the preparations were fun and playful.

The day before Thanksgiving, the day his dad was scheduled to arrive, Lance got a phone call. I watched his face change from anticipatory joy to severe disappointment. "Why not?" I heard him say. "Everything is ready for you."

He frowned at me, and I took the phone. "Hello, there," I said to his dad. "I really hope you can make it to dinner. We've been cooking for quite a while, and I know Lance is really looking forward to seeing you. And so am I."

"I'm not coming," was his reply. He didn't say why, and he didn't apologize to me or to Lance. I handed the phone back to Lance.

We had a lovely dinner with Lance's siblings.

By the time I was ready to go back to work, more changes had occurred in Lance's life. After being offered a great position in another city, Lance asked me what I thought about this new opportunity—he always consulted me about his changes—and I encouraged him to go for it. He wanted a change, and this looked like it had real possibilities. But soon enough, a load of in-house corporate fighting occurred and it all blew up. As I began to shoot a new season of *The L Word*, Lance left his job and moved into my home in Colorado. He had no job now, and the first time I ever saw him in jeans and a T-shirt was at my ranch.

With Lance living at the ranch, taking care of things for me, I immersed myself in the work. *The L Word*'s popularity was growing faster than any of us had imagined, and we held our season premieres in large nightclubs in twenty-five major cities, ranging from New York to San Francisco. They sent one of us to each premiere, and we attracted so many people that it was a common occurrence for the venue to run out of food before the night was over. Thousands of women and a load of curious men watched *The L Word* in various clubs all over the country, and we were all stunned at how well the show was holding its own.

Lance, however, was in a transitional phase. I encouraged him to take this time and write that novel he'd always dreamed about. I really loved him, I knew that he loved me, and when he got a great new job, I was thrilled.

The turning point came when a wealthy friend of the family invited Lance to vacation in the south of France. God knew Lance needed a vacation, and so did I, but there was a catch.

"I've just been invited to sail through the south of France," he said.

"Wow," I said, "that sounds amazing. When do we leave?"

"We don't," he said glumly.

"I wasn't invited, was I?" I asked him.

"I'm not going," was all he said.

I felt a sinking feeling. I knew he wanted to love me, and I had hoped he would remain my hero and allow me to love him back.

But after much dissent and arguing, Lance was so frustrated, he blurted out, "Pam, you're just not country club. I've lost too much because of you. You're just not my marrying kind or even a life partner."

I was furious and humiliated. "After this many years, you just figured out I'm not your marrying kind? I asked you years ago if I were a sexual fetish. You could have been honest and we could have just had some fun. But instead of saying good-bye as friends, you led me on," I retorted.

"I still love you," he said.

"Well, I guess that isn't enough."

If being with me was not going to work out, it was time to look elsewhere. I only regretted having wasted so much time.

CHAPTER 39

You Say Good-bye, I Say Hello

While I watched my relationship with Lance fall apart, we got the news that the sixth season of *The L Word* would be our last. We were all disappointed, because there were so many issues that we had not yet taken on. I could envision at least two more seasons full of sizzling topics that were both current and controversial.

For example, I read an article about a Middle Eastern lesbian couple in Toronto who were on the run from their families. Their families' staunch Middle Eastern views on life considered lesbianism an absolute disgrace, punishable by death, and these women feared for their lives. Unfortunately, being on the run from societal and gender prejudices was a common theme among women in general, and lesbians in particular.

Then there was the California lawmaker who was determined to dissolve the fifteen thousand legal gay marriages performed in 2008 and repeal the "equal rights for all" law. It would have been a great episode to see the reactions of same-sex newlyweds across the state, but that was not to be.

While we filmed our last season of *The L Word*, we were all keenly aware of an imminent loss. It was a bittersweet period of deep introspection, as I had constant sentimental reflections about a family of people who were as close to me as anyone I had ever known. We had shared deep intimacies, we had given each other advice, we truly cared about each other's families, and we were part of each other's dreams. Not a day went by, even when we were on hiatus, that I didn't think about Kate's new kitchen or Jennifer's triathlon or Laurel's marriage and the birth of her child, or Mia's book, or Ilene's children. I also deeply cared about the Showtime executives who put their reputations on the line during each season to continue this revolutionary show about women.

Now we were being canceled, and it felt like someone was stripping away my family. And yet, I still had my memories. The idea of the end of the series was a deeply meaningful and emotional experience for all of us, so to cope, I increased my volunteer work. It seemed that despite my disappointments and gargantuan challenges, I had reached a point in life where I felt mostly gratitude.

I was grateful to my mother for raising me with the right values.

I was grateful to the military for having exposed me to so many different experiences and cultures during my childhood.

I was grateful to the men in my life for the lessons I learned and the inner strength I mustered to deal with them in a direct and honest way.

I was grateful for the roles I was offered and the lessons I learned from other actors and directors along the way.

Most of all, I was grateful for my life. I was a cancer survivor, and I got to wake up every day, take a deep breath, and create beauty.

In the wake of so much to feel good about, it was only natural that I would also feel the urge to give back. I continued my work with the no-kill animal shelter People and Animals Living Synergistically (PAALS), where Lance and I had offered our services starting a few years back. PAALS needed so much, like towels, sheets, kitchen appliances, pet food, and money, to keep their doors open, and I did what I could. I met with the owners of a very successful horse show who for many years had donated their proceedings to PAALS for these unfortunate abandoned pets and homeless people who cared for the animals. I had felt like an abandoned creature myself more times than

I cared to remember, so I really understood the agony of being left out in the cold.

I also joined a group who rescued horses for an inner-city riding program to help build self-esteem in physically challenged and underprivileged kids and adults. The miraculous woman who ran this program, Bonnie, had been stricken with multiple sclerosis, epilepsy, and cancer, and she was 80 percent blind. Still, she stood out in the hot sun when need be, working with people, both ill and well, who wanted desperately to get up on the back of a powerful horse.

While on *The L Word,* I met a rep named Pam Derderian from a product placement company who convinced Subaru to donate an Outback SUV to the horse program. They donated one to PAALS as well (hell, I could have used a free Outback!), and as I observed Bonnie weakening by the day, I realized that we were all one unexpected bump on the head away from where she was. Each time I saw her, I gained more courage to go on, always asking myself, If I were her, how would I deal with it? In the end I learned to fly from the wings of this amazing angel.

I had another opportunity to give back when I shot *Holy Smoke* with Kate Winslet. I got a call from a marketing man who had shot several rap videos for some huge hip-hop stars. I had met Snoop Dogg along my travels, and many of the hip-hop artists had recognized me and helped to keep me a visible icon and encouraged me with my career. When the marketer Chris Latimer told me about his charity, Hip Hop 4 Humanity, I asked how I could help.

Our first outreach was to raise funds to feed the homeless a Thanksgiving dinner in Manhattan. I called around to the various record companies and asked for donations. They were generous. Then I called the Weinstein brothers, Harvey and Bob, who had produced *Jackie Brown* at Miramax Films. Would they be interested in giving a small donation, like five hundred dollars or so, to our cause? The Weinsteins not only said yes, but they matched the donations from all the record companies. In the end, with the help of prison chefs from Rikers Island, we fed as many as twenty-five thousand people on Thanksgiving, with food left over for two more days.

There I was with a group of world-famous hip-hop artists in downtown Manhattan, feeding dinner to people who were desperately hungry and asked for extra food to take back to their loved ones. I gave them as much as they could carry, knowing that I could just as easily have been that desperate myself. When a crippled woman with only one glove recognized me, she said, "Aren't you that movie star?"

She was waiting in line to eat, and I said, "Not today I'm not. Today I'm here to serve you. Would you like some mashed potatoes, fried chicken, and green beans with biscuits?"

My volunteer work, a mainstay in my life, helped me cope with the loss of both a great love, Lance, and a family of women, the cast of *The L Word*. Our show had had such success—what other series' premieres were attended across the nation by sold-out crowds? I was proud to have been a part of a project that woke people up to a world about which they knew very little. The women demonstrated their commitment to being women first and lesbians second, so I always felt like I was in the mix. As part of a force to help people feel less threatened by something that was different, I was honored to help establish an image of character, integrity, and dignity among all women, no matter our sexual persuasion.

While I shot the last season of *The L Word* and went on the never-ending publicity interviews and personal appearances, I felt my losses keenly. I had hoped for more time with Lance and the show, but we don't get to choose the cards we're dealt. We do get to choose how we feel about it, though, and how we get through it.

Today, I have to admit that I was hugely disappointed in Lance. But I was even more disappointed in myself for not digging deep enough to have gotten the message sooner. True, Lance and I had interesting discussions about life and love. We read and debated the book *John Adams*, and we also read the contemporary works of Henry Louis Gates Jr. I began to fill in missing parts of an education I had been denied when I was growing up, and I have to say that Lance was instrumental in changing the way I looked at the world. But I have a hard time reconciling the time I spent with him, years that I could have been building a foundation with someone who could truly be a partner.

As for my career, while I regretted the end of a fantastic series, I could only look forward to what was coming next. Experience taught me that my best roles had come suddenly, in circumstances that were often mysterious and beyond my imagination. While I was waiting, there was no place like home.

As we women all said good-bye for the last time, vowing never to lose touch, I was ready to go back home, groom my horses, shovel snow, grieve my losses, celebrate my joys, and anticipate what might be coming down the road. Life had always been relatively good to me, offering me some pretty intense lessons as well as new situations and opportunities that were mine for the taking. I usually took them, anxious for the next experience, since leaving one phase of life with no bitterness usually leads to the wonder of the next one. It just keeps on coming, and we have only to stand up and embrace the newness with positive anticipation and a good sense of humor. When the world seems to be getting gray and shutting down, the next day always comes, bringing with it a whole new set of possibilities, which hopefully we can meet with an open heart.

In the words of the fabulous Beatles:

You say good-bye.

I say hello.

Epilogue

It's 6:00 a.m. and I just headed from my house to the barn under the rising sun. I miss the times when Lance used to bring us two cups of tea, and we would sit in front of the barn under the rising sun. The light is beginning to poke its head above the horizon, and I can hear my sweet horses neighing for me. I smile as I watch my dogs chasing bunnies across the field. Most mornings, before breakfast, I'm in the habit of visiting the barn, feeding my rescued horses, and stroking their beautiful long manes and the soft spots on their muzzles.

When the sun and moon are switching places in the sky, it's a perfect time to think about my life and how it might unfold over the coming years. When I look back, I can say without hesitation that I have stepped up and met my challenges with as much courage as I could muster. I have had my share of tragedies, but I also have had amazing opportunities in life, most of which I turned into great achievements as a single woman, always doing my best to avoid being grandiose or arrogant. I have gained whatever knowledge I could, I have come to know a variety of cultures from around the world, and I have survived as a human being and a woman as I lived up to my strengths and my imperfections.

"Don't mess with imperfection," the late Conrad L. Hall, Oscar-winning cinematographer several times over, told a friend of mine. I took his words to heart and have always strived to be the best me I could be, perfect and imperfect.

My humble ranch in Colorado continues to be my sanctuary for family and friends in a chaotic world. I like being out of the mainstream, with my mother, sister, and brother all living about an hour away, and my bout with cancer helped me gain strength and a much greater passion for living healthy—by necessity. I have had to toughen up both mentally and physically to thrive in a rural and agricultural environment. But while I give up some of the amenities and services that we get in the city, I reap great benefits from drinking fresh well water without chemicals, eating nutritious food, and breathing good clean air. When I saw how the chlorine and pollution dried up my hair and caused it to break off when I lived in the city, I could only imagine what these impurities were doing to me internally.

I walk back to the house in the burgeoning light and brew some South African red bush tea, my favorite at the moment. I never imagined my life would be like this when I was still young, eager to conquer the world and learn about everything in it. I thought that by now I would have a husband, some wonderful children, and an Ivy League education. These were my dreams, but the fact that they did not come true does not discourage me.

To be perfectly honest, some days I feel like I missed out on having children and creating my own nuclear family. On other days, I'm so overwhelmed with writing, acting, and caring for my home and my animals, I wonder how I would ever manage having children. Either way, my life has been full and exciting. It's never too late for love, and there are always children who need parents, a good home, and an education. I also have my sister's and other friends' children to help raise.

I do not feel embittered by anything in my life, partly because my mother made sure I knew better and partly because I see life as a classroom and the experiences within it as lessons. All I can hope is that I use those lessons to be better prepared for what is still to come. I believe we can dream until we take our last breath, and I have plenty of dreams that can still come true. I see life as a free-form dance, and we are the choreographers. One day, you're strong and lean, running six miles a day. You don't drink, smoke, or do drugs. And then, all of a sudden, you have cancer. There's no way to prepare for it, but now that you're in it, a saving grace is to be grateful for what you have.

I see it all in the form of seasons: a season to plant and a season to grow, a season to do personal preparation and a season to reap the benefits of life and give back to others. Whichever season I'm in, however, I look to my heroes to inspire me.

My list of heroes begins with my mother, Gwendolyn, who taught me to forgive discrimination. Without that lesson, I might have turned into a bitter woman, a victim of life, instead of becoming the strong-willed, compassionate, individual thinker that I am today. My mother showed me that while prejudice may be alive and kicking in some areas of the world, we are in reality a multiracial world that requires great patience and understanding.

President Barack Obama and First Lady Michelle Obama are my heroes, too, as they exhibit the desire and the ability to listen to others and to respect them. They appear to be curious and intelligent people who have a great level of selflessness and are deeply committed to the creation of a kinder, more compassionate, and color-blind world.

I owe a great deal to Oprah Winfrey, another hero of mine, who graced me with an invitation to her Legends Luncheon, where I sat across from Michelle Obama. That afternoon, Mrs. Obama told me that her husband, Barack (had I ever heard of him?), was considering a run for president. During that luncheon, I learned from and mingled with some of the most powerful African American women of our time. I admire Oprah for being a catalyst in creating an inclusive world while encouraging millions of people worldwide to do the same. May her efforts help melt the walls of discrimination, racial hatred, and gender bias.

I also see feminists Gloria Steinem and the late Bella Abzug as heroes, as well as Shirley Chisholm and the late Barbara Jordan. They supported women in breaking down the walls between them and making decisions for themselves, instead of letting men decide things for them. They showed me that I had choices, that I could get married or not, that I could have children or not, and that society does not have the right to judge me as inferior because I don't have a husband or live in a more traditional manner.

With inspiration from many people along the way, I have learned to look at the world and say, "This is what is inside of *me*. This is my life, which I am free to create for myself. I had only a year of college but I take online courses to further my education. I didn't get married but I have wonderful men and lovers in my life, anyway. I learned that I am capable of loving someone with everything in me. I didn't have children but there are too many children without parents in the world, as it is."

Perhaps the greatest gift of all is my freedom—freedom is to wake up each day and take it as it comes. I intend to keep on acting. I still have the artistic passion for it, which now has extended past just acting and has gone on to writing, directing, and developing shows. I never intend to retire unless illness forces me to, because I love having a purpose. The greatest part of being an artist is that we never retire. We can continue to create our art until we take our last breath.

These days, I love sitting down in a coffee shop in Sonoma with my dear friend Paula Gentry, overlooking the vineyards and chatting and discussing politics. I love hiking, biking, fishing, and enjoying the beauty of the countryside. I also love running through Central Park with my dogs. What if I had been born in the Sudan? What if I'd lived my whole life on a dirt floor, afraid of the militia rushing through and murdering my family?

I consider myself one of the most fortunate women in the world, and I'd like to leave my readers with a few pearls of wisdom that I learned the hard way:

Never take a gift for granted.

Pay attention to and respect other people, cultures, and lifestyles.

Never lose your curiosity.

Apologize sincerely when you're wrong, and ask for forgiveness. When you don't, it gets worse. When you do, it gets better.

Be excited about life, claim your place in the big picture, and always follow your passion.

I sip my tea and watch the sky turning into pastel streaks, warming up the heavens. The sun is up, and God only knows what's in store. As I head to the bedroom to get dressed and meet the day, I am reminded that when I was small, I dreamed of a world without discrimination, a world where people helped each other, just because we were all human beings. A world where the doors were all left open.

For our children today, those doors are finally open most of the way, and I say:

Run through them! The world is waiting!

Acknowledgments

With profound gratitude to Grand Central Publishing, publisher Jamie Raab, and executive editor Karen R. Thomas for their guidance, wisdom, and humor in helping me to discover what was lost and now found and nurtured. Thanks to Matthew Rolston for his brilliant photography.

Heartfelt thanks to Dad and the Family of Angels.

Matt Blank, Robert Greenblatt, Jerry Offsay, everyone at Showtime Networks.

Andrea Cagan, who suffered hair loss working with me. She taught me volumes. I thank her for the shared discipline of an exciting journey.

Quentin Tarantino, Harvey and Bob Weinstein, Lawrence Bender, Kelly Bush, Alfred Sapse, Jim Stein, Steve LaMana, Scott Harris, Scott Miller.

Aunt Mignonne, Beth Klein, Pearlina Igbokwe.

Roger Corman, Oprah Winfrey, Ilene Chaiken, Rose Lam.

The L Word family, Jennifer Beals.

All of my teachers, shamans, talismen, agents, stuntpeople, especially Bob Minor and Jadie David, and my casting directors.

Jeff Corey, Tamar and Josh Hoffs, Carl Gottlieb, and Seth Riggs.

Gloria Steinem, Bethanne Hardison, Annie Leibovitz, Greg Gorman.

Andrew Davis, John and Sandy Carpenter, Michael Mann, Steven Seagal.

Wilford Brimley, Paula Gentry, Lani Groves, Bobby Womack, Sylvester Stewart, Warrington Hudlin.

Eve Ensler, Valerie Scott, the Ryan Family, Haywood Hobbs.

Denver Center for the Performing Arts, Crossroads Theatre, Terrence McNally, Sam Shepard, Julie Hubert, Will Smith, David Alan Grier, Jay Leno, Eddie Murphy, Spike Lee, Martin Lawrence, Adrianna Trigianni, Bonnie Seligson, Diane Benedict, Mike Davis, Alan Lande, Debra Martin Chase, Joel Lachman, Whoopi Goldberg, Andrew J. Epstein.

Grand Master Doo Wai, Pam Derderian, Tim Bennet, Tim Mahoney, and Abana Jacobs, Subaru USA, Chris Latimer, Cynthia Summers, Joanne Fowler, Paul Edwards, Faye Katz, Howard Sherman, Robin McMillan, Rich Licatta, Danielle Gelbert.

The *Linc's* family, Tim and Daphne Reid, Susan Fales-Hill, Charles Randolph-Wright.

Thanks to Herman, Wanda, Debby, and Tom and family. Tim Burton, Dorothea Petrie, David Moss, Maggie Charnas, Sharon and Greg Dreyden, Diana Gradiska, Bob and Angela Egerton, Phillip and Brenda Kruse, Irv Schecter, Glenn Leira, Harry Gold, Marlee Matlin, Darryl Marshak, Gail Poindexter, Glenn Riggberg, Larry Kinnar, Erin Daniels, Daniella Sea.

Mia Kirshner, Laurel Holloman, Leisha Hailey, Cybill Shepherd, Snoop Dogg and family, Ernie and Ashley Smatt, Kate Moening, Rose Rollins, Angela Robinson, Amy and Gloria Hempel, Bonnie and Jamie Schaefer, Elizabeth and Amy Ziff, Betty, Minaz, Hennessey USA, Rose Troche, Kirk Montgomery, Tricia Brock, Scott Peacock.

Wayan brothers, Dr. Joel Gendleman, Geoff and Valerie Young, Bill Pickett, Rodeo Inc.

Lu Vason and family, TZR, and Tony.

Producers and casting directors who hired me for many years.

My physicians, who have managed to save my life many times over.

In memory of
David Baumgarten, Minnie Riperton, Odessa Oma, Altovise Davis, Aunt Mignonne, and Fritz Baskett